Mountain Holidays in Norway

COMPILED BY
PER PRAG

PUBLISHED BY
NORWAY TRAVEL ASSOCIATION
OSLO, NORWAY

J. S. Kaye,

For details of first ascents etc.
made on expeditions to Lofoten,
Tysfjord region and Lyngen see
pages:-

TYSFJORD ↓ NARVIK
$\begin{cases} 103 \\ 104 \\ 106 \\ 107 \quad 1956 \\ 110 \\ 110 \\ 112 \\ 113 \end{cases}$

LOFOTEN
$\begin{cases} 115 \\ 120 \\ 124 \\ 131 \end{cases}$ 1956 & 1958

LYNGEN
$\begin{cases} 144 \\ 149 \end{cases}$ 1958

CONTENTS

See back pages for alphabetical index.

EIKESDAL

① KVANDALS-
TIND

KALSKRA-
TIND

EIKESDALSVATN

MARDALSBOTN

VENGE-
TINDANE
1843

VENGEDAL

VERMEDAL ⑦

⑥

ROMSDALS-
HORN
1555

TROLLTIN
1794

⑥

NESAKSLA

RAUMA

GRØVDAL
HOEM

④ ISFJORDEN

⑤ STRANDAFJELL

③

②

Leif Lundgren
1961

ÅNDALSNES

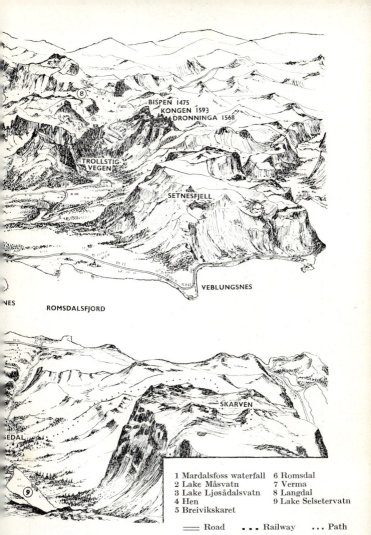

BISPEN 1475
KONGEN 1593
DRONNINGA 1568

TROLLSTIG-
VEGEN

SETNESFJELL

VEBLUNGSNES

NES

ROMSDALSFJORD

SKARVEN

EDAL

1 Mardalsfoss waterfall 6 Romsdal
2 Lake Måsvatn   7 Verma
3 Lake Ljøsådalsvatn 8 Langdal
4 Hen   9 Lake Selsetervatn
5 Breivikskaret

═══ Road ••• Railway ••• Path

D ENVIRONS

We cannot supply you

with crampons

but should you

require a tanker

or a bulkfreighter

drop us a line.

GÖTAVERKEN NORSK A/S

General Information

MOUNTAIN HOLIDAYS IN NORWAY

The vast mountain ranges of Norway provide an ideal playground for holiday-makers. The scenery is truly magnificent — giant peaks, glistening glaciers, remote mountain valleys, thundering waterfalls, peaceful lakes and blue fjords cutting deep into the mountain ranges. Above all, perhaps, the real charm of Norway lies in the people you meet. Norwegians are easy-going, informal and friendly. You are among real friends all the time. Do not bother to learn Norwegian before you go, because practically every Norwegian you meet will be very disappointed if he or she doesn't get the chance of showing off that English is taught in all Norwegian schools! The friendly and helpful attitude of the Norwegians and the beautiful scenery that meets the eye everywhere, combine to make your Norway holiday into something you will always remember.

The informality of Norwegians is never more characteristic than when you sit around the open-hearth fire in the evening in a youth hostel or a tourist lodge. Comradeship and friendship is the hallmark of these evenings. Conversation flows in a never-ending stream, only interrupted by a sing-song and an occasional yarn. On such evenings you will probably find that you are right in the middle of a miniature "united nations", where visitors from all parts of the world exchange news and tales of what they have seen and what they intend to do the following day. But beware! This is where your laboriously planned itinerary goes haywire. When you find yourself listening to a group of enthusiasts, who seem to have experienced all the thrills of a whole holiday in one single day, and they suggest that you should join them, you forget all about your own itinerary and you join your new friends. By all means, do it — unless you have already booked a room somewhere else!

The purpose of this book is to give you an idea of what the mountain ranges of Norway can offer. It cannot be more than a vague outline, because a description of this incredibly elongated country and its vast mountain expanses would require a thick volume to do them justice.

TRAVEL FACTS

All details of passports, currency and customs regulations
etc, also a description of how to get to Norway, are found
in a free booklet entitled "Travel Facts on Norway",
available together with an illustrated tourist map, from
the nearest Norwegian National Tourist Office, addresses
as follows:

Britain: Norwegian National Tourist Office, 20 Pall Mall,
London SW 1.
USA: Norwegian National Travel Office, 290 Madison
Ave, New York 17, NY.
France: Office National du Tourisme en Norvége, 10
rue Auber, Paris (9e).
Belgium: Office National Norvegien du Tourisme, 16
Place Surlet de Chokier, Bruxelles.
Denmark: Norges Officielle Turistkontor, Borgergade 16,
København K.
Sweden: Norska Turistbyrån, Strandvägen 113, Stock-
holm NO.
Norway: Norway Travel Association, H Heyerdahlsgate 1,
Oslo.

HOLIDAY SEASON

Although the summer season in Norway extends from
early May until late September, the season is fairly
short in the mountain ranges, owing to the altitude.
In areas higher than about 3500 ft, the holiday season
is only from the last week in June until about September
10.

TOURIST LODGES AND "DNT"

Inexpensive tourist lodges are found in all the principal
mountain ranges. They are situated at convenient distances of about a day's walk from one to another, and are
well staffed. Good meals are provided. There are also
some unstaffed huts, which are only meant to provide
shelter for a night. If your route takes you to any of
these huts, you should take packed lunch with you from
the lodge you leave in the morning. All lodges provide
bedding, china and cutlery, but towels and soap should
be taken. It is cheaper if you bring your own sheet
sleeping bag. Travellers' cheques are accepted.
A number of tourist lodges and unstaffed huts are owned
by the Norwegian Touring Club (called DNT). You will
save money by becoming a member of the DNT, because
they offer reduced terms at their lodges and huts for
members who have paid the current subscription. Similar

Spiterstulen lodge in Jotunheimen (Photo: Normann)

reductions also apply to DNT members when staying at
certain other lodges, owned by associated clubs or even
by private individuals. Membership cards are issued by all
Norwegian national tourist offices. Ask for their circular
on DNT membership, which also contains details of
tourist lodge charges. The DNT takes pride in announcing
that not only do they dislike advance bookings, but they
also claim that, so far, no visitor has ever been turned
away from any of their lodges. Even if all beds are taken
for the night, the warden will provide bunks on the floor
in dormitories.

YOUTH HOSTELS

Over 200 youth hostels with more than 6000 beds are at
your disposal in Norway. Some hostels are entirely new,
built especially for the purpose; others are located in
farmhouses or in schools, but they are all clean though
simply furnished. Meals are generally available, either
at the hostel or at a reasonable cafe nearby. Always bring
your own towel and sheet sleeping bag, although the
latter is often available at a small charge. If you wish to
do your own cooking in the members' kitchen, you must
use your own cutlery, but pots and pans are provided.
Norwegian youth hostels are usually open from May or
June to mid-September, but some are open all the year
round. Advance bookings are essential for groups and
advisable for others, particularly during the peak season
in July and August. Write direct to each hostel in
question. Your membership card from your own YHA
will admit you to any youth hostel in Norway. All
youth hostels in Norway are listed in the international

YHA handbook which is available from the YHA head-
quarters in your own country, but a complete list is
also available (free) from any Norwegian national tourist office, together with a list of current prices, which,
of course, are scaled to suit young visitors. The
Norwegian YHA, Dronningensgate 26 Oslo, will also
be glad to assist in suggesting an itinerary for your
Norway holiday. They have a useful sketch map which
indicates the location of all hostels in Norway. You
can nearly always cycle from one hostel to another in
a day. Motorists and motor cyclists are also admitted
to youth hostels in Norway. Several hostels have "family
rooms", which are designed for young couples with small
children. Although most visitors prefer to travel from
one hostel to another, there is also a number of hostels
which are ideal for a stay-put holiday. These hostels
provide everything including full board. The most popular
hostels in this category are located at Eidfjord, Geilo,
Gjøvik, Hamar, Lillehammer, Mjølfjell, Nesflaten, Oslo,
Rjukan, Stavanger and Voss. Several of these hostels
are also ideal for winter sports holidays.

PRIVATE LOG CABINS

When travelling in a small group, it may be an idea to
hire a private log cabin and stay put all the time. A great
number of privately owned log cabins in the mountain
ranges are available for shorter or longer periods at a
reasonable rent. All are situated amidst grand scenery,
and there is invariably great scope for delightful walks,
trout fishing, boating and bathing in lakes, etc. Private
log cabins are generally well equipped, but linen and
cutlery should be taken. Write for further information
and details of prices to Hytteformidlingen, Kierschows-
gate 7, Oslo.

CAMPING HOLIDAYS

Camping conditions can never be more ideal than they are
in Norway, with fascinating camping sites almost everywhere. Whether travelling by car or bike, it is never
difficult to find a suitable camping site when the evening
draws near. Nobody will mind if you make your home
for a night or two anywhere you care to choose. Even in the
environs of Oslo, Bergen or Stavanger and many other
towns you will find suitable camping grounds. There are
regular camping sites along all the main roads, where
a small fee is payable.
If you wish to pitch your tent in the field of a nearby

farm, it is customary first to ask the farmer for his permission, which is almost sure to be forthcoming. When buying milk or other farm produce from him, you pay on delivery; otherwise there is no charge for the actual camping site if the party consists of boys or girls, but motorists are usually supposed to give a tip — dependent on how flashy the car looks! However, the farmer will appreciate it if you say goodbye to him before leaving. And remember to leave the place just as tidy as you found it. Be careful with fire! It is illegal to make an open fire in wooded country. You may safely drink water anywhere, provided you can see it is not stagnant. You will find rivers or brooks anywhere.

CYCLING HOLIDAYS

Although Norway is a mountainous country, it is well suited for cycling. There is never a tedious journey to reach your destination, because in Norway you are there all the time. Something new turns up around every twist and bend of the road, and the scenery is constantly changing in an endless series of vistas.

The roads are not as good as in flat countries — and one would be surprised if they were — because road construction in Norway is more difficult than in most other countries. In fact, you will wonder often how on earth they did manage to build roads through mountains or along precipices. Most roads are gravel surfaced. Generally, you should not calculate on covering more than about 50 miles a day. Of course, the hills are not always against you, but any cycling tour of Norway is certainly also a combined walking holiday. However, it is always good to know that when you have to walk uphill, you can always coast downhill. Cyclists will find much useful information in a booklet called "Motoring in Norway", available at a small charge from the NNTO in London.

WALKING TOURS

By building lodges and marking trails, the Norwegian Touring Club has opened up the vast mountain ranges of Norway so that all can safely enjoy their beauty and grandeur. Valley paths and mountain trails are clearly marked by cairns, which are placed at regular intervals, often with a red "T" painted on them, so that anyone can follow the route without difficulty.

Guides are generally not required for ordinary walking tours, but for rock climbs and glacier walks, guides are available in the most popular mountain ranges, particu-

Trout fishing and mountain hiking is a wonderful combination

larly in Jotunheimen and on the Jostedal glacier. These
are contacted through the local tourist lodges.

Your may be puzzled why Norwegians measure mountain
journeys in hours instead of kilometres. The fact is that
the trails climb up and down, in and out, in order to
avoid the natural obstacles of rock and river, so that
linear measurement becomes altogether irrelevant. There-
fore, you will find that the walking tour between any two
lodges is always stated in hours on the sketch maps
which are published by the DNT in respect of the various
mountain ranges. Remember that the number of walking
hours quoted on these sketch maps, is the actual walking
time; any resting stop must be added.

PONY TREKKING HOLIDAYS

This is a type of holiday, which is rapidly growing in
popularity from year to year. Pony trekking holidays
are organized every summer on the Hardanger mountain
plateau, trekking from one tourist lodge to another. Each
party has a Norwegian leader, who also acts as a riding
instructor. In Norway, there are two hardy breeds which
make good saddle ponies — the "fjording", which is bred
in the Fjord Country, and the "dølahest", which hails
from the eastern valleys. These ponies are friendly, sturdy
and reliable. Even children can be safely taken on these
trips. Programs with itineraries and prices are available
from the Norwegian Touring Club, Stortingsgaten 28, Oslo,
or from the West Norway Youth Hostels Association,
Strandgaten 4, Bergen.

ROCK CAVE EXPLORING

There are over 20 rock caves in Norway, particularly beyond the Arctic Circle. Most of them are more or less unexplored, as Norwegians seem to take very little interest in them. As there is no speleological society or potholers clubs in Norway, there is not much information available, either. Some of the most famous rock caves are described in this book — such as the Little Hell cave (Finse-Bygdin ranges), the Troll Church near Molde (Romsdal), the Cathedral cave on Trena island (Below the Artic Circle), the Grønli and Plurdal stalactite caves near Mo i Rana (Svartisen glacier), and the Gråttådal grotto in Beiarn (Bodø region).

CLIMBING HOLIDAYS

Although most peaks have been climbed, there is certainly still scope for further exploring. New routes are made every year, and there are walls and ridges which will yield good sport, but which have never been climbed. The scope for new climbs of all standards of difficulty, particularly in Arctic Norway, is still considerable, and several problems of a high order of difficulty remain.

Most of the popular rock climbs are well cairned, thus making these ideal for parties of some experience, wishing to learn guideless climbing. The ice and snow work encountered is generally easy and suitable to novices. Descriptions of rock climbs in this book are based upon the six climbing booklets which were published in 1953, plus scores of personal reports from climbers. It would be greatly appreciated if details of new ascents — and indeed any comment regarding routes already described — be sent to the NTTO in London for inclusion in any subsequent issue of this book.

CLOTHING AND EQUIPMENT

For walking tours or cycling holidays in Norway, wear whatever you wear on similar tours in your own country — only remember that sunglasses are usually more necessary than oilskins. Norway is certainly more solar than polar! Shorts and open-neck shirts are usual in the Norwegian mountain ranges — even for glacier walks. Warmer clothing may be handy after sunset, when it is apt to get chilly. However, the country is rough, and boots are much better than shoes, with a lighter pair for indoor comfort. Take heavy boots for glacier walks. Rubber shoes are unnecessary for all the straightforward climbs; triconnies or clinker nailed boots are adequate.

Cairned trails and comfortable lodges have opened up Norway's mountain ranges
(Photo: Gunnar Raabe)

Norwegian camping equipment of all kinds is of high quality and also inexpensive. Specialized climbing equipment may not be available in sports shops on short notice, so it is wise to bring your own equipment. There are no customs formalities in respect of climbing gear. Useful addresses of good sports shops in Norway: A Gresvig, Storgaten 20, Oslo, and J Berstad, Strandgaten 20, Bergen.

PROVISIONS

Provisions for camping holidays and climbing expeditions can be bought in any town or village before you move into the mountain ranges. Norwegian canned foods are delicious and inexpensive. For bread, try Norwegian "flatbrød" or "knekkebrød", packed in airtight containers, which hold good for months. If you enjoy smoking and drinking, it is just as well to stock up on the boat or aircraft coming over, when you can buy duty-free cigarettes and liquor. When bringing your own provisions for larger expeditions, you should apply for an import licence from Direktoratet for Import, Fr Nansens plass 5, Oslo (but send it through your own Embassy in Oslo), giving details of quantities, port of arrival, destination and duration of stay, also number of members in the party. If you intend to visit isolated mountain ranges, it is essential that you also take medical supplies including first-aid kit, and that at least one member of the party is versed in the use of first aid. Mosquitoes seldom make a nuisance of themselves in western or central Norway, but they can be bad in Arctic Norway. However, there is now an efficient mosquito repellant available from chemists all over Norway.

14

CLIMBING PERMIT

There are no formalities in respect of ordinary climbing expeditions to any area south of Narvik, but if you wish to climb anywhere north of Narvik, you are advised to obtain prior consent through the nearest Norwegian Embassy, as certain areas in Arctic Norway are restricted for military reasons.

Scientific expeditions are requested to apply to the Norwegian Embassy for permission. The application should state the nature and location of the research, also approx number of members of the group. Before leaving, a list of the members of the party should be submitted to the Embassy with details of date of arrival. Land surveying will not normally be permitted.

SAFETY RULES

The general "rule of the road" for walking tours in any mountain range is that you are perfectly safe as long as you follow the cairned trails, but you should never try to make short-cuts unless you are accompanied by experienced Norwegians who are familiar with that particular terrain. Also make it an unbreakable rule that you never cross any glacier without a guide, and never unless there are at least three persons in the party, and always use a rope whenever you cross a glacier. There is very little danger of avalanches, but certain glaciers are rather crevassed. No member of any expedition should set out on walks without first informing the leader of destination and estimated time of return.

MAPS

Norwegian survey maps are generally good and up-to-date. The scale is usually 1 in 100.000 or 1 cm to 1 km, which by comparison means that 1 inch on the map represents 100.000 inches on the ground, or the equivalent to 1,58 miles. However, there are still certain areas where only old-fashioned and unreliable maps are available — such as the Jostedal and Ålfot glaciers, Sunnmøre, Romsdal and Nordmøre. It is hoped that new maps will replace the old ones in near future. The Lyngen area is now covered by excellent new maps.

All maps listed in this booklet can be bought from the NTTO in London. Please send stamped addressed envelope for their circular on maps with prices.

Principal Mountain Ranges

THE ROGALAND—SETESDAL HIGHLANDS

This is a vast area of unspoilt country to the N and E of Stavanger, forming the southernmost part of the Fjord Country. The scenery is a fine blend of mountains, valleys, rivers and fjords. Large herds of wild reindeer roam about in the mountains, and most rivers and lakes afford good trout fishing.

The Stavanger Touring Club owns 16 inexpensive lodges and huts in the Rogaland mountains, situated at convenient distances of about a day's walk from one another, and the trails are clearly marked. Before starting on any walking tour in this area, visitors are invited to call for further information at the office of the Stavanger Touring Club, Skagenkaien 18, Stavanger. Here are details of 3 popular lodges which are recommended for a longer stay, as they are all situated in delightful countryside, which affords a series of interesting walks and excursions:

The "Pulpit" with a sheer precipice of 1700 ft in the Lyse fjord (Photo: Ellingsen)

The Prekestol Lodge (map E 412 Hunnedal), alt 815 ft, 70 beds, built in 1950, the best and most comfortable tourist lodge in this area, full board, reached from Stavanger by fjord steamer to Jørpeland in just over an hour, then 10 miles by bus or taxi to the lodge. A delightful walk of 2 hrs takes you to the very summit of the Pulpit, a famous flat-topped peak with a sheer precipice of 1700 ft into the Lyse fjord. Free trout fishing for those staying at the lodge. Fly fishing and spinning, bank casting or boat fishing.

The Nilsebu Lodge (map E 447 Jøsenfjord), alt 2300 ft, 36 beds, modernized in 1955, full board, reached from Stavanger by fjord steamer to Lysebotn in 4-5 hrs, then 1 hour by bus to lake Nilsebu and across the lake by motor boat to Nilsebu in 20 mins. Free trout fishing for visitors staying at the lodge. Fly fishing is considered better than spinning. Rowing boats are available, but bank casting is preferred.

The Ådneram Lodge (map K 480 Setesdal), alt 1950 ft, 34 beds, rebuilt in 1954, full board, reached from Stavanger by bus to Fidjeland in 3 hrs. Also open for winter sports, when the bus journey via the Gyadal takes 5 hrs.

A Fine Mountain Holiday (maps E 447 Jøsenfjord, E 690 Ombo, E 412 Hunnedal): (1) Morning steamer from Stavanger to Lysebotn in 4-5 hrs, bus to lake Nilsebu in 1 hr, motor boat to Nilsebu lodge in 20 mins. (2 & 3) Stay at Nilsebu. Excursion to the Lyse hydro-electric plant and back. (4) By motor boat and bus to Lysebotn as above, then by steamer to Refsås in 2 hrs and walk to lake Refsvatn in less than an hour. Motor boat across the lake or walk around it in 45 mins to the Prekestol Lodge. (5 & 6) Stay at Prekestol. Excursion to the Pulpit mountain and back. (7) Take bus to Jørpeland in 25 mins and afternoon steamer to Stavanger in 1 hr.

Round Trip of the Rogaland Mountains (maps E 447 Jøsenfjord, E 763 Sand, K 480 Setesdal): (1) From Stavanger to Nilsebu Lodge as described above. 2) Stay at Nilsebu. (3) Walk to the Blåfjell hut (12 beds), a tour of about 8 hrs. This hut is unstaffed, but provisions are available. (4) Follow cairned trail from Blåfjell to the Undeknut hut (12 beds) in 5-6 hrs. Unstaffed hut, built in 1953, but provisions are available. (5) Walk in 6 hrs to the Stranddal Lodge (30 beds). (6) Spend day at Stranddal. (7) Walk in 6 hrs to the Sandsa Lodge (42 beds). (8) Walk to Suldalsosen on road No 505 in 4 hrs. Bus to Sand in 1 hr and afternoon steamer on the beautiful Ryfylke fjords to Stavanger in 4-5 hrs.

THE FOLGEFONN GLACIER

Although the Folgefonn glacier is the third largest ice-field in Europe, it is not often visited by tourists, in spite of the fact that its glistening white snow dome looks exceedingly inviting when seen from practically every angle from every main route in the Hardanger fjord district. It covers an area of 108 sq miles and attains a max altitude of 5423 ft. Particularly the eastern fringe is most impressive, as the ice brim covers completely the sheer precipices facing the Hardanger fjord. There are three main starting points for the traverse of the glacier. Mauranger, also called Sundal, lies on the W side and is reached by steamer from Bergen in 8 hrs; Krossdal (Jondal) on the W side is reached by bus from Bergen to Torvikbygd and ferry to Jondal in 5 hrs; Odda lies on the E side of the glacier at the head of the narrow Hardanger fjord and is reached by steamer from Bergen in 12 hrs, alternatively by bus and ferry from Bergen via Utne in 6 hrs. Good accommodation is available at all three centres. Maps E 275 Folgefonn and E 253 Fjæra.

Several interesting glacier walks can be made from Mauranger, Krossdal and Odda, but when making a complete traverse, a guide is always required. This can be arranged in Mauranger or Odda. The 1st passage of the glacier with horse and sledge was made in 7/1888 by Yngvar Nielsen and J Vibe, from Gjerde to Tokheim, and the 1st (and only) passage by reindeer and sledge was made in 7/1895 by A and G Schibsted with S A Gjerde, from Gjerde to Tokheim. It is also perfectly feasible to make short or long excursions on to the glacier plateau from either side, but remember always to obtain local advice about routes and snow conditions.

Glacier Traverse Mauranger — Odda (map E 275 Folgefonn): Follow road up Bondhus valley, but turn left over bridge somewhat below lake Bondhus (190). A cairned footpath then leads past lake Botna (837) and up to Breidablik (1323), which is a small log cabin, available to wayfarers. It takes 5 hrs to reach it, and another half hour takes you to the glacier snout. Aim first at the highest point, but before reaching it, turn L and walk towards Tokheimnuten (1345). Descend through the Tokheim valley, reaching the main road about 3 km N of Odda. A fine tour with magnificent views. Time, about 11 hrs, of which the glacier crossing itself takes 3 hrs. Guide required.

THE HARDANGER MOUNTAIN PLATEAU

The vast expanses of the Hardanger mountain plateau cover an area of more than 7500 sq km, situated at an altitude of 3500 to 4500 ft. It lies E of the Hardanger fjord and is bounded to the N by the Bergen railway. By a freak of nature, this mountain plateau which is larger than Wales, has none of the fertile valleys which usually traverse the mountain ranges of Norway, and the whole area is almost void of forests. Only on the outer fringes of the plateau can one find small valleys and wood-clad hills.

The Hardanger mountain road runs right across the plateau between Vøringfoss and Geilo. Travel by bus from Bergen to Kvanndal, ferry to Kinsarvik and by bus up the stupenduous hair-pin bends of the Måbødal to any starting point between Vøringfoss and Geilo — a day's journey of great scenic beauty. From Bergen or Oslo one can also travel by train to Finse, Ustaoset or Geilo. From Stavanger, by fjord steamer to Sand, bus to Solheimsvik, ferry to Nesflaten and bus to Breifonn or beyond in one day. Map J 400 Hardangervidda covers the whole range, and sketch map C 110 Hardangervidda gives a good summary of lodges and routes, very useful when planning itineraries.

Pony Trekking Holidays: Norwegian "fjord ponies" are available for treks across the Hardanger mountain plateau, staying at various tourist lodges en route. On these expeditions you will be accompanied by experienced guides and horsemen, who will take you safely across all obstacles. Write to DNT for further details or to West Norway Youth Hostels Association, Strandgaten 4, Bergen.

The Waterfall Excursion (map J 400 Hardangervidda): This is a fine day's outing from Odda and back. Travel by car along the fjord to Tyssedal and then up to Skjeggedal, where a cable-car whisks you up to Topp (900). Then by motor boat across lake Ringedal to the famous Tyssestrengene waterfalls with a sheer drop of about 1000 ft, also to the Skjeggedal waterfall which is equally impressive. Return by the same route. This excursion can be booked through Odda Travel Bureau, Torget, Odda. How to reach Odda' see previous chapter.

A Recommended Route (map J 400 Hardangervidda): (1) Travel by train from Bergen or Oslo to Finse, which is the highest railway station in northern Europe at 4010 ft. Stay at Finse Lodge, owned by DNT. (2) Walk to Krekja

Hårteigen — a peculiar rock massif on the Hardanger mountain plateau
(Photo: Gunnar Raabe)

Lodge in 7 hrs. (3) Walk to Stigstuv Lodge in 5 hrs. (4) To Rauhellern Lodge in 4 hrs. (5) To Sandhaug Lodge in 6 hrs. This is the central point on the plateau, and Sandhaug is also the largest lodge in the area. (6) Walk to Hallarskar Lodge in 6 hrs. (7) To Stavali Lodge in 7 hrs. (8) Descend to Kinsarvik on the fjord in 7 hrs and stay at Lofthus Youth Hostel. (9) By fjord steamer to Norheimsund and bus to Bergen, or by bus to Kinsarvik, ferry to Kvanndal and bus to Bergen.

Another Fine Route (maps K 480 Setesdal & J 400 Hardangervidda): (1) From Stavanger by fjord steamer to Sand, bus to Solheimsvik and lake ferry to Nesflaten. Stay at Nesflaten Youth Hostel. (2) By bus through the fascinating Bratlandsdal to Breifonn in 1 hr and then a walk of 2-3 hrs to Valldal Seter. (3) Walk to Litlos Lodge in 7 hrs. (4) To Sandhaug Lodge in 7 hrs. (5) To Bjoreidal Lodge in 5 hrs. (6) Walk due N for 1 hr to the mountain road, then take bus westwards, past the Vøringfoss waterfall and down the zig-zag bends of the Måbødal to Eidfjord. Stay at Eidfjord Youth Hostel. (7) Travel by bus to Kinsarvik, ferry across the fjord to Kvanndal and bus to Bergen.

Rock Climbs (map J 400 Hardangervidda): There is very little scope for rock climbs on the Hardanger mountain plateau, but there is one solitary peak which can be seen for miles in all directions: *Hårteigen* (1691) is a peculiar rock massif between Hallaskar Lodge and Litlos Lodge, rising 650 ft above the plateau. In spite of its bulky size, it affords only one route, although many attempts have been made to make new routes. 1st asc 8/1812 by N Hertzberg and C Smith, up by the NE side. From Litlos or Hallarskar, follow cairned footpath to the gorge on the NE side. Danger from falling boulders. The gully narrows higher up and a glacier tongue is encountered. There is one airy passage where a fixed rope serves as hand railing. Time from foot to top, 1 hr. The 1st winter asc was made in 3/1959 by E Bagge-Lund, O Fjellestad, J Haukås, E Myrseth and Chr Nielsen. One rope, 2 ice axes, crampons.

THE MJØLFJELL RANGES

The Mjølfjell mountain ranges are situated on either side of the Bergen railway at Mjølfjell station, southwards to the Hardanger fjord and northwards to the Sogne fjord. The scenery is an impressive combination of mountains, valleys, lakes and waterfalls. Mjølfjell is reached by train from Bergen in 3 hrs, from Oslo in 8 hrs. It is known as the "British Holiday Centre", because the popular Mjølfjell Youth Hostel draws more visitors from

Great Britain than from all other nations combined. It is one of the finest youth hostels in Norway, modern and comfortable, famous for its friendly and international atmosphere.

Mjølfjell is also a splendid centre for day excursions — such as for instance the 7 hr return trip to Skåra mountain (5200 ft); to Vosseskavl glacier and back in 9 hrs; to Øykjafonn mountain (6100 ft) in 7 hrs, and so on. Many interesting walks can also be combined with a rail journey, for instance to Reimegrend, Myrdal, Hallingskeid and Flåm, returning on foot — or vice versa. Map E 270 Flåmsdal covers the main surroundings, and C 120 Finse—Bygdin is a useful sketch map of routes and lodges in the area.

Mjølfjell—Voss (maps E 270 Flåmsdal & E 994 Vossestrand): Narrow road passable by car, or easy downhill walking all the way in 7-8 hrs. Voss is a well known tourist centre, and you should look around for a few hours and spend the night at Skulestad YH. Retur by rail the next morning.

Mjølfjell—Ulvik (maps E 270 Flåmsdal & E 935 Ulvik): Walk across the river to Urdlandstøl and up through birch scrub, past several lakes and then through Trygla Skar, which is a rugged mountain pass with magnificent surroundings. Amazing scenery with visible traces from the Ice Age. Steep descent through Fadlet into the Tyssedal and down to the Hardanger fjord at Ulvik, which is a famous tourist centre. Time about 8 hrs. Cairned footpath all the way.

Mjølfjell—Flåm (map E 270 Flåmsdal): Follow mountain road across bridge to Ljosanddal and continue through pleasant and greatly varied countryside, through a fine mountain pass and then steeply down the Flåmsdal, reaching the road about 3 miles S of Fretheim Hotel at Flåm. Time about 10-12 hrs. Bus service from Flåm to Aurland (half an hour) with a good youth hostel and several pensions.

THE FINSE—BYGDIN RANGES

Is is hard to beat the Finse—Bygdin mountain ranges when it comes to grand scenery, interesting travel and comfortable lodges. This area lies N of the Bergen railway and extends to the Sogne fjord and Jotunheimen. Its main feature is the Hallingskarv ridge, which stretches for several miles along the railway and is one of the outstanding tourist attractions on the rail journey between Bergen and Oslo.

Finse is the usual starting point. It is the highest railway station in northern Europe (4010 ft) and is reached from Bergen in 4 hrs, from Oslo in 7 hrs. Finse Lodge is entirely modern and is owned by the DNT. Many interesting walking tours can be made in this area, but there is one route in particular, which seems to be the most popular of all walking tours:

The "British route" (maps E 345 Hardangerjøkel, E 120 Aurlandsdal & E 270 Flåmsdal): (1) Travel by train from Bergen or Oslo to Finse and stay at Finse Lodge. Excursion to the "Blue Ice" glacier, 3 hrs. (2) Follow cairned footpath northwards to the right of the Finsenut (5250 ft) and walk up to St Paul, which is the western outlier of the Hallingskarv rock massif. Grand views. Avoid the Storfonn glacier by following cairns E of St Paul.

You should reach Geiterygg Lodge in 5 hrs. (3) Walk to Steinbergdal Lodge in 3 hrs and stay for lunch. Continue up and down steep slopes for another 3 hrs to Øvstebø Lodge. The scenery is indescribably grand, the track following a chain of small lakes, connected by a river which sets off a series of wonderful waterfalls. (4) Walk from Øvstebø, below the Bjørnesteg (Bear's Ladder), past the Little Hell's cave and Svartetjern (Black Tarn) and down to the Veum Lodge at Steine in 6 hrs. The scenery is most fascinating, and you are now below the tree line, with lush vegetation and many lovely mountain flowers. (5) Take local bus down to Aurland in half an hour — or walk in 2-3 hrs — to Aurland Youth Hostel or Wangen Hotel. (6) Travel by fjord steamer through Aurland fjord and the narrow Nerøy fjord to Gudvangen and then by bus up the terrific hair-pin bends of the Stalheim gorge to Skulestad Youth Hostel near Voss. (7) Continue by bus to Voss and train to Bergen or Oslo. Try this route once — and you will return to Norway for your next holiday!

Vetlehelvete cave (maps as above): This cave is very little known, but it is a real attraction on its own merit. It lies between Øvstebø and Steine (4th day on above tour), only slightly off the cairned footpath. When walking past the Black Tarn, there is a small bog to L. At its end, turn sharp L and walk for about 300 yds to the cave entrance. The "Little Hell's Cave" has been formed through centuries by a peculiar process of erosion. It consists of a large dome inside a colossal block of gneiss. The cave bottom is filled with murky still water, and the walls are smoothly polished, arched in Gothic style, leaving a narrow open space at the top, which allows a glimmer of light to penetrate into the cave.

The Hallingskarv (1933) (map J 400 Hardangervidda) stretches N of the Bergen railway between Finse and Geilo. Its top is almost flat, with a series of glaciers and snowdrifts, quite steep on most sides, particularly the S face which can be seen from the railway. The rock face is about 1000 ft in height, but in several places it is gashed by huge gaps which render easy access to the top. Only one 1st asc is recorded, namely the S face of *Tvergasteinskarv*, which was climbed in 1937 by A Næss.

The Aurland Ranges (map J 300 Aurlandsdal): *Blåskavl* (1770) is a fine snow dome NE of Aurland. From Aurland village, follow road northwards to Kvam farm and ascend by mountain path to Stegastein. Fine views. Continue towards glacier and ascend by one of western glacier tongues. The first known ascent of this glacier was made in 10/1177 by the Viking king, Sverre (1150-1202), when he lost his way between Lærdal and Voss. When descending towards Skjerdal seter, a peculiar flat stone can be seen near the path. It is called Kongshella, because king Sverre is supposed to have rested there. Time from Aurland and back, 10 hrs. Guide and rope recommended. *Honnsnipa* (1660) is a peculiar peak on the E fringe of the Blåskavl ice-cap, resembling a buck's horn. For centuries it has been used as a landmark by those walking or riding on the ancient Viking road between Aurland and Lærdal. Surveyor's cairn.

JOTUNHEIMEN

What the Lake District means to the British and the Yosemite Valley to the Americans, that is what Jotunheimen means to the Norwegians — an enormous expanse of mountains, glaciers, highlands, valleys, lakes and waterfalls. There are peaks rising to over 8000 ft — the real "Home of the Giants". Jotunheimen has over 60 glaciers and more than 250 peaks over 6000 ft in height. It is ideal country for walking tours, rock climbs and glacier walks, facilitated by a great number of good tourist lodges.

Jotunheimen lies E of the Sogne fjord and is reached easily in one day from Bergen or Oslo. Several routes lead into Jotunheimen, but most visitors seem to prefer the route by fjord steamer from Bergen to Hermansverk and then by bus to any starting point on the Sognefjell

road — Norway's highest mountain pass — such as
Turtagrø, Elveseter or Røysheim. From Oslo, the Sognefjell road is reached by train to Otta and then by bus.

Visit the Giants (maps E 550 Lom, E 305 Gjende, E 775 Sjodalen, E 965
Vangsmjøsi): This is a popular walking tour, which includes the two highest
peaks in Norway. (1) Start from Røysheim Hotel on the Sognefjell road, the
first few miles by jeep, and walk to Spiterstul Lodge at the head of a valley
with a profusion of sharp peaks and ridges, black rock walls, white snow and
blue ice all around. (2) Scramble to the very top of Galdhøpiggen (8095 ft)
in 4 hrs and return to Spiterstul. (3) Walk to Glitterheim Lodge in 5 hrs
direct — or spend an extra 2-3 hrs on ascending the Glittertind (8010 ft)
on the way to Glitterheim. (4) Walk to Gjendesheim Lodge in 8 hrs. (5)
Follow Peer Gynt's route across Besseggen ridge, fantastic views, to Memurubu Lodge in 5-6 hrs. You can send your rucksack by motor boat from
Gjendesheim to Memurubu. (6) Walk to Gjendebu Lodge in 6 hrs — or
travel by motor boat. (7) Walk to Eidsbugaren Hotel in 5 hrs. (8) Return
by bus to Lærdal and express steamer to Bergen, or by bus to Fagernes and
train to Oslo.

Three Glaciers in One Day (map E 305 Gjende):This grand route starts from
Leirvassbu Lodge, which is reached by car from Elveseter Hotel on the
Sognefjell road. Walk via Leirhaug (1657) and ascend to Leirløyftet, which is
the col between 2113 and 2162. Through the col and across the S Illå glacier
to col 2053, which leads to Bukkehol glacier. Follow its W fringe in a northerly direction and cross over to the Tverrå glacier between 2168 and 2149.
Walk across Tverrå glacier, aiming at the col between 2309 and 2166, but
turn right before reaching it, and follow the N fringe of the glacier, down to
Tverrådalen and onwards to the Spiterstul Lodge. A safe route on level
glaciers. Time, 9-10 hrs. Rope required and guide recommended.

THE HURRUNGANE GROUP (map E 870 Sygnefjell)
is a grand rock massif of majestic peaks, jagged ridges
and glistening glaciers. There is good rock climbing on
perfect gabbro rock, and several popular rock climbs
are well cairned, thus making these climbs ideal for
parties of some experience wishing to learn guideless
climbing. Turtagrø Hotel on the Sognefjell road is the
most popular starting point. If setting out before 8 am,
most expeditions should be completed before nightfall.
The best season is from July 15 to Aug 15 — or later.
Guides may be available at Turtagrø Hotel, which also
operates the "Norwegian Climbing school".

Old reports are confusing by referring to the "hut" as starting point for
many routes, because there are really two huts — the Skagastøl hut by
the first lake in the Skagastøl valley, reached in 2 hrs from Turtagrø, owned
by Norsk Tindeklub (NTK) and available to members only, and the Bandet
hut (Skagastølsbu) at the foot of Store Skagastølstind, owned by the Norwegian Touring Club (DNT). The latter hut has now been rebuilt and is
well equipped, but is rather small and often full in mid-season. The hut is
locked, but DNT members may get the key from Turtagrø Hotel.

Nordre Skagastølstind (2168) is the northernmost peak on
the Skagastøl ridge. 1st asc 7/1820 by C P B Boeck and
B M Keilhau, up by the NW ridge. Follow cairned
footpath from Turtagrø, but turn L at the first Skagastøl tarn and follow the NW ridge to the top. Steep
scramble, magnificent views. Time, 4 hrs up, 3 down.
Its E face also provides an easy scramble. The 1st winter
asc of Nordre and Nebbet was made in 1959 by A R
Heen, I Huse and B Ugelvik.

Midtre Skagastølstind (2286): Its N ridge from Nordre runs across a subsidiary peak called *Nebbet*, whose S wall forms the spectacular *V-Gap*. The S wall of this gap is about 250 ft high, topped by a remarkably flat rock platform called *Berges Stol*, of some 200 sq yds. Steep crags lead from Berges Stol to Midtre's summit. Its S ridge towards Vesle Skagastølstind includes 5 peaklets, each separated by a small col. This ridge is narrow and offers magnificent resistance — particularly in two places: *Halls Hammer* is an absolutely vertical crag of 25 ft which blocks the ridge. It was climbed in 1905 by E Ullen. *Patchells Sva* is a smooth slab which is crossed in order to avoid Halls Hammer. The 1st asc of Midtre was made in 8/1884 by C Hall, M Soggemoen and Vetti, up by the NW face from Skagastøl glacier. C Hall and Matias also climbed it in 7/1894 by the S ridge from Vesle Skagastølstind, abseiling Halls Hammer into the gap, a traverse of 2 hrs. The E face from Styggedal glacier was climbed in 8/1897 by C E Ashford, H Kempson and O Øiene, thus avoiding the long walk up rough scree which leads to the NW face. The N ridge from Nordre was climbed in 8/1900 by Wm C Slingsby, E Sundt, O Berge and E Hogrenning. The same party also made a descent from the V-gap to the Styggedal glacier. A new route from Skagastøl glacier via Halls Hammer was made in 1942 by E Kierulf and L Onsager, a severe route which should not be chosen in the ordinary way.

Midtre by NW Face from Skagastøl Glacier — Up by lower part of gully below V-gap, then turn R and climb chimney. Up steep smooth slab with small crack. From top of this slab (Nils Hammer), turn L, up on easy ledges to ridge just S of summit. Time from glacier to top, 4 hrs. When descending, be sure to get into gully below V-gap, as gully below Nils Hammer is difficult further down.

Midtre by E Face from Styggedal Glacier — Cut up steep slope to avoid ice-swept rocks at bottom and then follow R buttress of 2 buttresses which strike arete S of summit.

Midtre by N Ridge from Nordre — Follow ridge across Nebbet and descend into V-gap. Climb up S wall to good belay, then horizontally to R and over easier rock to Berges Stol, then follow L side of ridge to Midtre. Time 1½ hrs.

Vesle Skagastølstind (2325) is a summit ridge, only 7 — 8 ft wide, from the highest point of which a gradually sloping ridge stretches E to Centraltind, whereas the main ridge continues S to a col named *Mohns Skar*, which lies below the summit of Storen. Vesle was cairned in 8/1885 by C Hall and Matias, climbing the S arete from Mohns Skar, a strenuous climb but no real difficulty. Its N ridge from Midtre was traversed in 8/1896 by H C Bowen, C W Patchell and J Vigdal. A slight variation was made in 1901 by T Bertheau, G Pauss, K Tandberg, O Berge and P Bjerk. The NE face from Styggedal glacier was climbed in 7/1902 by J Lowrey and O Øiene,

Store Skagastølstind — the finest gem of the Hurrung group
(Photo: NTK)

following snow and ice patches from glacier to top. Favourable snow conditions are essential for this route. The 1st winter asc of Vesle was made in Easter 1960 by A R Heen, O Mork and B Ugelvik, from Mohns Skar.

Vesle by N Ridge from Midtre — Traverse from Midtre across 4 subsidiary peaks to Halls Hammer. Climb round its L corner, descend to small platform and then another 5 ft down to roomy step. Traverse across Patchells Sva and continue horizontally to broken chimney which leads up to ridge just S of Halls Hammer. Finally by easy rock to top. Time, 2 hrs.

Store Skagastølstind (2405) is the finest gem of the Hurrung group, a real "must" for all rock climbers. This outstanding peak is crowned by twin summits, of which the northern is called Slingsbys Fortopp. Storen was cairned on July 21, 1876, by Wm C Slingsby. He was accompanied by E Mohn to Mohns Skar. This ascent made climbing history in Norway. Although the usual route now differs from Slingsby's line of ascent, it is still a good climb. The present "highway" from Hjørnet offers several alternatives which were explored as follows: Heftyes Renne in 8/1880 by J T Heftye, J Klingenberg and P Melheim; Vigdals Sva in 7/1890 by Johannes Vigdal; Andrews Renne in 8/1899 by A W Andrews, O K Williamson and O Berge; Tandbergs Renne in 7/1903 by T Bertheau, K Tandberg and E Ullen; Sørvestveien in 7/1904 by E & O Rostrup, H Tønsberg and E Ullen; Ullens Veg in 8/1904 by T Bertheau, E Ullen and S Williams, and the W ridge in 1935 by A Næss and H Tønsberg.

The NW wall from Skagastøl glacier was climbed in 8/1904 by E Ullen and K Fortun. This route leads up to Mohns Skar and thence to the top by the usual route. Nordvestveien was made in 1906 by Tandberg and Rostrup, a fine climb of 4000 ft. The 1st winter asc was made in 3/1923 by F Lorentzen and B Schlytter, up by Andrews Renne and down via Heftyes Renne. The S face from Slingsby glacier was climbed in 7/1927 by O H Furuseth, A Gunneng and B Schlytter. This steep and almost overhanging face has been compared with that of Grepon, and it yields fine sport on firm rock, except on the first couple of rope lengths. The W buttress was climbed in 1927 by E Jensen, C W Ruben. son and E Sundt. It provides an alternative to the first part of the usual route to Hjørnet. Slingsbys Fortopp was climbed by its NW wall in 1935 by O H Furuseth, A Næss and H Tønsberg, and its NW ridge was climbed in 1943 by B Christiansen and E Hoff Hansen.

Storen by Slingsby's Route — From Bandet hut at foot of Storen, descend glacier towards Midtmaradal to distinct gallery which leads to Slingsby glacier. Step cutting may be required occasionally in its upper parts towards Mohns Skar. If there is little snow, keep close to wall below Centraltind. From Mohns Skar, follow ridge to top, first keeping R, afterwards L. Time from hut to top, 5 hrs. At least 2 ice axes.

Storen from Hjørnet — From Bandet hut, follow cairned footpath near precipice above Skagastøl glacier. Avoid keeping too far to R, where you may get stuck on steep slabs. After nearly 1¹/₂ hrs' easy climbing, you will reach a broad ledge which leads to R, below the highest and steepest part of peak. The ledge terminates at Hjørnet (corner) where you get first glimpse of Slingsby glacier. This corner should not be confused with another which is situated 450 ft lower down. Alternative routes from Hjørnet: *Via Heftyes Renne* — After short and steep ascent from Hjørnet, traverse R, on to E face above Slingsby glacier. Continue along gallery and up 2 steep slopes to conspicuous ledge. Heftyes Renne begins as a narrow crack 9 ft up a smooth vertical face above this ledge. Difficult to get into chimney without help. Easiest to climb when facing R side of chimney. Then on to wide ledge. Follow distinct depression to S summit. Across small but steep gap and up to final top. Time from hut to top, 3-4 hrs. The chimney is v. diff. *Via Ullens Veg* — This variation leads up by the face between Heftyes Renne and Vigdals Sva. It is more difficult than the other variations and is seldom used. *Via Vigdals Sva* — From Hjørnet to ledge below Heftyes Renne. Traverse 9 ft L across Vigdals Sva (steep slab) to bottom of steep gully. Vigdals Sva is severe, and knee friction has to make up for absence of footholds. The handhold is none too good and is frequently wet, if not iced. The gully above Vigdals Sva is 25 ft high and affords good holds. At top of gully,

25

Heftye's and Vigdal's routes converge on wide ledge. Time from hut to top, 3-4 hrs. *Via Andrews Renne* — On the way to Hjørnet, turn sharp L when 80 ft below Hjørnet and follow depression which leads to well-defined chimney called Andrews Renne. It leads straight up to small gap between both summits. The climb commences on L side of chimney, but after 50 ft cross over to R and continue to top. Steep but with good holds. Time from hut to top, 3-4 hrs. *Via W Ridge* — From Hjørnet, follow route via Andrews Renne until about 350 ft below Andrews Renne, then traverse westwards to W ridge which is followed for 3 rope lengths to steep crag. Up through centre of crag to small sloping shelf. Good belay. Follow shelf 10 ft towards R and then easy to top. Time, 2 hrs. 3 belays. V. diff. *Via Tandbergs Renne* — From Hjørnet to ledge below Heftyes Renne. Turn R, up on slabs to steep short gully (Tandbergs Renne) which leads to easier rocks. The gully itself is too narrow to be climbed, but there is a little jagged ridge to L of it, up which the ascent is fairly comfortable, although steep and airy. *Via Sørvestveien* (SW Arete) — From Hjørnet, up 2 steep pitches to foot of large block. Climb up it either by its L corner or by crack between block and peak or by small ledges and cracks in R corner. Continue L from block, over slab with poor holds, then straight up over small rock. Continue upwards on L side of slab, into hollow behind large rock. From hollow, follow steep chimney straight up to S summit. Time from hut to top, 3-4 hrs. 80 ft rope.

Storen by NW Wall from Skagastøl Glacier — From Skagastøl glacier below permanent snow patch on NW wall, follow scree ledges towards snow patch. Up on snow for about 200 ft, then take ridge to R and follow it towards upper section of snow gully. Cross it just above snow and climb to R, up by distinct ledges and cracks to a corner. Turn sharp L, crossing small snow patch to foot of steep wall below Mohns Skar. Climb up crack between large blocks to ridge, which is reached 100 ft S of Mohns Skar. Time from glacier to Mohns Skar, 3 hrs. At least 1 ice axe.

Storen by Nordvestveien — From Skagastøl glacier, follow a ridge on L side of big snow patch, from top of which a distinct gully (usually wet) leads to foot of large slabs. Try to follow bottom of gully, but if ice-filled, climb its R side. Above gully, some slabs afford various routes. Start preferably to R, up steep chimney, good belay 80 ft up. Move slightly towards L, then up by short steep crack to foot of long chimney which leads directly to summit ridge. Do not climb this chimney, but climb 80 ft up slightly to R, then turn L across distinct square-cut ledges, back to chimney. Cross it and follow wide sloping slab which leads to summit ridge between both tops. Time from glacier to top, 3-5 hrs. 80 ft rope per man.

Storen by S Face from Slingsby Glacier — From Bandet hut to Slingsby glacier to a point between 2 long parallel chimneys. Cross slopes to foot of R chimney, which is climbed 80 ft to hollow below overhanging slabs. Leftwards to stone block. Good belay. Traverse 50 ft on grassy ledges to small platform (1 sq ft). Belay. Climb 8 ft straight up, then across to L into bottom of chimney. 20 ft straight up chimney to big block. Belay. Follow bottom of chimney 35 ft up to steep boulder which blocks chimney. Past boulder to large sloping plateau below overhanging slabs. Turn R from upper side of plateau, cross chimney and traverse 80 ft round sharp corner into big gully which leads towards Hjørnet. Straight up ridge on L. Follow bottom of gully for 300 ft, then leave gully and continue upwards to R on wide ledges and blocks to upper part of light grey patch, visible from glacier. Upwards to R, across steep slabs and up steep airy chimney. From its top, ascend steep slab with handholds in small cracks to R, under large overhanging rocks. Go round these into steep partly overhanging chimney which leads right up to summit ridge. Follow chimney for 200 ft, then turn R and on to big yellow slab. From its top, it is easy to reach summit ridge between both tops. Time from glacier to top, 5-7 hrs. At least 1 ice axe. 80 ft rope per man. Severe.

Storen by W Buttress — When starting from Skagastøl glacier, the route lies up the first prominent buttress to R of the cliff to R of NW ridge. The buttress is about 600 ft high and provides a severe climb of 4 hrs. There is some snow and ice on it. The route starts up the centre for 100 ft, then up to R flank for a further 100 ft. After crossing over to L, it continues up on L to 100 ft from buttress top, where a steep rake is followed up round buttress to top on R. Except for the first pitch on R, the rock is sound and the route is recommended as an excellent climb. (Report from S Stewart Orr). Very severe.

Slingsbys Fortopp by NW Wall — Follow route by NW wall from Skagastøl glacier until the climb commences under steep slabs. Turn L towards projecting buttress (Knatten). Traverse L to small ditch below little crag. Straight up (belays) and then leftwards to chimney which is followed to L edge of large shelf. 2 rope lengths up to slab to L of chimney. Follow chimney until it terminates below crag which is bypassed to L. Belay. Then straight up to top. Time, 3 hrs. 15 belays. Solid rock and safe route. 2 very severe pitches.

Slingsbys Fortopp by NW Ridge — This route leads mainly by the ridge from Skagastøl glacier and right up to top. It lies considerably more towards N than the route by the NW wall. Good belays. Partly loose rocks in lower section. Severe.

THE STYGGEDALSTINDER (2387) This fine ridge stretches eastwards from the Skagastøl ridge with 3 peaks and a skar. *Centraltind* (2347) is usually included in a number of different routes. Three grand ridges radiate from its summit. It was cairned in 8/1885 by C Hall, T Sulheim and M Soggemoen, ascending by the W ridge from Vesle Skagastølstind. This is the ridge which separates Styggedal glacier from Slingsby glacier. The traverse from Styggedalstind is also quite easy, and ascents have been made from Slingsby glacier as well as from Maradal glacier. The 1st winter asc was made from Mohns Skar in Easter 1960 by A R Heen, O Mork and B Ugelvik, probably the most tricky winter asc which can be made in Jotunheimen.

Styggedalstind (2387): 1st asc 8/1883 by C Hall and Matias by the S (N ?) face from Gjertvass glacier. This route is no longer used. The W ridge was climbed from Centraltind in 8/1885 by the same party in 1 hour. The E ridge was climbed from Gjertvass Skar in 8/1888 by M S Green, T Sulheim and A Eide. The S face was climbed from Maradal glacier in 1906 by E Ullen and K Fortun. The NW ridge was climbed in 8/1911 by V Jacob and H F Reid in 5—6 hrs from Turtagrø. At least 1 ice axe.

Gjertvass Skar is the gap between Styggedalstind and Gjertvasstind, connecting Gjertvass glacier with Maradal glacier, but whereas the former lies almost level with the skar, the latter lies some 2000 ft below the skar and is reached by a narrow snow gully. The upper section of Gjertvass glacier is very steep and rather crevassed. The skar can be reached from either glacier only under favourable snow conditions. 1 ice axe per man. Severe. 1st passage from Maradal to Gjertvass glacier in 8/1887 by C Hall and Matias.

Gjertvasstind (2352) was cairned in 7/1876 by Wm C Slingsby, E Mohn and K Lykken, up by the E ridge from Gjertvassnosi. The ridge is broad and easy. The W ridge was climbed from Gjertvass Skar in 1901 by T Bertheau, G Pauss, K Tandberg, O Berge and P Bjerk. At least 2 ice axes. A descent by the W ridge to Gjertvass Skar was made in 7/1891 by J J Hoddinot, T Sulheim and K Furås, but this is difficult and varies greatly with snow and ice conditions. The 1st winter asc was made in 4/1953 by E Bakke and A R Heen, up by the E ridge.

THE MARADALSTINDER (1958): This is probably the most difficult ridge in the Hurring group. In contrast to the more popular ridges, it is not much frequented by climbers, and it is very likely that unfinished work may still be found here. Carl Hall once said that "when everything else has been done, the Maradal ridge will still be there!" The *Nordre Maradalstinder* are a series of pinnacles on the N end of the ridge between Centraltind and Jernskartind. The traverse is easy in either direction. This ridge also affords a handy passage between Slingsby glacier and Maradal glacier. 1st asc 8/1890 by C Hall and Matias. *Jernskartind* (1958) is the highest point on the ridge. 1st asc 7/1904 by E Ullen and K Fortun, up by the SE ridge from *Jern Skar*, which is the large gap that separates Jernskartind from Kjerringa, facilitating the passage between Midtmaradal and Maradal glaciers. A very long chimney leads from Midtmaradal to Jern Skar.

Jernskartind by SE Ridge from Jern Skar — From the skar, follow gently sloping slabs towards L side of steep wall to vertical 15 ft high wall. Hand-holds in vertical cracks. Up another slab with vertical cracks to foot of overhanging wall. Good belay round rock flake. Traverse R, across slab into very steep chimney, the upper part of which is overhanging. Up chimney to roofed ledge below overhanging rock. Continue a little to R on wall above Maradal glacier, then up easier ledges and a slanting chimney to top. Time from gap to top, 1 hr. Severe. When descending, traverse ridge to Central-tind and follow gallery which leads down to Slingsby glacier. Time, 2 hrs. At least 1 ice axe.

Kjerringa (1938) was cairned in 7/1889 by F de Chazal, T Sulheim and J Urdahl, up by the NW ridge from Jern Skar. The SE ridge from Maradal Skar was climbed in 8/1908 by F Schjelderup, K & A Fortun. This is the trickiest part of the ridge. *Maradal Skar* is the deep gap between Kjerringa and Mannen. It is very steep and is 430 ft high. 1st asc from Midtmaradal 7/1904 by E Ullen, T Bertheau, J C Procter and K Fortun. A better route which leads up straight through the gorge was made in 1933 by A R Heen and K Oshaug. It was reached from Maradal glacier in 8/1911 by R P Bicknell, K Field and P Bjerk. There are 3 formidable bergschrunds, above which a long couloir leads to the top. Skogadalsbøen Lodge is the best starting point.

Kjerringa by SE Ridge from Maradal Skar — From bottom of skar, ascend 80 ft straight up on small ledges, then a long traverse to R on grassy ledges. Around corner on lowest ledge. Into short chimney up to good belay. Up another long, steep, rotten chimney. Good belay at top. Ascend 50 ft straight up and a little to L to large block. Good belay. Balancing 30 ft to L on narrow ledge to projecting rock. Continue up grass tufts to small horizontal crack which runs across wall to L. Spacious grass ledge on other side. Around small corner to L and up to small plateau. Up crag to L, up to roomy ledge with Raeburn's cairn. Turn R, along ledge and then 80 ft straight up to hollow, whence short steep chimney leads to top. Time from gap to top, 3-4 hrs. Rotten rocks in lower part. Severe.

Mannen (1951) is the southernmost peak on the ridge. 1st asc 8/1885 by R L Harrison, R Starr, C & H Wilson, T Sulheim, J Vigdal and L Jensen, up from Skogadals-bøen. The S face was climbed from Midtmaradal in 7/1903 by T Bertheau, K Tandberg, E Ullen, O Berge and K Fortun. The same party descended into Maradal Skar (severe) and then returned to the top via the NW ridge in 1 hr. Mannen was also reached from Maradal Skar via the NE corner in 1929 by S Løvenskiold, B Schlytter and H Tønsberg. Severe. The SE arete was climbed in 7/1956 by J H Barber and C A Simpson. Severe. They descended by the E face, made difficult by narrow grassy ledges and steep slabs.

Mannen by NE Face — Up by the NE angle of the terminal peak, diagonally up the NE face by steep rocks.

Mannen by S Face from Midtmaradal — From Bandet hut, descend into Midtmaradal, turn L, down a gully and continue to L, keeping well above steep smooth slabs. Time is saved by going all the way to bottom of valley, which follow short way down and turn gradually to L across foot of Mannen. Go round to S face which is climbed easily. Time from hut to top, 4 hrs.

Mannen from Maradal Skar — From bottom of skar, climb up sloping rocks to NW ridge which follow to top. Time 1 hr. The variation via NE corner leads up by a sloping ledge on NE corner for 1/2 rope length. Don rubbers. Then a steep climb up wall to top. Exposed route, but safe and solid rock. Time, 2 hrs. Severe.

Mannen by SE Arete — Start from foot of true arete (cairn). Slabs and flakes are climbed for 60 ft to small ledge. Traverse R, below awkward bulge to vertical open crack which is climbed to large ledge with good belay, below two vertical cracks. Climb R crack, then follow easier rock to junction of snow gully with arete crest (cairn). Broken rocks lead for about 200 ft to terrace below steep wall, marked at its extreme right by wet black rocks. A vertical crack and wall is climbed from cairn at extreme L of this terrace to good stance below 12 ft vertical chimney. Climb strenuous chimney or traverse R on slightly higher ledge and then upwards to L over smooth slabs to good belay. Thereafter the route is indefinite and easier. Time from foot to top, 2½ hrs. Severe. (Report from J H Barber).

THE DYRHAUGSTINDER (2149): This is a long and fine ridge with 3 distinct peaks and several lesser summits, S of Turtagrø. The traverse affords an interesting expedition of several hours with splendid views to both sides. The middle section of the ridge is very narrow with huge precipices to left and right. Søre Dyrhaugstind affords best sport.

Nordre Dyrhaugstind (2149) was cairned in 7/1820 by G Bohr, climbing the NW ridge. Time, 7 hrs from Turtagrø and back. Time may be saved by following the W bank of the stream issuing from Skagastølsdalen for some distance before climbing on to the NW ridge. The 1st asc of *Midtre Dyrhaugstind* (2134) was made in 8/1884 by C Hall and Matias Soggemoen, traversing from Nordre. Its N face from Skagastøl glacier was climbed in 1915 by A B Bryn and K Hanssen. Favourable snow conditions are essential for this route. The NE ridge from Skagastøl glacier was climbed in 8/1932 by A M Greenwood, J A Ramsay and E A Wedderburn. Time from foot to top, 3 hrs.

Søre Dyrhaugstind (2014): 1st asc 8/1886 by C Hall and Matias, up by the SW face from Riings glacier, following a tongue of snow to a shallow gully between Berges Skar and the summit. Its S face from Bandet was climbed in 8/1895 by C W Patchell, J Simpson and J Vigdal, now the usual route. The S face offers several interesting variations — (a) via Raeburns Sva, 8/1902 by G Pauss, H Raeburn and K Tandberg, following a narrow crack from the point where the S ridge joins the S face; (b) via Tønsbergs Hylle, 7/1905) by S Malm and H Tønsberg by an unsafe ledge which leads slightly upwards across the S face from the knee which seams the E ridge to the main peak; and (c) from Midtmaradal glacier, 1935 by A Næss and H Tønsberg, starting by the easternmost of 2 vertical cracks which can be seen clearly from the glacier. The large N face also affords various routes from the Skagastøl glacier, but favourable snow conditions are always essential: (1) via Ullens Route, 1906 by J Procter and E Ullen, up from the NE face by very steep ice slopes on the W side of huge outlier; (2) via Schlytters Route, 7/1932 by M Hansen, A Næss and B Schlytter, from a gorge which lies somewhat to the left of the distinct arete which stretches from the glacier to the top; (3) via Næss' Route, 1936 by E Holter and A Næss. This route leads up the sharpest arete between the usual route and the gorge where Schlytter's route commences. Strictly for ironmongers.

Søre Dyrhaugstind by S Face from Bandet (usual route) — From Bandet, follow broad and easy E ridge to foot of steep S wall. Follow ledge for 9 ft to L and climb up 25 ft high steep chimney to another ledge. Belay. Another chimney, but steeper and more difficult, leads up to wide ledge which is followed slantwise to R. Keep L and ascend to corner under large crag which is climbed, alternatively bypassed through easy chimney to L. Above crag, work about 60 ft horizontally towards L over a nose and around a sharp corner to small platform. Up steep and short chimney to ledge and follow steep crack to another but narrow ledge, 35 ft long. Follow this till within 7 ft of its end, then turn sharp L, across steep slab to foot of 6 ft high overhanging crag whose top affords good holds. Then easy to top through small chimneys. Time from Bandet to top, 2-3 hrs. 80 ft rope per man.

THE MIDTMARADALSTINDER (2063):

This fine ridge is separated from Søre Dyrhaugstind by Berges Skar and runs SE between Midtmaradal and Stølsmaradal glaciers. It affords interesting sport, suitable to novices and experts alike. *Berges Skar* is a difficult pass between Søre Dyrhaugstind and Nordre Midtmaradalstind. A steep couloir of 300 ft in height and at least 60 degrees in its upper part leads from Midtmaradal glacier up to the skar. This couloir is called *Berges Renne*. 1st descent 8/1899 by A W Andrews, A H Fox-Strangways and O Berge. Descent by the W side from Berges Skar in 8/1899 by A W Andrews, O K Williamson and O Berge, 1st asc by Berges Renne to Berges Skar and descent to Riings glacier in 1915 by K Hanssen and M S Manner. A rock fall in the upper part of Berges Renne has now made it virtually impossible to move about without dislodging loose rocks. There is, however, an overhanging rock at the top of the snow tongue and a large chockstone just over 100 ft further up, and by belaying to pitons beneath these two in turn, the climb can be completed without the second man being endangered by falling rock. (Report from R E Kendell). 120 ft rope, time 2 hrs, difficult.

Nordre Midtmaradalstind (2063) was cairned in 8/1886 by C Hall and Matias by the N ridge from Berges Skar. Time from Bandet hut to top, 3 hrs. From top via Riings glacier to Turtagrø, 3 hrs. The W face was climbed from Riings glacier in 1910 by A B Bryn, S Mortensen and F Schjelderup. Time from Turtagrø to top, 4 hrs. The E face from Midtmaradal glacier was climbed in 1910 by A B Bryn, K Hanssen and G N Sabro. An asc by Østkanten from Midtmaradal glacier was made in 1935 by O H Furuseth and A Næss, using 30 pitons in 5 hrs from glacier to top. *Nålene* are 4 pinnacles between Nordre and Lav Skar, facing a precipice of 1100 ft above the Midtmaradal. The 1st asc from Lav Skar and traverse of the pinnacles was made in 1906 by J C Procter, E & O Rostrup. The northernmost pinnacle was climbed direct from Midtmaradal glacier in 1938 by E Næss, K Tandberg and B Walther. *Lav Skar* is the lowest gap on the ridge between Nålene and Store Midtmaradalstind, affording easy passage between Midtmaradal and Stølsmaradal glaciers. 1st traverse 8/1887 by C Hall and Matias.

Store Midtmaradalstind (2057): 1st asc 8/1886 by C Hall and T Sulheim, up by the SW face from Stølsmaradal glacier. The NW arete from Lav Skar was climbed in 8/1897 by C C & R P Bicknell and O Berge. This route bypasses the high overhanging wall which is called the Hammer, but a variation was made in 7/1901 by E Rostrup and K Fortun by climbing the E face of the Hammer. The SE ridge was climbed in 7/1907 by M Hansen, H Tønsberg, N Vetti and Falch, following the crest of the ridge all the way. The E wall was climbed from Midtmaradal glacier in 7/1908 by A B Bryn, C Saxlund and H Tønsberg. This wall is extremely steep and rises from the glacier to the top in an almost unbroken sheet of slabs. Severe. The 1st winter asc was made from the S in 1958 by A Bekkelund, A R Heen and B Ugelvik.

Store Midtmaradalstind by NW Arete from Lav Skar — From Lav Skar, follow crest of ridge as far as a high wall about 300 ft from top. This is bypassed on the Stølsmaradal side by descending a gully for 80 ft and then turning L along ledges to a couloir which leads up to regain the ridge about 200 ft below summit. From here, straight along ridge to top. Rope only needed while bypassing high wall. Time from Lav Skar, 2 hrs up, 1½ hrs down. (Report from R. E Kendell).

View from the top of Søre Dyr-haugstind towards Store Midtmaradalstind (Photo: Oppi)

Store Midtmaradalstind by E Wall from Midtmaradal Glacier — From Bandet hut, walk across Midtmaradal glacier towards its highest crest below Store Midt-maradalstind. Leave snow slightly to L of its highest point and ascend by wide gully to L. From its top, traverse 150 ft to L and pass below 2 small snow patches. Turn straight up on L side of 2nd snow patch to large slabs which are climbed towards L. Up to distinct gallery, slantwise to corner above Midtmaradal, around overhanging rock to large sloping plateau, where several chimneys lead straight up. Follow westernmost chimney for 15 ft, then turn R, through small tunnel which terminates in narrow slanting ledge. Severe and airy, but good and safe belays. The ledge ends below 2 snow slopes towards small glacier below summit. Turn sharp R and follow broad ledges to top. Time from glacier to top, 3-5 hrs. 80 ft rope per man. At least 1 ice axe.

THE RIINGSTINDER (2124) are situated immediately W of the Midtmaradalstinder, reached from Turtagrø by way of Riings valley and up Riings glacier. At least 1 ice axe is required when climbing any of the Riings-tinder. *Austre Riingstind* (2004) connects with the Midt-maradalstinder to the E. It was cairned in 1891 by A Andrews and J Urdahl, up by the W ridge from Riings Skar. Time from Turtagrø to top, 8 hrs. The NE ridge was climbed in 1908 by B & T Kroepelien and F Schjel-derup. This ridge can be reached without difficulty from Nordre Midtmaradalstind or from Riings or Stølsmaradal glaciers. *Riings Skar* is the large gap between Midtre and Austre Riingstind, affording passage between Riings and Stølsmaradal glaciers. 1st passage 1874 by A Dew-hurst, G Girdlestone, Wm C Slingsby and W Worsley.

Midtre Riingstind (2026) connects with Viking Skar and Stølsmaradalstind to the S. It was cairned in 8/1878 by F R Green, H G Willink and J Vigdal by the W face from Gravdal Skar in 8 hrs from Turtagrø. The E face was climbed from Riings Skar in 8/1894 by H Congreve, G H Goodman, Wm C Slingsby and C Todd. A variation was made in 1907 by B Kroepelien and H Tønsberg. The 1st winter asc was made in Easter 1962 by A R Heen and Bodil Roland.

Midtre Riingstind by E Face from Riings Skar — Climb straight up from skar until just below top, then turn towards R and climb straight up. When descending, follow S ridge for about 90 ft to cairn on L and then straight down on ledges on E face until joining E ridge. Time from Turtagrø to top, 8 hrs.

Gravdal Skar lies immediately below the E face of Store
Riingstind, separating Riings glacier from Gravdal glacier. 1st passage 8/1908 by Wm C Slingsby and party.
Store Riingstind (2124) has a spectacular W arete from
Solei Skar which has never been climbed, although
attempts have been made. The summit ridge is 150 ft
long with 5 or 6 lesser points. 1st asc 8/1890 by C Hall
and O Berge, up by the SE ridge from Gravdal Skar.
Time from skar to top, 1 hr. Its S face from Gravdal
glacier was climbed in 7/1892 by B Goodfellow, J J Hoddinot, E J Woolley and T Sulheim. A gully runs up the
S face and joins the SW ridge about 100 ft below the
top. Time from glacier to top, 3 hrs. The 1st winter asc
was made in Easter 1944 by H C Bugge and B Schlytter,
on skis to the top. The W wall was climbed from Berdal
glacier in 1944 by H C Bugge and A R Heen. The route
leads up on small ledges with solid rock. Time from foot
to top, 2 hrs.

STØLSMARADALSTIND (2028) is a twin-capped peak S
of the Riingstinder. *Viking Skar* is the wide gap between
Midtre Riingstind and Stølsmaradalstind, connecting
Gravdal glacier with Stølsmaradal glacier. 1st passage
8/1878 by F R Green, H G Willink and J Vigdal. The 1st
asc of *Stølsmaradalstind* (2028) was made in 7/1891 by
J J Hoddinot, T Sulheim and K Furås by the SW ridge
from Gravdal glacier. Descent either by the same route
or by the SE ridge to Stølsmaradal glacier. The NW
ridge was climbed from Viking Skar in 9/1899 by A W
Andrews, O K Williamson and O Berge. A variation was
made in 1909 by A B Bryn, B & T Kroepelien, C W
Rubenson, C Saxlund and F Schjelderup. This is one of
the few places in the Hurrung group where the rocks are
really rotten. Time from Turtagrø and back, 10 hrs.
The 1st winter asc was made in Easter 1912 by W Eger,
C Saxlund, F Schjelderup and A Fortun.

THE SOLEITINDER (2082) are 3 peaks on a fine ridge
which makes ideal "first days climbs" from Turtagrø.
The traverse of Nordre and Store is a good expedition
for beginners. The usual route to *Nordre Soleitind* (2030)
lies up an extension of its NW ridge, which leads to a
narrow level section separated from the summit by a
gap, reached by descending a loose but easy pitch of 50
ft. From this gap it is usual to bypass Nordre's summit
by easy ledges on its W face, which lead to a col between
Nordre and Store. The descent to this col from Nordre
looks difficult. The true NE ridge is a snow ridge abutting
the narrow section of the NW ridge and ending in a steep

buttress which is bounded on its SE by a snow gully which leads to the narrow section of Nordre, and on its R by a high corrie (cairn). The corrie is best reached by following the Riings Skar track on the E bank of the stream, crossing the stream near the glacier snout and ascending a gully filled with fallen boulders (report from E A Bridle). The snow gully which leads to the narrow section of Nordre was climbed in 7/1902 by G Pauss, H Raeburn and K Tandberg. The E face was climbed from Riings glacier in 1908 by N Backer Grøndahl and F Schjelderup, descending by the W face to Solei glacier. The 1st winter asc was made in Easter 1911 by H Bugge and F Schjelderup.

Store (or Midtre) *Soleitind* (2082) was cairned in 8/1888 by M S Green, T Sulheim and K Furås, up by the SW face from Berdal glacier. The NE ridge via Nordre was climbed in 8/1894 by E V Mather, C W Patchell, J Simpson and J Vigdal. Time from Turtagrø and back, 9-10 hrs. *Søre Soleitind* (2049) rises between Store Soleitind and Solei Skar. It has been climbed. *Solei Skar* is a grand glacier and rock pass between Søre Soleitind and Store Riingstind, affording the one and only direct passage between Riings and Berdal glaciers. 1st passage 8/1899 by A W Andrews, O K Williamson and O Berge. As the Riings glacier has receded considerably during the last 50 years, the ascent of the skar is now a real climb.

THE AUSTABOTTINDER (2203) are situated S of the Soleitinder. The usual starting point is Fortun on the Sognefjell road. Only *Store Austabottind* (2203) provides real sport, as the other peaks are merely subsidiary summits. 1st asc 8/1883 by C Hall and Matias, up by the NW ridge from Berdal glacier. A variation of this route was made in 7/1892 by B Goodfellow, J J Hoddinot and E J Woolley, following Hall's route to the first summit, but then descending 200 ft, traversing S side of the NW ridge and regaining it just below final summit. The N ridge from Berdal glacier was climbed in 1901 by E Rostrup and K Fortun. A descent by this ridge had already been made in 8/1889 by E T Hartley, G Hastings, Wm C Slingsby and T Sulheim, when they made the 1st passage of Rabne Skar. The ascent by the N ridge is now the usual route, but the top can be reached easily by various routes up the N face, which is largely covered by the Berdal glacier. The SW ridge was climbed in 1908 by T Kroepelien, C W Rubenson and F Schjelderup. A descent by this ridge was made in 8/1899 by A W Andrews, O K Williamson and O Berge, when they traversed the

SW peaks. The SE ridge from Gravdal glacier was climbed in 7/1927 by O H Furuseth, A Gunneng and B Schlytter. The 1st winter asc was made from Berdalen via the W ridge in Easter 1962 by A R Heen, T Kleppen, O Mork and B Ugelvik.

Store Austabottind by SE Arete from Gravdal Glacier — Up by SE arete from glacier to narrow gap facing unclimbable crag. Bypass it by traversing to R and continue up 200 ft into grassy chimney. Climb it and then turn R, towards ridge which follow to yellow crag which is bypassed to L. Then climb ridge to top. Descent by usual route. Time from Turtagrø to foot of ridge, 4-5 hrs; from foot to top, 4-5 hrs. At least 1 ice axe. 80 ft rope per man.

THE FALKETIND GROUP (map E 870 Sygnefjell) is situated within the triangle Vetti—Eidsbugaren—Skogadalsbøen and can be reached from either tourist lodge by a walk of 3—4 hrs. *Hjelledalstind* (1990) rises N of the Koldedal glacier, an elegant peak which was cairned in 8/1884 by C Hall and Matias. *Falketind* (2067) separates Morka—Koldedalen from Fleskedalen. 1st asc 7/1820 by C P Boeck, B M Keilhau and O Urden, up by the N face. Its W face was climbed in 7/1878 by C Christensen and O Skattebo. The E ridge was climbed in 1941 by H C Bugge, D & R Dekke. This ridge is very sharp and runs across *Falkeungen*, which is a steep needle below the NE face. 1st asc 1915 by R Børsum and L Irgens Jensen. *Stølsnostind* (2073) stands NW of Falketind. Slingsby has compared it with Matterhorn, describing it as "one of the gems of Europe". Its W face has never been climbed but it is considered feasible. 1st asc 7/1877 by H H Reusch, Wm C Slingsby and A Vetti, ascending by the S side and E arete, returning same way.

THE MJØLKEDAL GROUP (maps E 870 Sygnefjell & E 305 Gjende) is situated between Eidsbugaren, Tyinholmen and Skogadalsbøen, reached from either in 3—4 hrs. *Urdanostind* (2157) is a sharp ridge with fearsome-looking precipices on both sides. The 1st asc of *Søre Urdanostind* (2048) was made in 8/1896 by C C B Moss and Dr & Mrs T K Rose, climbing the W ridge. The traverse from 2048 to *Urdanostind* (2157) is easy. 1st asc 7/1876 by E Mohn, Wm C Slingsby and K Løkken, up and down by the N face. Time from Eidsbugaren or Tyinholmen or Skogadalsbøen to top, 8 hrs. Its SE face has a 1000 ft high and very steep snow couloir which has never been climbed. Its W face is considered unassailable. *Slingsbytind* (2027) is reached by a ridge walk from 2157. 1st asc 7/1876 by Wm C Slingsby, traversing from 2157. *Sagi* (2041) is a saw-toothed ridge N of the Urdanostinder. The 1st asc of the N point was made in 7/1889 by F de Chazal and T Sulheim, ascending the W face and descending into Mjølkedalen. The 1st

asc of the S point was made in 7/1894 by T Bertheau and A Saxegaard, ascending from the SE. The *Mjølkedalstinder* (2136) are situated E of Sagi, reached from Olavsbu hut (unstaffed) in 3 hrs. The 1st asc of *Søre & Nordre Mjølkedalspigger* (1990 & 2041) was made in 8/1889 by G Hastings, Wm C Slingsby, A Aukrust and R Garmo, climbing pt 1990 by its NE ridge, then traversing to pt 2041. *Mjølkedalstind* (2136) was cairned in 9/1881 by Wm C Slingsby and J Vigdal, up by gully on the E face and then via a broad ledge to the SW and so to top.

THE SMØRSTABBTIND GROUP (map E 870 Sygne fjell) is situated between Krossbu on the Sognefjell road and Leirvassbu, which is reached by jeep from Elveseter. There is a walk of 2–3 hrs from Krossbu or Leirvassbu to the Smørstabbtinder. *Kalven* (2035) is the westernmost point, connected with *Skeia* (2118) by a narrow ridge. 1st asc of Skeia in 8/1894 by C Hall, M Soggemoen and O Fortun, up from Smørstabb glacier, down by the N face. Its W ridge from Kalven was climbed in 8/1911 by J Nordahl-Olsen, R Ødegaard and N Bakkeberg. Good sport on narrow ridge. The central peak is *Veslebjørn* (2152), very sharp and attractive. 1st asc 7/1877 by E Mohn and C Traaen, up by the S ridge. There is probably still scope for further exploring here. *Storebjørn* (2223) is the highest and southernmost peak, a square-topped rock which rises with a 2000 ft precipice from glacier to top. 1st asc 8/1885 by C Hall and Matias, up by the W side. The usual route is up by the S side. The SW ridge has also been climbed. *Saksa* (2191) rises N of Veslebjørn. 1st asc 8/1886 by C Hall and Matias, up by the NW ridge. *Geita* (2001) is merely an eminence on the NE ridge of Saksa. *Kniven* (2133) is a summit on the knife-edge ridge N of Saksa. 1st asc 8/1891 by C Hall and Matias and boy Anders, up from the Smørstabb glacier. *Store Smørstabbtind* (2208) is the northernmost peak. Its SE ridge affords a severe route. A complete traverse from Krossbu was made in 8/1911 by J Nordahl-Olsen and party via Veslebjørn, Skeia by the E ridge, Saksa by the S face and descent by the NW ridge, then via Geita (1st asc), Kniven and Store Smørstabbtind with descent by the W face and return to Krossbu, a magnificent expedition of 12 hrs. Winter ascents of all peaks in the Smørstabbtind group were made during Easter 1962 by T Kleppen and O Mork.

Store Smørstabbtind by SE Ridge — Follow true ridge, which starts with 100 ft of VD climbing to small cave — a good stance but poor belay. Escape from cave by L side of overhang. Good handholds. Easier rock follows for about 200 ft to foot of steep wall. Climb diagonally R, then traverse L to good belay. Here the rock is sound but of high angle. Thereafter the climbing is of standard difficulty. In view of the first 2 pitches and the steep wall pitch, this route should be graded severe. An easy descent to the skar between this mountain and Kniven is to be had by a stone gully on the S face. (Report from J H Barber).

Stetind (2019) is a solitary peak situated SW of Leirvassbu. 1st asc 8/1890 by C Hall and Matias. It is reached from Leirvassbu in 3 hrs. Further N of the Smørstabbtind group, near Bøvertun, lies *Loftet* (2170). 1st asc 1875 by surveyor J N Hertzberg and party.

THE BYGDIN – GJENDE RANGES (map E 305 Gjende) are situated N of lake Bygdin and S of lake Gjende, reached either from Torfinnsbu Lodge or from Gjendebu Lodge. The westernmost peaks can also be reached from Eidsbugaren Hotel. *Galdebergtind* (2047) is a snowy peak between Eidsbugaren and Torfinnsbu. 1st asc 7/1876 by E Mohn, Wm C Slingsby and K Løkken, up from the glacier. *Slettmarkpiggen* (2163) is an elegant pyramid, 3 miles SW of Gjendebu. Its SE wall has never been climbed and may offer scope for an interesting route. 1st asc 8/1885 by R L Harrison, C & H Wilson and J Vigdal, up by the W ridge. Its E arete was climbed in 1942 by E Hoff-Hansen and P Hohle, a very narrow ridge with 2 difficult buttresses. *Svartdalspiggen* (2143) is a jagged ridge S of Gjendebu. 1st asc 1842 by surveyor H N Wergeland and party. Merely a scramble. *Mesmogtind* (2270) is one of the real gems of Jotunheimen, situated between Gjendebu and Torfinnsbu. 1st asc 8/1885 by R L Harrison, C & H Wilson and J Vigdal, up by the N face and down by the S side of the W arete. Its SW ridge was climbed in 7/1904 by K S Klingenberg, M Følsvik and P Skjolden. This is the easiest and most natural route. The E wall was climbed in 7/1943 by P Hohle, E Nørregaard and P Skavang. A strenuous but interesting route. Descent by snowdrifts on the SW side. A new route from the E was made in 1955 by E W

Norwegian Touring Club's lodge Gjendesheim on lake Gjende (Photo: Normann)

Eriksen and P Vigerust. The *Torfinnstind Ridge* rises immediately above Torfinnsbu Lodge. It is capped by 3 rugged peaks which afford good sport. *Austre Torfinnstind* (2113) is the southernmost peak. 1st asc 7/1876 by E Mohn, Wm C Slingsby and K Løkken, up by the easternmost gully on the S face. Time from Torfinnsbu to top, 3 hrs, down 2 hrs. Its N face was climbed in 1933 by L Henschke and B Ræder. This is a risky route owing to loose rock. The E face was climbed by a fine chimney in 1941 by P Hohle and E Rothman. The NE face was climbed in 1943 by P Hohle and E Nørregaard. Very exposed climbing and a severe route. *Vestre Torfinnstind* is the lowest peak on the ridge. 1st asc 1912 by R Ødegaard. *Midtre Torfinnstind* was cairned in 7/1894 by T Bertheau and A Saxegaard, traversing from Austre in 2 hrs.

Kvitskartind (2193) is the northernmost peak. 1st asc 8/1911 by R Ødegaard. A complete N−S traverse of the ridge from Langedal glacier to Torfinnsbu was made in 8/1920 by F Lorentzen, R Ødegaard and B Schlytter.

Knutsholstind (2340) is a grand rock massif SE of Gjendebu. Fine sport. 1st asc of *Store Knutsholstind* (2340) 1875 by J T Heftye and K Løkken, up by the very steep S ridge. The 1st winter asc by this ridge was made in 1960 by W Dyås and B Halvorsen. Its NW face was climbed from Svartdal in 8/1881 by Wm C Slingsby, M Sønstenes and J Vigdal. Merely a scramble. Its E side from Knutsholet cirque was climbed in 8/1885 by C Wilson, N Storstensrusten and J Vigdal, a grand rock climb. The 1st asc of *Nordligste Knutsholstind* (2140)

was made in 8/1947 by D B Burchardt, up by the N
ridge, down towards the *SW. Leirungstind* (2294 & 2288)
is a continuation of the Knutsholstind ridge. Both
summits have been climbed. The S wall of Vestre Leirungstind (2294) was climbed in 1943 by E Nørregaard
and P Skavang, a difficult route. *Kalvåhøgdi* (2182)
is situated NE of Torfinnstind, overlooking Leirungs-
botn, which is one of the most fantastic cirques in Norway,
enclosed by sheer walls of over 1500 ft. The 1st asc of
Kalvåhøgdi was made in 7/1820 by C Boeck and B M
Keilhau, from the SW via the W col of Rasletind (2108)
and so to the top. A new route from the SW was made in
7/1876 by E Mohn and Wm C Slingsby. *Tjørnholstind*
(2329) rises SE of Gjendebu between 2 famous cirques —
N and S Tjørnholet. 1st asc of *Vestre Tjørnholstind*
(2329), 7/1878 by H Graff, E Mohn and A Rusnes, up by
the W edge of the cirque. Its S face was climbed in 7/1910
by E Randers and party. *Steinflytind* rises E of Tjørnholstind, but is not denoted on the map. 1st asc 1898 by
E A Thomle and K Storstensrusten, up by the S wall
with traverse to the E face. Attempts have been made to
reach it from Tjørnholstind. A complete traverse was
made in 14 hrs in 7/1934 by D B Burchardt and R Ødegaard — from Gjendebu via Knutsholet — Skarvfly
glacier — Vestre & Midtre Tjørnholstind — Steinflytind
and descent to Gjendesheim.

THE RAUDDALEN GROUP (map E 305 Gjende) is
situated W of Gjendebu Lodge, halfway between Eidsbugaren and Leirvassbu. Olavsbu hut (unstaffed) is the
best starting point. *Sjogholstind* (2142) is an easy peak S
of Rauddalen. 1st asc 1875 by J N Hertzberg. It adjoins
the Mjølkedalstinder, described in previous paragraph.
The *Rauddalstinder* are worth a visit. *Rauddalseggen*
(2155), also called Store Austre Rauddalstind, has a 180
ft long summit ridge, very narrow with a steep precipice
to the W. 1st asc 8/1906 by A Jakhelln and F Schjelderup, up by the E ridge. The 1st asc of *Midtre Rauddalstind* (2087) was made in 8/1935 by R Ødegaard and G N
Sabro. *Store Rauddalstind* (2154) is very impressive with
sheer precipices on 3 sides. 1st asc 8/1890 by C Hall
and Matias, traversing from Vestre Rauddalstind (2056).
Skardalstind (2159) rises on a long and narrow ridge.
1st asc 1841 by H N Wergeland.

THE LEIRVASSBU E RANGES (map E 305 Gjende)
are situated E and NE of Leirvassbu Lodge. *Kyrkja*
(2032) is a fine pyramid, a sharp conical peak of black
rock, very much like the Eiger when seen from the

Leirvassbu – Spiterstul footpath. The easiest route is from
Leirvassbu to the S gap, then follow the S ridge to the top
in 2 hrs. *Tverrbotthorn* (2153) is a crescent-shaped ridge NE
of Leirvassbu. The 1st asc of *Austre Tverrbotthorn* (2104)
was made in 7/1885 by A Walnum from the glacier
cirque and up by the N face. The 1st asc of *Vestre Tverrbotthorn* (2101) was made in 8/1890 by C Hall and Matias
from the col between 1970 and 2101. *Nordre Tverrbotthorn*
(2153) was cairned in 1935 by R Ødegaard and G N
Sabro. Peaks 2162 and 2113 are reached easily from
Leirløyftet, which is a popular pass, used during the glacier
walk from Leirvassbu to Elveseter, Juvvass or Spiterstul.
Semmelholstind (2149) rises E of Kyrkja. 1st asc 8/1881
by Wm C Slingsby and J Vigdal, up by the SW face from
Vis glacier which separates it from *Visbretind* (2235),
cairned by the same party. The easiest route is up by the
NW ridge or by the S face. The *Urdadalstinder* are 5 pretty
aiguilles rising out of small glaciers with steep icefalls,
situated on a long S-shaped ridge. The southernmost
peak (1990 or 2012?) was cairned in 8/1870 by T L &
W R Brown and J F H Saunders, up by the E face.
Midtre Urdadalstind (2071 or 2012?) was cairned in 8/1939
by R Ødegaard and R Raabe, up by the S ridge. *Nordligste and Nordre Urdadalstind* (2104 & 2061) were cairned
in 1937 by R Ødegaard.

THE GALDHØPIGGEN RANGES (map E 305 Gjende):
This is the real heart of the "Home of the Giants",
situated S of Juvvass Lodge and W of Spiterstul Lodge.
Galdhøpiggen (2469) is Norway's highest peak, the westernmost point on a long ridge with fearsome-looking precipices towards S & W & N. It can be reached by a steep
scramble on a cairned footpath from Spiterstul in 4 hrs
up, 2 down. *Keilhaus Topp* (2351) is a subsidiary peak,
cairned by B M Keilhau and surveyor Andresen in 1844,
ascending from Visdalen. The 1st asc of *Galdhøpiggen*
(2469) was made in 7/1850 by L Arnesen, S Flotten and
S Sulheim, ascending from the E from Spiterstul. Its
NE ridge was climbed from the Stygge glacier in 1857
by Ole Røisheim. Its W face was climbed in 8/1886 by
R F Ball and J Vigdal, an exposed route up by a broad
gully from Stygge glacier. The 1st winter asc was made
in 12/1887 by K Borchgrevink, J T Heftye and K Vole.
The SW ridge from Svellnos glacier was climbed in
1906 by K Lous and E Ofigsbø, a good climb. Its NW
ridge which separates Storjuv from Stygge glacier, is the
sharpest ridge of this rock massif, climbed in 1912 by
N Backer Grøndahl and H Horn, an interesting climb,
but severe. *Vesle Galdhøpiggen* (2369) rises NW of the

The usual route to Galdhøpiggen across the Stygge glacier (Photo: Normann)

main peak. 1st asc 8/1897 by E Lindbäch, N A Lindhult and K Vole, up from the point where its ridge joins the Stygge glacier. Descent towards E, combined with the ascent of Galdhøpiggen by the usual route.

Galdhøpiggen from E from Spiterstul — Walk up the steep Piggebakk hills, zig-zagging up to plateau (1700) below Svellnose. Up on snow and rocks, across Svellnose and Keilhaus Topp (2351). Slight descent to Pigg glacier and then up to main summit. Time from Spiterstul, 4 hrs up, 2 down. Cairned footpath between Spiterstul and glacier.

Galdhøpiggen from NE from Stygge Glacier — Follow cairned footpath from Juvvass Lodge and traverse fringe of Vetljuv glacier on to Stygge glacier. Crevasses, often covered by snow. Rope. Follow ridge to top, final pitch on snow or ice. Keep away from W precipice. Time from Juvvass to top, 3 hrs up, 2 down. Guide with rope and ice axe.

Galdhøpiggen by NW Ridge — The route commences from skar called Porten, between Storjuv and Stygge glaciers. Easier to get on to ridge from Stygge glacier. From Juvvass Lodge, ascend Stygge glacier towards NW ridge, which follow to top.

Skarstind (2373) is a grand peak W of Galdhøpiggen. Its E and S walls are very steep and the NE arete is a knife-edge ridge. Its very steep E ridge has never been climbed, although several attempts have been made. The 1st asc was made in 1884 by O Kristiansen, S Thor and S Wleugel, up by the S face. Its NW ridge was climbed in 8/1886 by R F Ball and J Vigdal, and the NE ridge in 7/1946 by John Poole and party. The W ridge affords the easiest way to the summit. The 1st asc of *Austre Skarstind* was made in 8/1892 by C Hall and Matias. *Storgrovtind* (2259) is a distinct peak N of Skarstind. Its S face has never been climbed. The 1st asc was made in 7/1946 by D B Burchardt and R Ødegaard, from the gap below the N face. The same party also made the 1st asc of pt 2170 from the S from Storgrov glacier. The *Ymestinder*, also called Storgjuvtinder, are situated on the ridge which

4

intervenes between Storgjuv and Svellnos glaciers. The
1st asc of both peaks (2343 & 2303) was made in 1927 by
M Hansen and A Næss. The *Tverråtinder* (2309) stand
between Svellnos and Tverrå glaciers. The 1st asc of
Vestre Tverråtind (2309) and *Austre Tverråtind* (2301)
was made in 8/1906 by F Schjelderup and E Ofigsbø.
Styggehø (2214) is a long ridge S of Tverrå glacier and SW
of Spiterstul. The 1st traverse was made in 8/1886 by E
Vestermarch and L Sulheim, merely a steep scramble. The
Bukkeholstind ridge rises between Leirvassbu and Spiter-
stul. The 1st asc of *Store Bukkeholstind* (2212) was made
in 8/1887 by A Walnum and L Sulheim, up by the S face
to the col between Austre and Store, and so to top.
Søraustre Bukkeholstind (2053) was climbed in 1941 by
D B Burchardt and R Ødegaard. The 1st asc of *Nordre*
(2149) and *Nordvestre* (2168) *Bukkeholstind* and 4 lesser
Vestre peaks was made in 7/1906 by A Jakhelln, C W
Rubenson and F Schjelderup.

THE MEMURU GROUP (map E 305 Gjende) is situated
E of Urdadalen, halfway between Gjendebu and Spiterstul. *Semmeltind* (2236) presents a magnificent view from
Urdadalen — a sharp needle and scarped on its E face
into one unbroken precipice rivalling that of the Fins-
teraarhorn, which it somewhat resembles. The 1st asc was
made by an Englishman up the W side, a tiring trudge
over loose boulders. The steep and sharp SW arete was
climbed in 8/1885 by R L Harrison, R Starr, C Wilson,
J Vigdal and L Jensen. The SE arete was climbed in
7/1956 by J H Barber and C A Simpson.

Semmeltind by SE Arete — The start from the glacier is indefinite and the
best climbing is to be had on the E face of the ridge; 200 ft of standard diff.
Thereafter the arete becomes no more than a walk, and is followed to the
foot of the steep upper section, directly upwards to crest of arete which
follow to summit. The rock is not difficult but requires considerable care.
Probably an easier route is to traverse left to crest of arete and then to top.
Time from glacier to top, 2½ hrs. (Report from J H Barber).

The *Heilstugutinder* form the E boundary of Urdadalen.
In 9/1881, Wm C Slingsby and J Vigdal climbed peak
2188 by its W face and peak 2255 by its S ridge. Peak
2346 was climbed in 8/1886 by E Vestermarck and L
Sulheim from Heilstugu glacier. F Schjelderup traversed
the whole ridge from N to S in 8/1906. The *Memurutinder*
are splendid peaks which offer good sport. The 1st asc of
Sydligste Memurutind (2143) was made in Easter 1939
by R Ødegaard and J Randen on skis up the N face from
Austre Memuru glacier. The 1st asc of *Vestre Memurutind*
(2245) was made in 8/1881 by J T Heftye and K Vole.
The highest *Vestre Memurutind* (2290) was climbed in
1874 by A Dewhurst, J T Heftye, Wm C Slingsby and

R Alfsen, up by the steep N ridge from Heilstugu glacier. The 2nd-highest *Vestre Memurutind* (2243) was climbed in 8/1939 by H Kolberg, R Ødegaard, R Raabe and R Rosendahl, up by the W face from the highest point of Heilstugu glacier. *Store Memurutind* (2364) is reached in 5 hrs from Spiterstul via Heilstugu glacier and Veo Skar. The gap E of Store Memurutind is called Memuru Skar, a much used tourist route. The 1st asc of *Store Memurutind* (2364) was made in 7/1881 by J H Heftye and K Vole, probably up by the S face. It was climbed from Leirhø in 8/1884 by O Kristiansen, S Thor and S Wleugel. The 1st winter asc was made in Easter 1906 by F Schjelderup on skis up the S face. A new route from the E from Memuru Skar was made in 3/1907 by T Ravnsborg and H Tønsberg. The 1st asc of *Austre Memurutind* (2296) was made in 1939 by R Ødegaard and R Raabe, up by the N side from Veo glacier. *Leirhø* (2328) is the snow peak SE of Spiterstul. 1st asc 1875 by J N Hertzberg, up by the N side in 4 hrs from Spiterstul. The 1st winter asc was made in 3/1906 by T Ravnsborg and H Tønsberg. An Austrian party climbed it from Skautfly in 1937. The ascent from the S from Veo Skar is easy.

The *Veotinder* (2265) are situated on a ridge between Veo and Stygge glaciers. *Nordre Veotind* (2116) was cairned in 8/1886 by E Vestermarck, L Sulheim and K Vole. The E face of *Midtre Veotind* (2240, surveyors' cairn) was climbed in 1958 by H Lombert and K Pearce. The descent by the W face is an easy walk. *Søre Veotind* (2265) was cairned in 7/1906 by A Jakhelln, C W Rubenson and F Schjelderup.

Midtre Veotind (2240) by E Face — Up glacier and across bergschrund between peak and R edge. A series of pitches leads to sloping ledge, about level with ridge to R. A route may go to L of this ledge, commencing from large block. Up to R to ledge on corner where Veo glacier can be seen. Up ridge, finally crossing under peak on E face by loose ledge to finish 50 ft below top. Time from Glitterheim to rock face, 3 hrs, time on face 5½ hrs, time from top to Glitterheim 2½ hrs. Mild severe. (Report from H Lombert & K Pearce).

Store (2167) and *Austre* (2234) *Styggebretind* on the Stygge glacier were cairned in 7/1906 by A Jakhelln, C W Rubenson and F Schjelderup. Further S stands *Surtningssuen* (2368), the 5th highest peak in Norway, best reached from Memurubu Lodge. Very little climbing, except on the E face. The 1st asc was made in 1840 by Johan Sverdrup and party, up by the NE side. A cairned footpath leads from Memurubu to the top, a walk of 5 hrs. 1st winter asc in Easter 1906 by F Schjelderup and party. *Besshø* (2258) rises NE of Memurubu. 1st asc 7/1813 by C Smith, an easy scramble.

THE GLITTERTIND (2442) (map E305 Gjende) is Norway's second-highest peak, situated NW of Glitterheim Lodge. The highest point of the snowdrift which covers the top plateau, was measured to be 2469,70 metres in 1959 — a fraction higher than Galdhøpiggen which is Norway's highest peak. The usual route is an easy scramble by cairned footpath from Glitterheim to the top in 3 hrs, 2 down. The 1st asc was made in 1842 by H N Wergeland and H Sletten, up from Visdalen. The 1st winter asc was made in 1890 by O Elveseter, H Jacobsen and K Vole. A descent from Glittertind into Glittertindbotn cirque was made in 9/1893 by P A Øyen, Olaf & Ole Vole.

THE HOLÅ—HESTBRE RANGES (map E 793 Skjåk): This area lies N of Høydal Seter (tourist lodge), which can be reached by car from Bøvertun or Elveseter on the Sognefjell road. The 1st asc of *Vestre Holåtind* (2038) was made in 1937 by D B Burchardt and R Ødegaard. *Midtre Holåtind* (2047) or Arentz Topp was cairned in 7/1897 by J Aarestrup, E Arentz and S Kvitingen. *Austre Holåtind* (2043) or Tussetind was cairned in 8/1896 by F Arentz, T Bertheau and T Sulheim, up by the W face, down by the N ridge. The *Hestbrepigger* (2171) are situated E of Holåtind. The 1st asc of *Sulheimspiggen* (2139) was made in 8/1896 by F Arentz, T Berteau and T Sulheim, up by the narrow W ridge, down by the SW face. The 1st winter asc was made by K S Klingenberg and party. The 1st asc of *Store Hestbrepigg* (2144) was made in 7/1897 by F Arentz and S Kvitingen, up by the S ridge from Lomseggen. A traverse from Sulheimspiggen was made in 8/1897 by J Aarestrup, F Arentz and S Kvitingen. The 1st asc of *Nordre Hestbrepigg* (2171) was made in 1938 by J Falkenberg and R Ødegaard. A complete traverse was made in 7/1947 by C F Heber and G Røhn, from Høydal Seter via Sulheimspiggen, Store Hestbrepigg, Nordre Hestbrepigg by S face, Austre Hestbrepigg (2104) and down to Netto Seter, an expedition of 15 hrs.

THE JOSTEDAL GLACIER

Covering an area of 812 sq km or 480 sq miles, the Jostedal glacier is Europe's largest icefield, a glistening white ocean of eternal snow and ice, situated between Sogne fjord and Nord fjord. The main ice cap lies at about 6500 ft and is believed to be over 1000 ft thick. Glacier tongues extend from the main ice cap and many of them are

Aerial view of a Jostedal glacier tongue (Photo: Widerøe)

famous tourist attractions on their own merit. There are 24 glacier tongues, of which the Tunsbergdal is the longest, Nigard the prettiest and Austerdal the wildest. All glacier tongues surge into the valleys at varying speeds. The Bøya moves at the rate of half a metre every 24 hours. Today, most glaciers are about the same size as in 1700, but they then increased enormously until 1750, when much damage was done to farmlands. Between 1850 and 1880 the ice receded quickly, and the process is still going on at varying speeds. The Tunsbergdal glacier embraces a giant crater, which triggered a sad flood disaster in the Jostedal valley several years ago. A glacier trek right across the Jostedal glacier is one of the most exciting walking tours to be had. However dangerous it may seem, the glacier trek is always strenuous but without danger if assisted by guides. These are available at Åmot, Fjerland, Loen, Lunde and Stryn. It is cheaper if several visitors join into one party and hire a guide to take them across. Write to DNT for details of fees.

When crossing the main ice field from W or E, there is always a steep and laborious ascent and a corresponding descent on the other side. The actual time spent on the glacier plateau proper seldom exceeds 4 to 6 hrs. Whereas the Jotunheimen glaciers are located between the peaks, the Jostedal ice field is located above the peaks and forms a plateau such as is known in Iceland or Greenland. This limits the scope for rock climbs, but there are several peaks which yield good sport. The only existing map — K430 Jostedal — is old and inadequate, and the glaciers have receded considerably since it was drawn.

Across Jostedal Glacier, Fjœrland—Lunde (map K430 Jostedal): Fjerland village is reached by fjord steamer from Bergen via Balestrand in one day. From Oslo by train via Myrdal to Flåm and fjord steamer to Fjerland. Good accommodation. A fine excursion by bus will take you to the two local glacier tongues — Bøya and Suphelle glaciers. From Fjerland, 9 km by car to the foot of Bøya glacier. Follow cairned footpath up to the bergschrund and on to the glacier plateau through col and onwards to Kvitvarden (1350) which is the highest point on the route. Westwards to Mara glacier which is crossed. Past 2 Troll lakes with Trollbotn cirque to L. Across river Lunde on bridge and descent through steep and narrow Lunde Skar. Take care to follow footpath and avoid snowdrifts. Down to Lunde farm and then by car to Skei Hotel in Jølster on the main road Vadheim—Jølster—Olden—Loen. A full day's walking tour. Guide with ice axe and rope required. Guide charge less on Sundays.

Rcok Climbs from Fjerland (map K430 Jostedal): *Romhesten* (4000 ft) rises sheer out of the E side of Fjerland fjord. Its E side from Romedal was climbed in 1868 by J R Campbell. *Skeidsnipa* (1439) is Fjerland's "Sunday peak" which gives a good outing of 7 hrs incl a glacier crossing. 1st asc 5/1868 by K Lorange,·H and L Bøyum. *Suphellenipa* (1732) rises on the Suphelle glacier, N of Fjerland. 1st asc 7/1864 by F Sejersted and party. *Kalde-Kari* is a long ridge E of Suphelle glacier, a magnificent viewpoint. 1st asc 8/1894 by K Bing and O Dale, up from Suphelle glacier. An ascent from Snauedal glacier was made in 8/1910 by B Huun and A Mundal.

Rock Climbs from Olden & Loen (map K430 Jostedal): These are two popular tourist centres on the Nord fjord, reached by fjord steamer from Bergen to Vadheim and then by bus in one day. From Oslo by train to Otta and bus via Grotli in one day. A fine excursion can be had by bus from Olden to Briksdal glacier and from Loen to Kjenndal glacier. *Ceciliekruna* (1717) stands W of lake Olden and provides a good "first day climb". *Snønipa* (1827) is a nunatak on the NW ice field W of lake Olden. Surveyed in 1865 by F Sejersted and party.

Ravnefjell (1778) rises abruptly out of lake Loen. 1st asc 7/1870 by K Lorange and guides. It was this mountain that caused the disastrous avalanches into lake Loen in 1906 and 1936. *Skåla* (1938) is a famous peak and a favourite viewpoint E of Loen. Said to be "like a bigger Ben Nevis", having a stony W slope and a fine NW precipice dropping from the flat top to a glacier basin. The Kloumann tower is a stone hut (8 beds) built on the very top of Skåla (key from Tjugen farm). Time from Loen to top, 6 hrs. *Tindefjell* (1774) or Havald-Trede is a long and jagged ridge with a fine group of pinnacles rising from vertical cliffs above its glacier between lake Loen and Erdalen in Stryn. Its NE and E walls are fearsome-looking precipices. The ridge is reached easily from Loen via Skåla or from the road at lake Stryn. *Stor-Havalden* (1774) is the highest peak on the ridge. The ascent is said to be difficult. *Tafsehydna* (1731) rises on the same ridge. 1st asc 8/1893 by K Bing and party, up the W side. The S ridge was climbed in 1906 by E Rostrup and H Tønsberg. A complete W-E traverse of Tindefjell was made in 7/1956 by R M Middleton and R J Wathen, a fine climb of difficulty and exposure, somewhat marred by loose rock. The traverse might be better done E-W. "I am only slightly exaggerating when I say that if a climber were to stand at certain points on this knife-edge ridge and stretch his arms sideways, stones dropped from his hands would fall straight to the snowfields on either side without touching the rock walls!" (R J Wathen).

Tindefjell, W-E Traverse — Ascend R of stream from Sandvik, leave Skåla path high up, cross stream and ascend long snow slopes to col. Follow high ground of ridge for about a mile to Tindefjell. Descend a loose and exposed ridge into sharply defined V-gap. Exit by groove leading up R 30 ft to small cairn. To avoid difficult pitch below summit, traverse out R to ridge overlooking S snowfield and on to exposed S face. Traverse up past small cairn towards 2 horned crags on main ridge with large cairn. Continue ridge eastwards by an abseil down chimney to platform under vertical wall of next pinnacle, which is bypassed by abseiling down a chimney L, and traversing N face past ribs and gully till able to regain ridge by loose chimney L or severe wall R. Next pinnacle easy, and then a very loose ridge to final pinnacle and descent by its S ridge to skar on snowfield. Time from W of V-gap, 8 hrs. (R J Wathen).

Veslekåpa is a smaller peak SE of lake Loen. 1st asc 7/1820 by G Bohr. It stands immediately S of *Lodalskåpa* (2083) which is a bluntly truncated obelisk, 3 sides of which rise with walls of terrific steepness some 700 ft out of the snowfields, while the SW side has been broken into a deep hollow which holds a little glacier tongue, providing easy access to the top. 1st asc 1844 by G Rustøen and party, up by the SW side from Bødalen, the usual route. Guide is required and is available at Loen. The W side was climbed from Veslekåpa in 8/1884 by T Anderson, Wm Ecroyd, Wm C Slingsby and wife, L Jensen and J Rustøen. An uninteresting route. The N ridge from Kaupevatn was climbed in 8/1885 by R Starr and J Vigdal, up a very steep couloir which leads to a small glacier whose snow tongue runs far up the mountain, to a rocky tooth on the N ridge, a really good climb. The N ridge forms a skar by which the ascent can be made from Stryn. The NE face was climbed in 8/1889 by G Hastings, Wm C Slingsby and a porter. This face is very steep and consists of huge smooth slabs of gneiss, many of which partly overhang the precipice. The top of the slabs forms narrow ledges, some flat but others tilted. An occasional narrow chimney is to be found. The S wall from Lodal glacier was climbed in 1933 by A Backer and R Myrhaug. This route is severe and is only for experts on ice work. The E face was climbed in 8/1934 by Mrs A M S Shannon, R Myrhaug and J Orheim. A strenuous route. The E ridge was climbed in 1942 by H Giverholt and C J Koren, up by the crevassed Strup glacier and another steep glacier to the foot of the E ridge which provides a fine rubber climb to the top. The 1st winter asc was made in 1959 by H Chr Bugge and C M Haug.

A peak and 2 nunataks on the Mjølkevoll glacier S of lake Olden and E of Åmot were cairned in 8/1884 by Wm Ecroyd, Wm C Clingsby, J Lensen and J Rustøen. *Middagsnipa* (6000 ft) is the fine peak and *Onsdagsnipa* and *Larsnipa* (5600 ft) are the nunataks. The latter rises with grand precipices. Its summit is wholly composed of giant blocks of detached rocks. The ascent from the glacier takes only half an hour.

Kvitevarden is a peak on the Austerdal glacier, W of Jostedalen and SE on the main icefield. 1st asc 8/1894 by K Bing and D Søknesand, up by the W side. An hour afterwards it was climbed from the E by Wm C Slingsby and party. *Røykedalsfjell* (Vetlenibba on the map) stands on the Røykedal glacier, E of Tunsbergdal glacier. 1st asc 8/1899 by C W Patchell and J Vigdal.

Jostedal Glacier, N-S or S-N Traverse (map K430 Jostedal): This is the longest glacier traverse one can undertake in the whole of Europe, the distance being 44 miles as the crow flies. The first N-S crossing was made in 1898 in 47 hrs. In recent years, skiers have crossed the glacier in both directions, but this is still a grand feat. A recommended S-N route goes from Fjerland via the Flatbre hut (alt 3300 ft) to Jostedal, descending by the Fåbergstøl glacier. This tour must be made on skis and the skiers are roped all the way. Guide, rope and ice axes — and good weather. Time, 24 hrs, preferably early in the summer.

THE ÅLFOT GLACIER

This is the "unknown glacier", a huge icefield which covers an area of 68 sq km, situated S of Nord fjord, reached by fjord steamer from Bergen in 8—10 hours, either to Svelgen on the W side of the glacier, or to Hyen which lies SE of the glacier. Svelgen is an industrial centre with a giant hydro-electric plant built inside the mountain. Plain accommodation available at Svelgen and Hyen. There are very seldom any expeditions to Ålfoten glacier, and there are no details of routes. Climbers should *never* venture up on the glacier plateau without being roped together. Existing maps are very oldfashioned and inexact.

Hornelen (896) (map B 29/30 Fjordane) is a stupenduous sea cliff, situated at Bremanger, NW of Ålfoten glacier, at the S entrance to Nord fjord, seen in all its grandeur from the coastal express steamers, which sail close to it. The usual route leads up by the SW side from Berle. The steep E face has never been climbed. *Juratind* is a rock tower below Hornelen's N point. It has never been climbed.

The Svelgen Sector (map B 29/30 Fjordane): These peaks are reached easily from Svelgen. *Kjeipen* (1365) rises on the SW fringe of Ålfoten glacier. The usual route up is via lake Hjelmevatn. *Plogen* and *Saksa* are two smaller peaks E of Kjeipen. 1st asc 9/1885 by C Hopkinson, Wm C Slingsby and Lars Jensen. *Maritind* rises between Plogen and Saksa. It is a huge ruined tower. 1st asc 7/1894 by K Bing, up by the W ridge. He also cairned *Kompassnipa*.

The Hyen Sector (map B 29/30 Fjordane): *Gjegnalund* (1723) is the highest peak on the Ålfot glacier, called Blånitta on the map, situated N of Hyen. The SW ridge provides a long rock climb. Its W and NE walls are very steep and have never been climbed. *Bjørnetind* is a small peak E of Gjegnalund. 1st asc 9/1885 by C Hopkinson, Wm C Slingsby and Lars Jensen. *Bukkenipa* (1600) and *Storehesten* (1421) are situated W of Gjegnalund. Both were cairned in 7/1894 by K Bing.

Øye — mountaineering centre in the Sunnmøre Alps (Photo- Lystad)

SUNNMØRE

The "Sunnmøre Alps" are famous among rock climbers. Owing to the absence of high, connecting ridges, almost every peak commands a magnificent view, and there is a feeling of isolation about each top. Their general abruptness and shapeliness is most attractive. Ålesund is the chief town in Sunnmøre, reached by coastal express steamer from Bergen in 13 hrs, or from Oslo by train and bus via Åndalsnes in one day. There are also air services from Oslo and Bergen to Ålesund.

Ørsta and Øye are the main centres for walking tours and rock climbs, both villages affording good hotel accommodation. Ørsta is reached by bus or boat from Ålesund in 2 —3 hrs. Øye is reached by boat from Ålesund in 4 hrs or by bus and ferry from Ørsta in an hour. From Oslo, travel by train to Otta and bus to Geiranger in one day, next morning by ferry to Hellesylt and bus to Øye in 2 hrs. The road distance from Bergen via Voss and Vangsnes (ferry, 30 min) to Øye is 325 miles, or by ferry from Bergen to Vadheim (6 hrs) and then by road to Øye, 137 miles. From Oslo via Geiranger (ferry, 1 hr) 307 miles, or via Otta and Stryn (no ferry) 351 miles. Maps of the Sunnmøre ranges are rather oldfashioned and inaccurate. Several peaks are not even mentioned. Patchell's old sketch map is no longer available.

THE AUSTEFJORD — SAEBØ SECTOR (maps B 27/28 Ålesund & C 28/29 Stryn) is the root of the large peninsula E of Ålesund, between Auste fjord and Hjørund fjord, bounded to the N by the main road between Ørsta and Saebø. The bus journey from Ørsta to Saebø takes 1 hr, from Ørsta via Auste fjord to Bjørke, 2 hrs. Accommodation at Ørsta and Saebø. *Matøskja* rises between Auste fjord and lake Bjørkedal. The 1st asc of its E foretop was made in 1958 by R Bjørkedal and O Helset. *Krokfannfjell* (1446), called Storetind locally, is a pinnacled peak in Kvandalen, SW of Saebø. Its NW ridge was climbed in 1935 by E F Eckhoff, H Hagen and R Tønnesen.

Krokfannfjell (Storetind) by NW Ridge — From Bjørdal seter up to W side of ridge. Up between sharp pinnacle and small needle, then over another pinnacle, or steep gully on R, and follow ridge to top. Descend via Marijonstigen and E side of lake Kvandal. Time from Bjørdal seter and back, 8 hrs. (A Dagfinn Hovden).

Skårtind (1500) is a long ridge S of Saebø. "It would take about a week to do the entire ridge!" There is good sport, and one can have as much or as little as one likes, since it is always possible to turn difficult parts on the W face. 1st ascents of peaks and pinnacles on this ridge have been made by G Arbuthnot, W D Capjon, O H Furuseth, S Løvenskiold, O T Messelt, M Moss, B Schlytter and J Vigdal. The usual route is up from Skår on the Hjørund fjord, via Skår seter across a small glacier and then by the S ridge to the top of Søre Skårtind, followed by a traverse. The S ridge can also be reached from Bondalen. *Skårkongen* is the most difficult pinnacle on the N ridge. 1st asc 1933 by M Flem and H Hagen, up from the NW gap to a distinct gully in the centre of the W wall, then either up the gully, or turn R and climb up on narrow cracks. Severe. *Jeksla* pinnacle rises N of Skårkongen. 1st asc 8/1933 by H Hagen and E Heen, from plateau below the S wall, proceed towards the E wall across small slab and up to spacious platform, where a steep gully with good holds leads to the top.

Litle Toren is an elegant peak on the promontory between Dals fjord and lake Bjørkedal. A new route was made in 1959 by E & J Bjørkedal and O Helset.

THE ØRSTA — SAEBØ — STORE STANDAL SECTOR (map C28/29) Stryn) lies between the roads Ørsta-Saebø and Ørsta-Store Standal. The usual starting point is Saebø on the Hjørund fjord, reached by bus from Ørsta in 1 hr. The *Miendalstinder* (1402) make a splendid "first day climb", exceptionally suitable for beginners. This range is situated halfway between Saebø and Standaleid, and the main summit is in sight during the whole ascent. The avalanche of 1924 has planed the ground quite smooth up to the snow. The 1st asc was made in 8/1899 by dr Richards, Wm C Slingsby and S Urke, up from Saebø by an easy snow slope and an easy rock ridge. Time from Saebø and back, 7 hrs. A route by the W side was made in 8/1953 by H Flook and W Tennant, a delightful and yet really easy ascent, the last part by a ridge to the top.

Blåtind (1085) is a pretty double-peaked ridge NW of Saebø and W of the Grøtdalstinder. The 1st asc of both peaks was made in 9/1895 by C W Patchell and J Simpson, from Kalvedalen and up by a gully to the gap, whence both peaks are reached easily. A traverse of Blåtind was made in 8/1903 by W P Haskett-Smith and C W Patchell via the gap N of Nordre Blåtind, up by the N ridge and traverse across Nordre and Søre Blåtind, descending by the SE ridge. From this point, N Grøtdalstind and Nevedalstind can be climbed with descent to Standaleid. The SW ridge of Søre Blåtind was climbed in 8/1955 by L Arentz-Hansen and J H Høye, an excellent climb, but severe. The 1st winter asc of Søre Blåtind was made in 2/1958 by A R Heen, A D Hovden and J H Høye, up by the SE ridge.

Søre Blåtind by SW Ridge — From the Standal hut, through Kalvedalen to the SW ridge which overlooks Bondalen. Follow ridge to foot of slab which is bypassed L by way of steep gully which terminates in chimney. Follow ridge to overhang which is turned L, up steep and short gullies. From top of overhang, turn slightly R and climb straight up steep slabs with cracks to top ridge. The uppermost crack is severe. The uppermost pitch is about 130 ft long and affords no resting place before summit is reached. Time from hut to foot, 2 hrs; from foot to top, 3 hrs; severe. (J H Høye)

The 3 *Grøtdalstinder* (1326) are situated N of Saebø and S of Nevedalstind. The 1st traverse was made in 7/1903 by W N Ling and H Raeburn, climbing Søre by its E face and then across Midtre and Nordre Grøtdalstind, descending by the NE ridge. Time from Saebø and back, 8 hrs. The easiest route to Søre and Midtre Grøtdalstind leads from Frøland farm in Bondalen and up by the W face.

Nevedalstind is a twin-topped peak between Saebø and Standaleid. 1st asc 8/1908 by A W S Brown and C W Patchell, up by a gully on the E ridge to the gap between the summit and the little E horn, then to the top by a short chimmy and easy rocks. The N ridge was climbed in 1939 by P Devold and H Hagen, across Lille Nevedalstind to the main summit. A good traverse is had from the highest Nevedalstind via Nordre Grøtdalstind and Søre and Nordre Blåtind; descent into Kalvedalen. The 1st winter asc of Store and Lille Nevedalstind was made in 1936 by C Amundsen and H Hagen.

Nevedalstind by W Face (usual route) — From Standaleid to Nevedalen, also called Kopsdalen. Up on E side of lake, across slabs to gully on W face, which terminates in gap between both summits. Then to highest top by steep rock and short chimney. (H Hagen).

THE ØRSTA — STORE STANDAL — VARTDAL
SECTOR (maps B 27/28) Ålesund & C 28/29 Stryn) is
the top of the peninsula, N of the road between Ørsta and
Store Standal. Ålesund Ski Club owns a fine hut at
Standaleid, below Setretind, reached by bus from Ørsta
in 1 hr. *Liadalsnipa* (946) rises out of Ørsta fjord, 3 miles
NW of Ørsta. Its E ridge was climbed in 1925 by A J
Velle and party. This ridge is easy with 2 diff pitches,
an exposed and interesting variation from the other routes.
Its W face was climbed in 7/1953 by A D Hovden, J H
Høye and O Simenstad. The easiest way lies straight up
the W ridge from Halse farm. *Saudehorn* (1320) is a
prominent peak N of Ørsta, said to resemble Svartdalspiggen in Jotunheimen. It was climbed in 8/1889 by G
Hastings in 3 hrs from Ørsta. Magnificent views. The E
ridge was climbed in 7/1962 by H Buset, O Helset, A D
Hovden and A Næss, from Velle via Skytjådalen and up
by the ridge between Kirketind and Saudehorn, following the ridge to the top, a good climb with clean firm
rock. Its E neighbor is *Vassdalstind* (1300), a pretty
aiguille. 1st asc 9/1895 by J Simpson and S Nupen, from
Nupedalen and up by the S arete, descent by a steep
gully on the N face into Vassdalen. It is easier to ascend
by the E face. The 1st winter asc was made in 3/1960 by
O Helset and A D Hovden, up by the E face.

The *Sveddalstinder* (1152) are situated W of Romedalen,
a fine ridge, capped by 5 peaks. *Årseterhorn* is the southernmost point, followed by *Kjerringa* (1152), which sets off
an E top called Høgehorn. Then follows *Heimste* and
Fremste Raufanndalstind, the latter connecting with
Sveddalstind, which is the northernmost point. Its narrow
E ridge which has never been attempted, runs from Stein-
støyl in Romedalen and straight to the summit. The
usual route is by the airy N ridge. Old reports are confusing, but it appears that Bowen, Haskett-Smith and
Patchell made a N—S traverse in 8/1903 of Kjerringa and
probably Heimste and Fremste Raufanndalstind. In
1959, O Helset and A D Hovden climbed Sveddalstind
by the N ridge and traversed via Fremste to Heimste
Raufanndalstind.

Kolåstind (1463) is a grand peak which Slingsby called the
"Monarch of Sunnmøre". Its main features are as follows:
(a) Kolåstind glacier on the E side, facing the Setre-
tinder, provides the usual route. Climbed in 8/1876 by Wm
C Slingsby, but he did not reach the final top. 1 asc in
1880 by A Hovden and Betzy Kjeldsberg with N Kolås.

(b) The E ridge, climbed in 7/1962 by H Buset, O Helset, A D Hovden and A Næss, an airy and interesting route on solid rock. (c) The S wall drops steeply down from the long E ridge, climbed in 7/1933 by H Hagen and E Heen. (d) The SW ridge drops steeply from the summit to Sylen, then continuing almost horizontally towards Fingeren and Gluggen, climbed in 1939 by E Kraus and R Morch, a severe route, repeated in 1956 by E Aasen, H Berg, T Engeseth, A D Hovden, J H Høye and G Monsen. (e) The W wall, facing the Romedal, climbed in 1925 by N Kolås and party. (f) The NE ridge, dropping N from the summit, then bending easterly, parallel with the E ridge. Part of this ridge is still unclimbed and is very severe.

Kolåstind by E Side (usual route) — From Myklebust seter and then up by Kolåstind glacier to the top. Time up and down, 6 hrs.

Kolåstind by S Wall — From skihut or Myklebust seter and up by gully near SW ridge. Turn L, to distinct gap. Over easy rocks, then 30 ft dead L and 2 rope lengths straight up to broad ledge. Turn R, across slab below projecting rock, to small hole under steep wall. Turn R again, down to gully which leads through pot-hole created by large, loose boulders (great care), to gap below final top. Climb 1 rope length towards L and then straight up to slightly inclining slab. Trough steep chimney to top. Time from foot to top, 5 hrs. (H Hagen).

The *Kolåstind Pinnacles* on the SW ridge provide good sport. Five of them were cairned in 1875 by E Mohn. *Fingeren* which is the westernmost pinnacle, was cairned in 9/1895 by C W Patchell and J Simpson. The exposed face above Sylen is Kolåstind's S wall. Fingeren presents obstacles on its SW side, which was climbed in 7/1953 by T Bersås, J H Høye and O Simenstad. The climb is about 4 rope lengths and should be made with the traverse from Fingeren to Sylen. Very severe. Fingeren's E face has never been attempted. The 1st asc of *Sylen* was made in 7/1933 by H Hagen and E Heen via the E gap and up on slabs on the N face, returning the same way. Severe. A traverse from the gap E of Fingeren and on to Sylen which was climbed by the usual route, was made in 1935 by E F Eckhoff, H Hagen and R Tønnesen. Severe, incl several abseils. The S wall of Sylen was climbed in 1938 by H Hagen and H Lystad, a very severe route. *Gobo Needle* near the NE ridge was cairned in 1960 by G Hestad, O Mork, O R Nesje and B Ugelvik. The 1st asc of *Munken* or Heklenåla and *Lille Kolåstind*, both pinnacles on the NE ridge, was made in 1957 by T Engeseth, A D Hovden and J H Høye.

Sylen by N Face — From Standaleid to foot of peak, then up by open gully on N face. Straight up 18 ft to small hollow with good belay. Up by steep crack to crag and across small slab to top. Return same way to gully and proceed to skar between Sylen and Kolåstind.

Romedalstind (1304) is situated N of Kolåstind, with narrow and jagged ridges. The 1st asc was made in 9/1894 by E V Mather, C W Patchell and J Simpson, up by the NW ridge. An easier route, up the E ridge, was made in 8/1903 by H C Bowen and C W Patchell. The 1st winter asc was made in 1960 by O Helset and D Hovden, up by the S ridge. *Setretind* (1402) is a 3-peaked ridge E of Kolåstind and N of Standal seter, rising above the Standal ski hut. The 1st asc and traverse was made in 7/1903 by W N Ling, H Priestman and H Raeburn, up by the E face of Nordre Setretind, then following the ridge to the N gap of Søre Setretind. Its N ridge forced the party out on to the glacier, from which they ascended the E face of Søre Setretind, descending by the same route. The N ridge of Søre Setretind has never been climbed. Patchell was supposed to have made it in 1904, but Hovden believes he followed Raeburn's route. The S wall (Sydpillaren) of Søre Setretind was climbed in 6/1953 by H Berg, J H Høye, R Øyen and O Simenstad. The 1st winter asc of Søre Setretind was made in 1956 by A R Heen, D Hovden and J H Høye. The *Setretind Pinnacles* are plentiful, and many afford good sport. 1st ascents: 1 in 1949 by P Hohle and S Solberg; Brynet, Kloa and Saga in 6/1953 by H Berg, J H Høye, R Øyen and O Simenstad.

Søre Setretind by Sydpillaren (S Wall) — From Standaleid, climb towards central ridge of 3 ridges on S face. Across crags and mossy ledges to grassy plateau below steep wall. First 1 rope length towards L, then follow centre of ridge. The climb is about 6 rope lengths. Easiest line of descent by glacier to Fladalen. Time from Standaleid across summit down to N gap, 7 hrs. (J H Høye).

Have you ever heard of a mountain which fires great salutes on summer days, accompanied by white smoke? This is true of *Isflåmannen* (850) or the "Saluting Mountain" at Vartdal on the N tip of the peninsula. There is a 350 ft high vertical wall near the top, and this is where the "shooting" comes from, especially in rainy weather with SW or W wind. The white smoke is ejaculated like steam from a boiler. A climbing expedition tried to solve the mystery in 1957, abseiling from the top, but the wall appeared to consist of perfectly ordinary gneiss. Similar phenomena also appear at Molaupsåta, St Olavs Dal and Litledalsmannen.

Jønshorn (1437) rises steeply out of the Hjørund fjord with frightening precipices, ice-filled cirques and a pinnacled ridge. Its NE face was climbed in 8/1889 by G Hastings, and it has also been climbed from the fjord direct. The usual route is up from Barstadvik to Ramtind and then by the W ridge to the summit. The 1st asc of

Slingsby and Randers tops seen from the Molladal valley (Photo: Lystad)

Molladalsgubben pinnacle on the N ridge was made in 7/1954 by D Hovden, J H Høye and O Simenstad. The Jønshorn massif sets off a series of interesting peaks. *Holtanna* is the southernmost peak. 1st asc 1932 by E-H-R Hagen, up from the N gap into open gully which turns into a chimmy, then across a steep slab to the top. A steep gap separates it from *Mohns Topp.* 1st asc 9/1904 by C W Patchell and E V Slater, traversing across snow and boulders from Randers Topp. The S wall of Mohns Topp was climbed in 7/1954 by D Hovden, J H Høye and O Simenstad. It has also been climbed from Jønshorn, a sharp ridge with many delightful pinnacles of which *Tårnet* is the highest. 1st asc 7/1936 by P Devold, E F Eckhoff and R Tønnesen. Tårn Skar separates Tårnet from *Randers Topp.* 1st asc 9/1904 by C W Patchell and E V Slater, up by distinct gully from Molladalen. Its W wall was climbed in 1953 by J H Høye and O Simenstad. *Slingsbys Topp* is separated from the others by a little valley, the Litlestandal. 1st asc 8/1908 by A W S Brown and C W Patchell, involving a 50 ft chimney topped by a large flat table-stone under which the exit has to be made, and which resembles that on the Shamrock on the Pillar.

Mohns Topp by S Wall — Climb towards L from gap between Holtanna and Mohns Topp, up mossy ledges to plateau. Up narrow gully to R towards spacious shelf. Straight up 1 rope length in open and partly overhanging gully to broad shelf. Continue straight up, then towards R to large plateau, then easy to the summit. Time from gap to top, 1 hr. 1 severe pitch. (J H Høye).

Randers Topp by W Wall — From Molladalen and up slabs directly below Tårn Skar, via crack to shelf beneath 13 ft high block. Up on block; good belay. One step to R and steeply up to upright position on small loose block below overhang. Piton belay. Then 13 ft up towards right to sloping shelf with narrow depression. Belay in small rock. Follow loosely defined gully on steep wall for about 1 rope length. Resting place on shelf with fixed piton.

Somewhat easier gradient towards gorge below Tårn Skar. Climb slabs high up to R and into bottom of gorge. This is the most diff pitch, about 300 ft. Steep rope length into Tårn Skar. Turn R and ascend steep snowdrifts, then up open gully to summit. Time from foot to top, 4 hrs. 7-8 pitons. Very severe. (J H Høye).

THE BJØRKE — NORANGDAL SECTOR (map C 28/29 Stryn) is the root of the large peninsula E of Hjørund fjord and W of Geiranger fjord, bounded to the N by the main road between Øye and Hellesylt. Bjørke or Øye are the usual starting points. The southernmost range is the *Laudalstinder* (1580), a ridge with many interesting pinnacles. 1st asc 1881 by Wm C Slingsby and J Vigdal. The 1st traverse of the whole ridge was made in 1933 by E F Eckhoff, M Midsem and F Moe. *Storhorn* (1583) rises S of Bjørke, a dome-shaped peak with a pinnacled N ridge. The 1st asc was made in 1876 by Wm C Slingsby, from E from the glacier. In 1881 he also made the 1st asc of one of the pinnacles which are called *Kjerringkjefter* (Sweetheart Lips). The N ridge of Storhorn was climbed in 8/1895 by J S New, J E Sunderland, W Wareing and S Bjerke. The same party also made the 1st asc of 2 adjacent peaks, *Kvithøvd* (1660) and *Rokkekjerringa*. The latter rises out of lake Tussevatn, opposite *Hornindals-rokken* (1588), which is a beautiful peak. Its precipitious W wall which has never been climbed, drops steeply into lake Tussevatn. The N ridge was climbed in 7/1903 by J N Ling and H Raeburn from Bjørke, descent by the S ridge. *Kvitegga* (1704) stands N of Hornindalsrokken. Slingsby and Vigdal climbed it in 1891 by a "horrible route" up the N face from Kvitelvdalen, but a variant which is now the usual route was made in 9/1894 by E V Mather, C W Patchell and J Simpson. Time from Fivel-stad, 5 hrs up, 2 down. A descent into Nebbedal was made in 8/1890 by C W Patchell and O Lillebø, but this is a dangerous route. The NE ridge was climbed in 7/1900 by G P Baker, H Priestman, Wm C Slingsby and L Haugen, at that time one of the best and longest climbs in Sunnmøre, but this ridge has since suffered from a severe avalanche and the lower half is covered with much vegetation.

Staven (1518) is a remarkable mountain with one of the great rock walls of Norway, rising nearly 5000 ft out of the narrowest part of the Norangdal, 6 miles E of Øye. This E wall has never been ascended, and experts say that it is not suitable for climbing. *Lillehorn* stands W of Staven. 1st asc 8/1908 by A W S Brown, C W Patchell, and P Scones, by an easy traverse from Isenåsi. *Jakta* (1593) is situated S of Øye. Its W face rises 5000 ft sheer out of the valley and has never been climbed. The 1st asc was made in 8/1896 by H C Bowen and C W Patchell scrambling up the E ridge. They also climbed the curiously shaped needle from the S. Time from Øye and back, 7 hrs. The S ridge was climbed in 7/1903 by W N Ling, H Priestman and H Raeburn in 4 hrs from Øye, 2½ down. *Konehorn* (1277) overlooks Norangdalen, S of Union Hotel at Øye. It can be reached by a heavy grind from the S. It was climbed from NE in 1955 by T Wibye, J R Wilkinson and J A Wood. Its N wall is a giant precipice, partly overhanging and not suitable for climbing.

THE URKE RANGES (map C 28/29 Stryn) are situated N of Urke, E of Hjørund fjord and W of Urkedalen-Sykkylven fjord. Urke is reached by bus from Øye in 20 min or by ferry from Saebø in 30 min. Local youth hostel. Straumgjerde is another climbing centre, situated at the head of Sykkylven fjord. Local pension. Frequent bus/ferry services from Ålesund via Sykkylven. The walk from Urke to Straumgjerde takes about 7 hours. *Saksa* (1073) is a twin-capped peak N of Urke. A cairned footpath leads from Urke to the S col. In climbing the last 200 ft below the summit one should keep to the extreme L, where a good track leads on to the top. Its N ridge leads to *Elsanntind* (1395). The SE ridge was climbed in 7/1899 by H Armstrong and J Vigdal. The usual route from Urke is by way of the N branch of the Urkedal to the E gap. *Urkedalstind* (1535) is the S peak of the Regndalstinder, presenting a S face of rugged and precipitous scree. 1st asc 7/1897 by G Arbuthnot, E C Oppenheim and J Vigdal, traversing from Velleseterhorn and ascending Urkedalstind by the E ridge. The S face can be climbed from Urkedalen by steep and loose gullies and buttresses.

Råna (1593) is a grand peak, a miniature Wengen Alp. Trandal Skar is the gap on the NE ridge. Skuffelsenes Skar is the greatest obstacle on the SW ridge — so steep that "only a dead man would descend from it into Lille Trandal on the other side!" It has never been ascended or descended. Råna's top is an inclined plain, sloping gradually upwards from S to N. It is broad enough for a fair-sized town, and is supported on all sides by precipitous cliffs and ridges bristling with towers and pinnacles. The 1st asc was made in 9/1899 by G Hastings by the W side, a mere scramble in 5 hrs from Urke or 4 hrs from Trandal (reached by rowing boat from Urke). The NE ridge was climbed in 8/1897 by G Arbuthnot, E C Oppenheim and J Vigdal, a long and very fine climb. The SE wall from Regndal glacier was climbed by O Hansen and party in 8 hrs from Urke, 4 down. The N wall was climbed in 7/1930 by E-H-R Hagen, a grand route but highly exposed and dangerous. Severe. Its SW ridge from Skuffelsenes Skar was climbed in 8/1937 by P Devold and H Hagen, a fine route with good sport.

Råna by NE Ridge — From Velle or Trandal via Trandal Skar to gap in NE ridge just above sharp pinnacle. This gap is only reached from the S. Follow ridge, bypassing crags on N face. The ridge terminates in a steep wall just below summit. It is turned to L, first by descending 20 ft and then steeply up again and so to top. Time from Velle to top, 7 hrs.

Råna by SE Wall from Regndal Glacier — From Urke via skar between Nonshorn and Urkedalstind, on to Regndal glacier which is very crevassed and about 3 miles long. The climb commences at a point about 500 ft SE of the top and follows an ill-defined gully. The bergschrund may be difficult, but the 60 ft long climb is easy. Time from Urke, 6 hrs up, 4 down. 2 ice axes. An alternative route leads from Straumgjerde by Hansen's gully to Regndal cirque and then across glacier to top.

Råna by N Wall — From glacier below N wall, about 250 yds E of the cairn and just below the "step" which is a distinct platform below and E of Råna's highest point. Good holds and safe belays at first, but higher up it is necessary to work towards SE wall. Bypass first gully, then take second gully to a little skar about 35 ft deep and situated 240 ft NE of cairn. Then to top. Time from foot to top, 6 hrs. Severe.

Råna by SW Ridge from Skuffelsenes Skar — From Trandal seter via Kjerringhodet and up W side of ridge to glacier below Råna's N wall. Climb up to gap. Here the ridge appears to be unassailable. However, climb 20 ft straight up to overhanging buttress which is turned to L. Into an open gully for 2 rope lengths. Then follow arete, partly to L, straight up to top. Time from foot to top, 3 hrs. More exposed than diff climbing.

Råna's evil-looking SW arete links it with *Tranhullstind*. 1st asc 7/1897 by G Arbuthnot, E C Oppenheim and J Vigdal, up by obvious gully on the W face to the SW ridge which is followed to the summit. Time from Trandal and back, 5 hrs. *Trandalshatten* (1548) is a pretty peak N of Trandalen, called the "Reiffelhorn of Sunnmøre". The usual route is up by the W ridge, down by the E side. Time from Trandal and back, 6 hrs. *Blåbretind* (1472) is situated NE of Trandal. 1st asc 8/1897 by E C Oppenheim and J Vigdal, up by the SW ridge which bristles with provoking little pinnacles, descent by the N ridge. Time from Trandal and back, 8 hrs. Its NW ridge leads to *Storevasstind* (1275). 1st asc 7/1897 by G Arbuthnot and E C Oppenheim, up by a tricky chimney on the S face. The best route is up by the E ridge to the easternmost summit. *Straumsheimshorn* (1430) is situated NE of Storvasstind. 1st asc 9/1897 by G Arbuthnot, E C Oppenheim and J Vigdal, making a N-S traverse from Straumgjerde. The usual route goes up by the SW face. Time from Trandal and back, 8 hrs. *Slettefjell* (1350) rises NW of Straumsheimshorn in Riksheim valley. Oppenheim has described it as a "virgin peak which looks as if it would afford some excellent rock climbing."

THE ØYE RANGES (maps C 28/29 Stryn & C 26/27 Molde) include some of the finest peaks in the whole of Sunnmøre. This is the area N of Norang fjord, E of Urkedalen and S of the main road between Straumgjerde and Stranda. Visitors will find many splendid mountain walks as well as a perfect feast of climbing. Union Hotel at Øye is one of the most popular mountaineering hotels in Norway. Its proprietor treasures a valuable and highly interesting "climbers' book", dating back to the era of Slingsby and Patchell. Almost every peak in the district can be reached and the return made to Øye the same day. Primitive overnight accommodation can be had in the unstaffed Patchell hut (4 beds), situated at 2500 ft in the triangle between Slogjen-Brekketind-Smörskredtind. A new tourist lodge is being built in Gullmordalen between Slogjen and Brekketind.

Slogjen (1588) which rises sheer out of the Norang fjord near Union Hotel at Øye, has provoked more lyrical outbursts than any other peak in Sunnmøre. Slingsby has called it the prettiest peak in Norway, and Raeburn has said that the Fjord Route affords more climbing than what is afforded from the Italian or Swiss side of the Matterhorn. The 1st asc was made in 1870 by John Klokk and brother, up by the SE ridge from Øye, now the usual route. A route up the NW face and E arete from Jente Skar (gap between Slogjen and Klokksegga) was made in 8/1899 by G Hastings, Wm C Slingsby, A & O Todd. This route is steep and toilsome. The famous Fjord Route by the SW face was made in 7/1903 by W N Ling and H Raeburn. This is a grand rock climb, essentially for experts only. The 1st winter asc was made in 12/1934 by A R Heen and T Krohn by the usual route. A descent by the E face has been made once, but this is a horrible and dangerous route which should not be repeated. An attempt to ascend by the W gully was halted about 100 ft below the col.

Slogjen by SE Ridge (usual route) — Leave road at Patchell monument, take path through farm to foot of peak, starting at large cairn. It is essential to keep to the ridge as much as possible until above the tree line, trying always to keep Øye in view until open ground is reached. Pleasant descent to Urke from the shoulder into the head of the Langeseterdal. Time from Øye and back to Urke, 8 hrs. No rope or ice axe. Well cairned route.

Slogjen by NW Face & E Arete from Jente Skar — From Urke via Langeseterdalen to Jente Skar (gap between Slogjen and Klokksegga), across frozen tarn, through small gorge up to gap below Slogjen. Proceed towards NW face to pinnacle on NE ridge about 450 ft below summit. The rest is easy. Time from Urke to top, 6 hrs.

Slogjen by the Fjord Route (SW Face) — From Lille Slogjen at Øye, go up L side of torrent in Armstrong—Vigdal gorge. Follow gorge for several hundred feet until steep wall which partly blocks gorge on R. Here is a broad cleft which turns into a chimney to L and a narrow gully to R. Up chimney until it terminates in an overhang. Out on to a slab to R of chimney, then on broad shelf, past loose block and steeply up to ridge. Easy climbing along ridge until angle eases and leads into gorge which is followed easily for several hundred feet to SW wall which rises towards the top. One rope length to R to section with easiest gradient. Follow a gully to a 10 ft high block, then

1 rope length to L and a steep somewhat open gully to the ridge. Over a couple of buttresses to L, around a corner and up by a steep short gully. Above it is a steep rock wall with several vertical cracks. The L crack is easiest and leads up to a plateau. Turn L, up a short vertical wall with a crack in the centre, and again to L up final gully to top. Time from foot to top, 8—10 hrs. Severe. (H Hagen).

Smørskredtind (1629) rivals Slogjen in popularity. The twin spires of this peak are so perfectly proportioned and so exquisitely balanced that even in Sunnmøre there is nothing to surpass them. Baedeker himself said that Smørskredtind resembles the Wetterhorn. It is Slogjen's near neighbour. There are five recognized routes, all good climbs, none quite easy, and two giving really fine rock work. The 1st asc was made in 8/1884 by Wm Eckroyd, Wm C Slingsby and Jon Klokk, up the E face from Langfonn, the usual route. Its NE ridge was climbed in 8/1899 by C W Patchell and A Todd. The W ridge was climbed in 8/1901 by H Kynaston and L Haugen. A variation was made in 1938 by F E O'Riordan and B Ruud, and another variation in 1954 by E Lloyd and party. The NW ridge from Habbostad was climbed

Smørskredtind near Øye (Photo: Lystad)

in 8/1932 by O H Furuseth and O T Messelt. They also made the 1st asc of 2 pinnacles on the W ridge. The SW wall was climbed in 8/1935 by E F Eckhoff, H Hagen and R Tønnesen, an exposed and impressive route with belays hard to find and sloping holds. A new variation "fra dalen" (?) was made in 1959 by B Fostervoll and B Ugelvik. The 1st winter asc was made in 4/1944 by H Berg and A R Heen. *Austre Smørskredtind* rises opposite the main summit. The 1st asc was made in 9/1908 by A W S Brown, C W Patchell and P Scones, up by the NE face.

Smørskredtind by E Face from Langfonn (usual route) — From Russedalen, up broad snow slope below summit and up wide gully to either summit. The two are connected by a sharp arete, easily passed by a traverse on the N side a little below it. Descent by gullies on S face. Rope and axe.

Smørskredtind by NE Ridge — From Patchell hut across steep glacier to NE skar, up steep ridge with good holds but loose rock. A steep crag below the top is bypassed towards L. Time from Øye to top, 6 hrs.

Smørskredtind by W Ridge — From Øye via Skylstadbrekka to W ridge, traverse R and upwards across face of large rock tower which is steepest part of W ridge, until reaching large and apparently unclimbable gully. Climb upwards to meet the ridge up a series of grooves, two of which are very diff, joining the ridge at its narrowest point. Very diff. It is also possible on the lower section to climb edge of L ridge of gully. This is very steep and exposed and gives fine climbing. (E Lloyd).

Smørskredtind by NW Side from Habbostad — From Patchell hut, climb up N side of W ridge, straight to top. Time from Øye to top, 5 hrs.

Smørskredtind by SW Wall — From Skylstadbrekka, turn R, below W ridge, on to steep SW face, start climbing near small snow patch 650 ft below summit. 3 rope lengths up a gully to steep slab of lighter colour. Bypass slab to L, 2 rope lengths. Then 4 rope lengths straight up to broad shelf which leads towards R to steep crag. Up on crag and around overhanging block. Traverse 1 rope length towards R, to small ledge. Then 18 ft straight up and 13 ft towards L on narrow inclining crack. Finally 1 rope length of easier climbing to hollow below top. Time from Øye to top, 8 hrs. 2 ropes for 3 climbers.

Austre Smørskredtind by NE Face — This peak rises opposite twin-peaked Smørskredtind. From foot of couloir, follow steep slopes of grass and scree towards base of final rocks. Cross steep little glacier up to NE ridge which follow to top. Time from Øye, 5 hrs up, 3 down.

Brekketind (1571) is a grand twin-peaked mountain forming a horse-shoe with 3 adjacent glaciers and 3 pinnacled aretes. The W ridge terminates towards N in Lille Brekketind and the E ridge terminates in Store Brekketind. Brekketind Skar is the fine pass W of Brekketind. The 1st asc of *Store Brekketind* (1571) was made in 9/1889 by G Hastings and Wm C Slingsby, up from Habbostad via the W gap, now the usual route. The N ridge was climbed in 7/1903 by W N Ling and H Raeburn. The E ridge was climbed in 8/1933 by C Amundsen, O Drabløs, R Frøland and R Sonneville. The S wall was climbed in 8/1937 by H Hagen and E Heen, choosing the easternmost of the 2 gullies which lead from glacier to top. The 1st winter asc was made in 12/1934 by H Hagen and A R Heen by the usual route. *Lille Brekketind* is approached via the glacier and up the sloping slabs to a col E of the summit. The traverse to Store Brekketind is interesting. Rope is required for all routes, and an ice axe will be found useful.

Store Brekketind from Habbostad (usual route) — From Patchell hut across moraine and glacier and little col to W gap, then easy climbing to cairn. Time from Øye and back, 8-9 hrs. It is an interesting climb to follow the ridge to Lille Brekketind.

Store Brekketind by N Ridge — This ridge can be reached either via Gullmordal glacier or by glacier E of the peak. Steep but easy climb. Time from Øye and back, 10 hrs.

Store Brekketind by E Ridge — Although this ridge runs S-N, it is usually called the E ridge. From Patchell hut across glacier to NE ridge which follow to first gap, using rope down to bottom and then turn R, towards sharp peak of next gap. Abseil again (90 ft rope), continue to R, across small slab and up past projecting rock. Past 3 smaller clefts to top.

Store Brekketind by S Wall — 2 gullies lead from glacier to top. Start up E gully, partly in it and partly to L. About halfway up, make an easy traverse to W gully, which leads nearly to top. Time from foot to top, 2 hrs.

Velleseterhorn (1523) is the highest point of 4 peaks on a long ridge NW of Brekketind. The 1st asc was made in 1890 by W Barrow and H Priestman, up from the glacier by the E ridge, following its extreme W end. Time from Urke and back, 8 hrs. Its S face was climbed in 7/1897 by G Arbuthnot, E C Oppenheim and J Vigdal, also making the 1st asc of the 3 remaining peaks. A traverse of the ridge was made in 7/1936 by B and M Lyche.

Brunstadhorn (1495) rises in splendid and wonderfully pinnacled precipices from Brunstad Skar, sending a long and gently sloping shoulder towards Habbostaddalen. The Brunstad Skar which leads from Brunstaddalen to Habbostaddalen, is a narrow and jagged mountain pass. Brunstadhorn is said to resemble a "petrified troll". Its N peak is highest. The 1st asc of *Søre Brunstadhorn* was made in 8/1899 by C W Patchell, Wm C Slingsby, A & O Todd from Brunstad Skar and down by a steep chimney to the snow-paved gorge below, then up grassy slopes and easy rocks to the top. The 1st asc of *Nordre Brunstadhorn* (1495) was made in 8/1903 by H C Bowen, W P Haskett-Smith and C W Patchell, up by the S face, a laborious route. The only difficulty is the crossing of a narrow and very steep snow gully. Time from Øye to top, 6 hrs.

The *Hammersettinder* (1216) are situated E of Straumgjerde and N of the Sykkylven—Stranda road. Only the northern peak affords real sport. 1st asc 1931 by C Amundsen and H Hagen, climbing from the S. It was climbed from the N in 1943 by H Hagen and R Ranes.

Nordre Hammersettind from S — From Straumgjerde into Gimsedalen and up to S gap of the peak. Up E side of gap on mossy shelves to gully leading to gap between the 2 first noteworthy pinnacles. Continue to last pinnacle, then abseil, so easy to top. The only difficulty lies in bypassing the last pinnacle. It is made on E side — or rope used for abseil can be left and used to climb steep N face of pinnacle. The ridge can also be descended to the N. From top to sharp pinnacle, abseil into gap and proceed on W side 60 ft down to plateau. Follow ledge which ends in a moulding, steep down the ridge just below pinnacle and follow ridge down to Gimsedal seter. Time from Straumgjerde and back, 8 hrs.

Nordre Hammersettind from N — From Straumgjerde via Gimsedal seter, follow N ridge to sharp pinnacle near top. Abseil on R side to moulding which leads to plateau. Up to gap S of pinnacle. Difficult from gap to ridge which is followed to top. Time from Straumgjerde and back, 8 hrs.

On the E side of Geiranger fjord, *Lauparen* (1449) rises E of Vaksvik, a fine conical peak with a very narrow E ridge which has never been climbed. The S and N faces present no difficulties. The 1st winter asc was made in 2/1954 by H Berg, J H Høye, A Næss and B Ugelvik, up by the N ridge.

ROMSDAL

Few tourist districts in Norway have evoked more lyrical outbursts than the Romsdal. The valley with its mountain ranges is said to be a worthy rival to the Yosemite itself, and the Romsdalshorn has been compared with the Matterhorn. The scenery is fascinating and the whole district is ideal for walking tours and rock climbs. Åndalsnes is the principal centre, facing the blue Romsdal fjord, reached by train from Oslo in 12 hrs. From Bergen by coastal express steamer to Ålesund in 16 hrs and then by bus to Åndalsnes in 4—5 hrs. The road distance from Oslo is 287 miles, from Bergen via Vadheim 171 miles plus 2 ferry crossings. Good accommodation is available at Åndalsnes.

One of Norway's best known rock climbers, Arne Randers Heen, lives at Åndalsnes. His experience ranges from all over Norway via the Alps to Himalaya, and he has made more 1st ascents, new routes and 1st winter ascents than most climbers are allotted in a lifetime. He runs a tailoring firm, but in his spare time he is prepared to assist climbers who want more information.

THE ISTERDAL RANGES (map G220 Setnesmoen or D 27/28 Romsdal): The famous hair-pin road from Åndalsnes to Valldal runs through the Isterdal valley with magnificent views of the Isterdal peaks. Trollstig Hotel on the top of the mountain pass (2790 ft) is reached by bus from Åndalsnes in 1 ½ hrs. *Bispen* (1475) is the southernmost peak and nearest to Trollstig Hotel. 1st asc 8/1882 by C Hall, M Soggemoen and E Norahagen, from Stegfoss via the hill SW of lake Bispevatn, then up by the SW gully. The least difficult route goes via the Bispevatn to the gap between Bispen and Kongen and then up by the N ridge, but the boulders along the lake are troublesome. Time from Stegfoss to top, 3 hrs. 1 rope. The S ridge was climbed in 11/1932 by A R Heen and T Krohn, thereby also making the 1st winter asc. A 9 ft crag above a spacious platform about halfway up should be turned to the right. Time from Stegfoss to top, 2—3 hrs. 100 ft rope. The E ridge was climbed in 1951 by A and S Gjendem and T Krohn. Time from Stegfoss to top, 4 hrs. The 1st winter asc by the E ridge was made in 1960 by T W Pattey and N H Stevenson. *Kongen* (1593) rises N of Bispen. 1st asc 8/1882 by C Hall, M Soggemoen and E Norahagen, by the S ridge. This route takes 3 hrs from Stegfoss via lake Bispevatn to the top. The traverse from Bispen to Kongen takes 2 hrs. The E face which drops steeply into the Isterdal, was climbed in

Kongen and Dronninga seen from the Isterdal valley (Photo: Normann)

8/1939 by A R Heen, T Krohn and S Nissen Meyer. This is a fine route, strictly for experts. The 1st winter asc was made in 11/1939 by A R Heen, up the usual route by the S ridge from lake Bispevatn.

Kongen by E Face from Isterdal — Start from the main road in Isterdal and walk up grassy slopes on the E side. Turn right, towards the gorge, when within 3 rope lengths of it. Difficult passage of a cavity. 2 rope lengths straight up on steep slabs broken by cracks. Belay. Along gallery towards gorge. Up by open gully to the left, to large plateau. Then easier climbing, leftwards to the top. Time from road near Knut seter to top, 7 hrs. 160 ft rope. Very diff.

Dronninga (1568) is a sharp summit ridge with many pinnacles, situated N of Kongen. The 1st asc of the N spur was made in 8/1882 by C Hall with Matias and Erik. The highest and southernmost pinnacle was cairned in 1928 by B Helseth and A Rypdal. The E wall direct from Isterdal was climbed in 8/1939 by R and S Nissen Meyer, a really grand route. The E ridge was climbed in 1941 by B Botolfsen, A R Heen and A Heyerdahl, another magnificent route, one of the most severe routes in Romsdal. A traverse from Kongen was made in 1946 by M Borg and A R Heen. They also cairned Prinsessa which is the westernmost pinnacle on the W ridge. It can be climbed from N or S and the ascent may be combined with any route. Time from foot to top and back, 30 min. No rope. The 1st winter asc of Dronninga was made in 12/1953 by A Næss and B Ugelvik, ascending from the W from Inn fjord.

Dronninga from Bispevatn — From Stegfoss to gap on L of Kongen's knee, slight descent on upper edge of snow glacier, diagonally upwards below Prinsessa pinnacle. Follow gullies to top ridge. Time from Stegfoss, 4 hrs up, 3 down. 1 rope.

Dronninga by N Ridge — From Isterdal seter up Urkleiva, across Karitind and up the N ridge. Time from seter to top, 5 hrs. 1 rope.

Dronninga by E Wall Direct from Isterdal — From the main road near Bø seter to the top of the birch slope on the E wall, up slabs to short open gully with holds in cracks. Steep crag to left. Half a rope length towards left and up on narrow distinct ledge. Up on long slabs to spacious gallery with large holed block. Up to broad cavity to the left of the block. Towards right to another gallery which leads horizontally to steep distinct gully which affords the only access to the wall. Up through gully, often with torrents, up to hollow below large projecting rock. Out on to the slabs to the left of gully, to point above 1st pinnacle on E ridge, which follow to top. Time from Bø seter to top, 14 hrs. 160 ft rope. Very diff.

Dronninga by E Ridge — From Bø seter to top of birch slope on E wall, then at slight left angle towards gorge to large open gully leading towards right. Cut sharp left across diff slab. Belays. Over small ridge to left, up to severe gully which terminates below large narrow gully. Good resting place in cave. Up on overhang, through chimney to grassy slope with drinking water. Long way up, steep and exposed climbing on right-hand side of E ridge. Then turn somewhat to the left and up on pinnacle and continue on ridge. Solid rock but spots for belays. Time from Bø seter to top, 15 hrs. 160 ft rope. Severe.

Dronninga from Kongen — Descend from Kongen by the W ridge to the knee and turn right, down through gorge and up by large open gully. Then follow Dronninga's SW ridge to top. Time, 2 hrs. 100 ft rope. Diff.

Karitind (1439) is an easy peak N of Dronninga. 1st recorded asc 8/1882 by C Hall with Matias and Erik. *Storgrovfjell* (1618), rises on the E side of the Isterdal, W of the Trolltinder. It provides magnificent views.

THE TROLLTIND RIDGE (1795) (map G 220 Setnesmoen or D 27/28 Romsdal): The Troll Peaks are the grandest of the Romsdal mountains. The fantastically jagged ridge baffles all descriptions. Its E face is for the most part absolutely perpendicular. This wonderful mountain wall is probably the highest overhang in Europe, a masterpiece of mountain architechture. A stone dropped from the top would touch nothing for nearly 5000 ft! Its N ridge is reached easily from Sogge bridge across Norafjell in 4 hrs from Åndalsnes, but the better routes are reached from Stegfoss near Trollstig Hotel, which is reached by bus from Åndalsnes in 1 hour. This is a S-N description of the Trolltind ridge:

Breitind is the southernmost peak. 1st asc 1880 by O K Lyngheim and the Speyer brothers. Time from Stegfoss to top, 3 hrs. No rope. Then follows *Stabben* which looks like a chimney stack, cairned in 1926 by E Birkeland and O Nygaard. Easy, no rope. *Trollryggen* (1742) is the ridge between Stabben and Trollspiret. 1st asc 1880 by Fieve and J Venge. It is reached from the S in 1 hour from the route to Store Trolltind. No rope. Trollryggen was the final goal for the dramatic ascent in 9/1958 by Arne Randers Heen and Ralph Höibakk, when they ascended its E side from Romsdal direct in 12 hrs, probably the most sensational ascent in northern Europe in this century. It was the 5th attempt and the 1st successful venture. The second ascent by this route was

made in 8/1959 by K Gottmann and M Obst, spending
2 nights on the wall. *Trollspiret* was cairned in 1929 by
M Hansen and A Næss. The top of this fine spire consists
of a large rock which looks as if it might topple over at
any moment — and probably will. The pinnacle is twin-
peaked and directly overhangs the stupenduous E wall,
facing the Romsdal. Best reached from Trollryggen.
Trollgubben is a peculiar pinnacle, its petrified troll face
looking eastwards. It was cairned in 1926 by O Broch
and E Fjeld. There is a choice of several routes from the
SE. The easiest route starts to the right. Traverse leftwards to the gap on spacious ledges. Turn left of another
pinnacle, then exposed climbing to the top. Time from
foot to top, 30 min. *Trollkjerringa* is one of the trickiest
pinnacles in Norway. Before reaching its top, it becomes
necessary to turn towards its N face, overlooking a
steep precipice of nearly 5000 ft. It was cairned in 1916
by A B Bryn, D B Burchardt, H Nygaard, E and L
Sundt, from E. It was climbed from the S in 1941 by
E Kierulf and L Onsager, and by the W wall in 1941 by
H Berg, A R Heen and J Undhjem.

Trollkjerringa from E Gap — Up through cleft in right-hand side of gap;
traverse a few ft towards left and up on shoulder. Up and out towards left
on loose flat rock. Up over severe crag (particularly when descending), then
easy to top. Time from foot to top, 30 min.

Trollkjerringa from S — Up on ridge facing lake Storgrov, climb 2 rope
lengths up its right-hand side. The last third is climbed on the ridge proper.
Time from foot to top, 45 min. Very diff.

Trollkjerringa by W Wall — Climb the wall at slight angle from the rocking
stone. Steep and exposed climbing, but good holds. Do not venture out on
the rock which sticks out from N wall. About halfway, there is a 6 ft high
projecting buttress which requires great care. Time from foot to top, 30
min. Severe.

Brurjentene are reached from SE in 15 min from the route
to Store Trolltind. No rope. The old *Brura* was cairned
in 8/1882 by C Hall with Matias and Erik, but most of
it toppled over the ridge with a big bang in 1946, leaving
a sharp needle which was cairned in 1947 by M Borg,
A R Heen and G Malones. Severe. *Brur Skar* is the lowest
gap on the ridge. Try to lie flat down and throw pebbles
into the Romsdal — a sheer drop of 4000 ft! *Brudgommen*
is an easy pinnacle, cairned in 8/1882 by C Hall, J Venge
and Matias. *Ugla* is a strange-looking needle, cairned in
1929 by M Hansen and A Næss in 15 min from foot to
top. *Spørsmålstegnet* is a sharp needle, climbed in 30
min. Then follows *Store Trolltind*, the big troll chief,
which was cairned in 8/1882 by C Hall, M Soggemoen
and J Venge, ascending from Isterdalen. It was climbed
from Adels glacier via Høg Skar in 9/1903 by H C Bowen
and C W Patchell. A route from Trollklørne was made
in 1922 by C Lysholm and H Nygaard. The N ridge from

Sogge via Nordre Trolltind was climbed in 1927 by E Fjeld and S Suhrke. The 1st winter asc was made in 1/1932 by H Hatlemark and K Oshaug, up from Lav Skar. The E wall from Romsdal direct was climbed in 1931 by A R Heen and E Heen, a long and impressive route, a first-rate climb involving an ascent of 6000 ft.

The Trolltind ridge seen from the Romsdal.
(Photo: NTK)

Store Trolltind from Isterdal (usual route) — From Stegfoss across glacier between Storgrovfjell and Breitind, up at slight angle towards Trollgubben. Time, 3 hrs. Follow cairns and footpath horizontally to Brur Skar. Past wide gorge to Storvarden. Bypass Brudgommen. Up through large gorge to left of Ugla, across Ugle Skar through hole in ridge, then keep below ridge, to L of summit plateau. Time from Stegfoss, 5 hrs up, 3 down. 1 rope. Alternative descent across W ridge via Trollklørne to Sogge, time 4 hrs.

Store Trolltind from Adels Glacier via Høg Skar — From Adels glacier and up by narrow gully to Høg Skar which lies W of Lav Skar. It may be difficult to reach the gully from the glacier. Time from Sogge, 6 hrs.

Store Trolltind by N Ridge — From Sogge to Adels glacier, then either via Nordre or directly up to ridge, SW of Nordre. The latter is shorter but more difficult. Past pinnacle and out on slab towards right. Up another slab to large rock. Further up and on to declining ledge towards right. Continue at slight angle, reaching summit to the right. Time from Sogge to top, 7 hrs. 100 ft rope.

Store Trolltind by E Wall from Romsdal — Leave road at Fiva, walk through woods to right of Storura (boulders), up easy slabs and grassy slopes to corner. Up through main gorge to snowdrift, halfway up. Follow ridge towards left until it rises steeply, then shift to gorge. Afterwards, follow another ridge towards right until it terminates below projecting crag. Turn right, pass under crag into main gorge. Up to large hole, through chimney up to Ugle Skar. Finally half an hour's easy traverse to Store Trolltind. Time from Fiva to top, 9 hrs. 180 ft rope. Very diff.

Nordre Trolltind was cairned in 1870 by General W Bromley-Davenport, MP, with J Venge. This ridge is reached from the main road at Sogge bridge and across Norafjell. Time from Sogge bridge to Nordre, 4 hrs. No rope. *Lav Skar* did connect with Adels glacier, but the gully from Adels glacier is now almost inaccessible owing to the recession of the glacier. The 1st asc of *Bjørka* pinnacle was made in 1930 by A R Heen and J F Strømme. 1 rope length from *Høg Skar* to the foot of Bjørka, then up its right-hand side from the gap in 15 min. *Søstrene* are sharp pinnacles on the S side of the ridge between Lav Skar and Trollklørne. Some were cairned in 1939 by E Birkeland, E H Falkenthal and S Hansen. *Trollklørne* are 3 sharp pinnacles, of which the highest was cairned in 1912 by C and J Lysholm. The lowest Trollklo is reached from Adels glacier, then up to S gap of central *Trollklo* which is climbed by its W side. Further up to highest Trollklo. Time from glacier to highest top, 2—3 hrs. These pinnacles should be included when returning from Store Trolltind. 100 ft rope.

THE ROMSDALSHORN (1555) (map G 220 Setnesmoen or D 27/28 Romsdal) is a dominating and majestic peak, well seen in all its elegant grandeur by everybody passing through the Romsdal, whether by rail, road or boat. It is said to resemble the Monte Faloria. Arne Randers Heen states categorically that it is Norway's most famous peak. It rises out of the Romsdal valley 10 miles S of Åndalsnes. Its twin peaks are called Storehorn and Lillehorn, the latter not to be confused with "Litlehorn" on old maps. The gap between Storehorn and Lillehorn is called Kløfta and the summit ridge S of Lillehorn is called Hornaksla. The 1st asc of Romsdalshorn was made dramatically in 1827 by Hans Bjermeland and Christen Hoel as a result of a dare during a merry drinking party. They reached the summit "by alternately pushing and pulling", probably up the E side, as A R Heen has since verified. They built the cairn which is there today. The 2nd asc was made in 9/1881 by C Hall with Matias Soggemoen and Erik Norahagen, up by the entire E side which is now the usual route. This is a jolly climb, not many difficulties, but a constant succession of minor ones. The N wall was climbed in 8/1920 by O H Furuseth, H Nygaard, R Ødegaard and G N Sabro, another grand route. The 1st descent by this route was made in 1915 by C and J Lysholm. The W wall via Altanen was made in 8/1928 by E Fjeld and S Suhrke. Its S wall via Hornaksla was climbed in 9/1929 by A R Heen. The 1st winter asc was made in 3/1930 by A R Heen, K & O Oshaug, up and down by the usual route. The W wall via Nasen was climbed in 1939 by R & S Nissen Meyer. The E arete was conquered in 1947 by H Berg, A R Heen and Ø Røed. The SW ridge from above Gjelet was made in 1957 by P Harvold and A R Heen. A new route by the W wall from above Gjelet

Romsdalshorn is a dominating and majestic peak (Photo: Birkeland)

was made in 8/1959 by R Høibakk, F Hørtnagl and A Mayr. Very severe.

Romsdalshorn by E Side (usual route) — From Venjadal seter, walk to lake Hånjvatn and follow steep path up boulders, aiming at gap to L of Yellow Patch (brightly coloured large slab below top between E ridge and N wall). When reaching steep black wall, traverse 2 rope lengths towards right and up on 7 ft high projecting crag. 1 rope length horizontally and up on small ledge. 1 rope length up on slabs, turn left. Upwards to craggy slab which bypass to left and get into Halls Renne (large gorge on E side). Follow it by its right-hand side until final rope length which is climbed on left-hand side. Ascend to gap between both peaks, then up on steep crags with good holds. Time from Venjadal seter, 4-5 hrs up, 3 down. 100 ft rope.

Romsdalshorn by E Arete — Up to craggy slab below Halls Renne (large gorge on E side) and turn right, towards Yellow Patch. Up on slab, 1 rope length leftwards and on to ridge. Around steep corner. Firm belay. Up steep short gully to small plateau. Up on small crag, through gently sloping gorge to summit. Good holds and firm belays. Time from seter to top, 4-5 hrs. The ridge proper takes 1 hr. 100 ft rope. Severe.

Romsdalshorn by N Wall — From gap in uppermost section of N ridge, turn slightly L up to steep wall. 1 rope length up open gully, terminating in small slab. Firm belay. Across projecting rock with good holds. Steeply up 1 rope length to spacious platform. Either to L across blocks, 4 rope lengths to white buttress — or turn R, up on awkward slab, up easy long gully. Continue towards right, to top. Time from Venjadal seter to top, 5 hrs. 100 ft rope.

Romsdalshorn by W Wall via Gjelet — Up to gap on N ridge, 1 rope length above gap, descend at slight angle, out on W wall to the cavity to R of, and below, Korset (yellow slab on W wall). From the cavity below Korset, climb directly up broad gully, upward R. Severe.

Romsdalshorn by W wall via Nasen — To cavity below Korset as described above, then 2 rope lengths towards R and 1 rope length steep up. Belay. Slightly towards L and 1 rope length straight up to convex shelf. Belay. Across small ridge towards L. Half rope length up on steep slabs to narrow platform. Belay. Turn projecting crag to L and up to large cavity, then easy to Kløfta, or turn L towards top. The wall proper is 650 ft high. Time from seter to top, 7 hrs. 160 ft rope. Severe.

Romsdalshorn by W wall via Altanen — To cavity below Korset as described above. Then 2 rope lengths towards R, 1 rope length dead R, across slab with ledges, to 6 ft high crag. Belay. Steep wall. Steeply 1 rope length up towards R. Across large shelves to Altanen (roomy platform on W wall, 150 ft S of Korset). Straight up towards R, into ill-defined gully, 1 rope length up it. This is the crux of the climb. Belay. Along gallery towards R. Up steep gully to plateau. Dead L and up to Kløfta (gap between both summits). Time from Venjadal seter to top, 7 hrs. 160 ft rope. Very severe. The cavity below Korset can also be reached from the Romsdal by zig-zagging up the grassy slope with some climbing towards cavity. Time from main road to cavity, 8 hrs.

Romsdalshorn by S Wall via Hornaksla — The easiest way is through Venjadal and up, E of the Horn, across Hornaksla to gap in S wall. Descend 30
ft from gap towards L and on to shelf. Up a 10 ft high crag. Diff. Then
easier up 25 ft to good belay. Up another tricky pitch, behind large square
rock. Slightly L and up to good belay. Another 12 ft exposed climbing towards R and up on to ridge. Time from gap to ridge, 2 hrs. Finally an easy
climb to Lillehorn. Time from seter to top, 6 hrs. 160 ft rope. Severe. It is
also possible to reach gap below S wall by taking route below N wall out
into W wall to cavity. 1 rope length downwards R. Difficult around a corner
up to long easy gallery to S wall.

Romsdalshorn by S Ridge — Up by the sharpest ridge directly from gap.
Critical point about 15 ft above gap. Severe.

The 1st asc of *Lillehorn* was made in 8/1884 by C Hall
with Erik and Matias, up from Kløfta, a direct route
without obstacles. The E ridge of Lillehorn was climbed in
1958 by D Dawes and R Høibakk.

Olaskartind (1428) is wrongly called Litlehorn on the map,
situated SE of Romsdalshorn. 1st asc 1929 by A R Heen.
Its is reached either from Romsdalshorn's E glacier or
from lake Olaskar. Time from Venjadal seter to top,
4 hrs. A large gap separates it from *Kalskråtind* (1797).
1st asc probably in 1865 by L Broch and party. 1st
winter asc 1957 by A Bækkelund, J Høye and A Næss.

THE VENJATINDER (1843) (map G 220 Setnesmoen or
D 27/28 Romsdal): This is a fine ridge with 3 good peaks
rising out of the Venjadal opposite Romsdalshorn. Travel
8 miles by car from Åndalsnes to Venjadal seter which
is the starting point for all routes. Store Venjatind
(1843) is the northernmost point, separated from Lille
Venjatind by a large gap called Skaret. Its long S ridge
connects with Søre Venjatind (1799). *Store Venjatind*
(1843) was cairned in 1881 by Wm C Slingsby and J
Vigdal, climbing the NE snowy side, an ugly route which
has never been repeated. Its N ridge was climbed in
8/1882 by C Hall with Matias and Erik. An asc from the
E was made in 1912 by C & J Lysholm, up by gullies and
slabs to the E of Slingsby's route. It was climbed from
Skaret via Galleriet in 1925 by E Birkeland and party.
The W ridge was climbed in 1930 by E Heen and K
Oshaug. The 1st winter asc was made in 1/1931 by A R
Heen and E Heen, up by the N ridge. A route by the S
wall with traverse to the E ridge was made in 8/1935
by A R Heen and K Grønlund. The S wall direct was
climbed in 1943 by O Hatlen, A R Heen and B Tokle.
A new route by the E wall was made in 1959 by O Mork
and O Nesje. The SW gully with traverse to the S wall
deirct was climbed in 1960 by T Engvig and R Høibakk.

Lille Venjatind was cairned in 8/1884 by Wm Ecroyd,
Wm C Slingsby and E Norahagen from Vestgjelet (W

The Venjatind ridge rises out of the Venjadal (Photo: Birkeland)

gorge up to Skaret) and up by the N ridge. Time from seter to top, 5 hrs. 100 ft rope. The 1st winter asc was made in 1/1933 by A R Heen and B Sæter, via Vestgjelet and the N ridge. The S ridge was climbed in 1935 by A R Heen and K Grønlund. Time from Skaret to top, 45 min. 1 rope. The W ridge was climbed in 1950. Time from seter to top, 5 hrs. 1 rope. The SW wall was climbed in 1943 by O Hatlen, A R Heen and B Tokle, a first-rate climb of high standard. *Søre Venjatind* (1799) is the southernmost peak on the long ridge S of Lille Venjatind. 1st asc 8/1898 by C Hall and Matias, up from lake Venjadalsvatn (526) to the southernmost outlier. From Søre they traversed to the Lille. Time from seter to top of Søre, 6 hrs.

Store Venjatind by N Ridge — From lake Venjadalsvatn through snow gorge to deep cleft on N ridge. Follow ridge, first half on left side, last half on right side. Actual climbing only a couple of rope lengths below top. Time from Venjadal seter, 5 hrs up, 2—3 hrs down. 100 ft rope.

Store Venjatind from Galleriet — Up through gorge to Skaret. An easy long gallery leads in a circle to E ridge, which follow to top. Time from seter to top, 5 hrs. 100 ft rope.

Store Venjatind by W Ridge — The best route from lake Venjadalsvatn leads towards gorge to right of ridge, following the ridge where gorge turns northwards. Easy but exposed traverse to ridge. Moderate climb to 5 ft high rock, where ridge rises steeply. Up 1 rope length, slightly towards left on steep slab with cracks. Straight towards right over small slab. Severe. Belay. 2 rope lengths up easy gully, then towards left across ridge to spacious shelf. 1 rope length steep up, across difficult slab. Up to small hollow, often wet. Up towards left across crag. Belay. Continue leftwards across steep crag. Past small pinnacle. Up the "7 meter" crag to right, across ridge and on to plateau. The last crag provides the most severe pitch, but it can be by-passed easily to L. Time from seter to top, 7 hrs. 160 ft rope. Severe.

Store Venjatind by S Wall Direct — Climb W gorge until 65 ft below Skaret. Up by slabby gully to plateau. Turn left of large brownish block. Up on diff crag, across 2 plateaux. Turn left across small uneven slab, up steep gully to another plateau. Descend 10 ft towards left and traverse wall on inclining ledge to plateau facing W ridge. Up on diff 20 ft crag to shelf. Up by narrow gully. Severe traverse to hollow for belay. Up on very severe projecting crag, reaching W ridge 25 ft below summit. Time from seter to top, 6 hrs. Time from Skaret to top, 2 hrs. 160 ft rope. Severe.

Store Venjatind by S Wall & Traverse to E Ridge — Follow first half of route "S wall direct" and continue from plateau in centre of wall above gully, upwards and out towards right, across large ledges to right of top. Time from seter to top, 6 hrs. Time from Skaret to top, 1¹/₂ hrs. 100 ft rope.

Lille Venjatind by SW Wall — Across Søre Venjatind to foot of wall, towards left under large brightly-coloured section from which SW wall rises steeply. Follow long gallery towards S ridge. Up on crag to gallery on left. Up steep gully with good holds. ¹/₂ rope length exposed climbing, then 1 rope length up towards left to final gully which leads to top. Drinking water is found below cairn after rainfall. Solid rock and good belays. Time, 2-3 hrs on the wall proper. 100 ft rope. Severe.

THE KVANNDALSTIND (1775) (map G 220 Setnesmoen or D 27/28 Romsdal):

This grand peak rises 5000 ft sheer out of Mjølner glacier and affords splendid sport. Slingsby has called it the "steepest mountain in Europe". It is situated SE of the Venjatinder. The easiest approach is by car from Åndalsnes to Dale in the Erstaddal (10 miles) and then walk up Kvanndalen. Kvanndalstind was cairned in 9/1885 by C Hopkinson, Wm C Slingsby and L Jensen, up by the N ridge, the usual route. The SE ridge was climbed in 8/1896 by H C Bowen and C W Patchell. They called it the "finest rock climb in Europe". The S face was made in 7/1897 by C C & R P Bicknell, W N Tribe and E Norahagen. The W ridge was climbed in 1920 by C & J Lysholm. The 1st winter asc was made in 2/1933 by A R Heen and T Krohn, up by the S face.

Torshammer is a peculiar 90 ft high pinnacle on the W ridge. It was cairned in 1925 by E Fjeld and S Suhrke, up by the E side on small ledges, or through narrow hole to L. Time from foot to top,

Torshammer is a peculiar 90 ft high pinnacle on the W ridge of Kvanndalstind (Photo: Birkeland)

15 min. Its W side was climbed in 1930 by E Birkeland and P Langdal, straight up, very steep but good holds. Time from foot to top, 15 min. The 1st winter asc was made in 1960 by A Bækkelund and O Mork.

Kvanndalstind by N Ridge (usual route) — From Dale, up Kvanndalen and climb straight up the ridge. Descent by S face or W ridge. Time from Dale to top, 5 hrs. A long but moderate climb.

Kvanndalstind by SE Ridge — From Kvanndalen, up by sloping glacier towards left to lowest point on ridge. A great tower about halfway up can be climbed or bypassed to the left. Time from Dale to top, 5 hrs. 100 ft. rope.

Kvanndalstind by S Face — Up glacier N of lake Svartevatn and get on to ridge in centre of S wall. Up to gorge, up to gap in E ridge. Follow ridge, 3 rope lengths to top. It is also feasible to follow shallow rock gully up to S face, reaching main ridge some 150 ft E of top, but this route is severe. Time from Svartevatn to top, 3—4 hrs. 100 ft rope.

Kvanndalstind by W ridge — Either up from Venjadalen via lake 1126 or up Kvanndalen if glacier conditions are favourable, or up Ola Skar from Horgheim, but the latter route is a heavy trudge. Follow S side of the ridge, past Torshammer, up on right-hand side of steep W ridge. Time from Venjadal seter to top, 6 hrs. 100 ft rope. If time permits, return via Søre and Store Venjatind. Time from Kvanndalstind to Store Venjatind, 3-4 hrs. The whole round trip is made in 14 hrs.

OTHER PEAKS NEAR ÅNDALSNES (map G 220

Setnesmoen or D 27/28 Romsdal): The W ridge of *Nesfjell* (842) drops right down to the Åndalsnes village. The ascent is an hour's scramble with magnificent views. No rope. *Setnesfjell* (1190) rises S of Veblungsnes, 2 miles by car from Åndalsnes. 1st asc 1872 by surveyor H C Due and party, from the E. Some climbs can be had on the peaks N of Hen at the head of Romsdal fjord. Travel 5 miles by car from Åndalsnes to Kavli farm and walk 4 hrs by cairned footpath across Loft Skar to Måsvassbu tourist hut at lake Måsvatn. *Kyrkjetaket* (1366) is an easy peak, reached in 3 hrs from Måsvassbu, or in 2 hrs from Kavli seter. *Klaua* (1500) stands N of Kyrkjetaket. 1st asc 1928 by C & J Lysholm, up by the SE ridge. The 1st winter asc was made in 3/1943 by H Berg, O Hatlen and A R Heen. *Blånibba* is reached by a 3 hrs' scramble from Vengedal seter. Splendid views. Some routes can be made on the S side.

Blånebba by S Wall — From ridge facing Romsdalshorn, traverse below S wall and up to grass shelf below steep slab, grooved by black cracks. Cairn. From shelf, slantwise to R, up 25 m in small gullies. Straight up steep gully (8 m). Up towards L in gully with projecting flakes, then a long way towards L. Straight up and later back to R towards bottom of distinct chimney. Up overhanging gully, slightly to R to bottom of chimney. Up its L side to spacious ledge below overhanging wall. From its L end, up 10 m high steep chimney, up gully towards R until it overhangs, then around corner to R and 3 m diagonally to L up steep slab to small shelf. Slantwise to R and up overhanging pitch to gully. Traverse back L to small triangular shelf below large overhang (piton left behind), around corner to L and into steep gully to top. This wall is 200 m high, very steep, but solid rock. 5—6 pitons, time 3½ hrs. Severe. (T Engvig and R Høibakk).

THE LAKE EIKESDAL RANGES (maps D 27/28

Romsdal & E 27/28 Lesja): Lake Eikesdal is one of the most beautiful mountain lakes in Norway. River Eira which runs from its N end to the fjord, is a famous salmon river. The Mardøla waterfall which is situated W of the lake, is Norway's highest waterfall with a free drop of 975 ft. Travel by bus from Åndalsnes to Øverås at the N end of the lake in 3 hrs, or from Molde in 2½ hrs. Accommodation. By motor boat across the lake to Eikesdal at its S end in 2 hrs. Accommodation. Hoem farm on the W side of the lake is reached from Åndalsnes direct by car via Grøvdal farm to Søredal seter (11 miles) and then a walk of 5 hrs by cairned footpath across the pass between Juratind and Nyheitind to Hoem. Vike farm lies on the E side of the lake, opposite Hoem, reached by motor boat from Eikesdal in 1 hour.

The Mardøla waterfall near lake Eikesdal. Norway's highest with a free drop of 975 ft. (Photo: Birkeland)

Hauduken (1730) is situated on the W side of the lake. 1st asc 1874 by H C Due and party. *Hoemstind* (1738) is a long ridge N of Hauduken. The 1st asc of its highest point was made in 8/1893 by C Hall, M Soggemoen and E Norahagen, up from Hoemsgjura. The E peak was cairned in 1939 by H H Aamot, E Birkeland, E H Falkenthal and A Hansen. The 1st winter asc was made in 1954 by E Kylling, A Næss and B Ugelvik. *Juratind* (1562) is a grand peak halfway between Eikesdal and Øverås. 1st asc 1880 by I Kavli, B Moen and 2 shepherd boys, up the NE ridge, which is now the usual route. Time from Søredal seter to top, 5 hrs. 100 ft rope. The SE ridge was climbed in 7/1889 by F M Beaumont, A Bill, R B Caldicott, R S Rotherham, A Øverås, Kristoffer & Kristian Vike. This is a jagged ridge with several towers. Time from Søredal seter to top, 6 hrs. 100 ft rope. The W ridge was climbed in 9/1903 by H C Bowen and C W Patchell, a better route than the NE ridge. Firm rock. Time from Søredal seter to top, 6 hrs. 100 ft rope. The 1st winter asc was made in 2/1931 by A R Heen and E Wille, up by the SE ridge. *Nyheitind* (1590) is situated N of Juratind. 1st asc 8/1874 by surveyor Iversen and party, up by the S face from Juratind's N gap. Time from Søredal seter to top, 5 hrs. 100 ft rope. The N face was climbed in 7/1899 by V H Gatty and E Hånde. Time from Nebba lake to top, 3 hrs. *Sjøvdøla* (1710) stands NE of Nyheitind. 1st asc 9/1874 by surveyor Iversen and party. The usual route is up by the SW face from Juratind's N gap. Time from Søredal seter to top, 5 hrs. A traverse from Nyheitind was made in 7/1899 by V H Gatty and E Hånde. The 1st winter asc

was made in 1957 by A R Heen and H Lange, up from
the NW. *Knorten* (1380) is the N spur of Sjøvdøla. 1st asc
1937 by A R Heen and S Rotevatn.

Ågottind (1588) on the E side of the lake is a veritable
knife-edge with 3 peaks, rising steeply out of the lake.
The best approach is from Vike, which lies N of the ridge.
The summit ridge is so narrow that it can be straddled
in places, with one leg dangling in the air. Some of the
rock is very loose. The 1st asc of *Nordre Ågottind* was
made in 7/1891 by a farmer from Eikesdal, scrambling up
from Vike. *Midtre Ågottind* (1388) was cairned in 9/1896
by H C Bowen and C W Patchell, starting from Vike
and traversing the whole ridge from Nordre via Midtre
to *Søre Ågottind*, which had been cairned in 7/1891 by
B Goodfellow and E J Woolley, ascending by the SE
ridge. The 1st winter asc was made in 1956 by S Lid,
A Næss and B Ugelvik. *Vikesaksa* (1990) is situated
N of Vike. 1st asc 1910 by Hoem & Vike. The ascent by
the N ridge is merely a steep scramble. 1st winter asc
1959 by J Hostad and B Ugelvik. *Fløttatind* (1654)
stands N of Vikesaksa, a long pinnacled ridge. 1st asc
7/1899 by V H Gatty and E Hånde, from Øverås and up
by the E side, descending by the S side. Time from Øverås
and back, 10 hrs. *Goksøyra* (1318) are two peculiar peaks
N of Øverås resembling a horse's ears. 1st asc 1874 by
J Iversen and party. *Skjorta* (1715) rises NE of Øverås.
Its E face forms a steep precipice which terminates in a
large cirque. The 1st asc was made in 1874 by J Iversen
and party, up by the N face. *Lille Skjorta* was cairned in
7/1899 by V H Gatty and E Hånde, up by the E ridge
from the E col, whence they returned to the col and
climbed the nameless E peak.

THE TROLLSTIG RANGES (map D27/28 Romsdal):
The main road between Åndalsnes and Valldal is the
usual starting point, reached by bus from Åndalsnes
in about 2 hrs. *Finnan* (1800) is a fine ridge behind
Bispen, reached from the main road near Trollstig Hotel.
The 1st traverse was made in 8/1898 by C Hall, M Soggemoen and E Norahagen. Time from Stegfoss to top, 3
hrs. 100 ft rope. The 1st winter asc was made in 11/1938
by A R Heen and P Sæter. *Storfjell* (1560) stands SW of
Trollstig Hotel, separated from Lillehesten by a large gap.
1st asc 8/1900 by C Hall and Matias, traversing from
Lillehesten. *Grønnfonntind* (1550) rises W of Storfjell.
1st asc 8/1899 by C Hall and Matias. They also cairned
Taskedalstind (1595), ascending Midtre peak first and
then traversing the whole ridge. In 8/1900 the same party

traversed *Seterfjell* (1516), which probably is the unnamed ridge between Taskedalstind and Grønnfonntind.

From Myklebust farm on the Åndalsnes—Valldal road, there is a walk of 6 hrs to Fokkhaug tourist hut Pusken seter on the map. *Trollvasstind* (1360) stands immediately N of Fokkhaug. The 1st asc of its twin-peaked ridge was made in 8/1897 by C Hall and Matias. Its N wall was climbed in 1959 by O Nesje. *Måsevasstind* (1349) is a long ridge in magnificent surroundings, E of Trollvasstind. 1st asc 1875 by surveyor F Jacobsen and L Skåre. They also cairned *Nonstind* (1688) which rises between Måsevasstind and Middagstind. The 1st traverse was made in 1897 by C Hall and Matias. *Middagstind* (1556) is situated NE of Fokkhaug and just N of Berildstøl. 1st asc 1895 by J E Furø and brothers Vold. An almost vertical rock tower on its N ridge is called *Middagshorn*. 1st asc 8/1897 by C Hall, M Soggemoen and L Skåre, up by the N ridge which is very narrow and yields good sport. The 1st asc of all Middagstind pinnacles was made in 1938 by E Aandahl, E Birkeland, E H Falkenthal and T Lundtvedt.

Trollstolen (1333) drops into Romsdal fjord just S of Vågstranda, which is reached by bus from Åndalsnes in 1 hour. 1st asc 1872 by F Jacobsen and party. He also cairned its neighbour, *Blåstolen* (1050).
The southernmost peaks in the Trollstig ranges can also be reached by travelling by bus from Åndalsnes to Valldal (2½ hrs), ferry to Tafjord (1 hr), car to Rauddalen (12 miles) and finally a walk of 5 hrs to Reindal seter (tourist hut). *Pytteggen* (1984) is the highest peak in the Romsdal, situated on the cairned footpath between Reindal seter and Pyttbua. The usual route is up by the E ridge from Pyttbua, descent to the S gap and walk to Reindal seter, an expedition of 8—9 hrs. No rope or ice axe. *Karitind* (1967) stands SE of Pytteggen, reached from Pyttbua in 3—4 hrs. *Benkehø* which rises NE of Pytteggen was always believed to be the highest peak in the district, but A R Heen has now verified that its height is 1900 metres.

THE TROLL CHURCH (maps C26/27 Molde & D25/26 Kristiansund) is a wonderful rock cave situated N of Molde, the "City of Roses", reached by bus and ferry from Åndalsnes in 2 hrs or by coastal express steamer from Ålesund in 2½ hrs. Good accommodation. Travel 17 miles by bus from Molde to Frena and walk 1½ hrs by cairned footpath via Nøsen seter to Brattfjell. There are

3 entrances into the fantastic stalactite grottoes, which contain a subterranean river and a 45 ft high waterfall which cascades into a giant "troll church" of glistening white marble. Torches are required.

NORDMØRE AND TROLLHEIMEN

Trollheimen is the "Home of the Trolls", a district of ancient sagas and fairy tales. The scenery is truly grand, and there is a fine network of cairned footpaths, also many good mountain lodges and tourist huts. The best access is by train from Oslo to Oppdal in 9 hours and then by bus to any starting point in the Sunndal valley.

For rock climbs and glacier walks, the best centres are in Nordmøre. The Nordmøre peaks have a distinct charm of their own, and there are climbs for experts and novices alike. Another attraction is that there are still impressive walls which have never been climbed as yet. The best centres are Sunndalsøra and Innerdal. Travel from Bergen by coastal express steamer to Molde in 19 hours and bus to Sunndalsøra in 3 hours. From Oslo by train to Oppdal in 9 hours and bus to Sunndalsøra in 2 hours. Good hotel accommodation at Sunndalsøra for climbs in the Lilledal and Sunndal ranges. The Innerdal Lodge and Rendøl seter can be reached by bus and car from Sunndalsøra in an hour, the final 4 km by jeep. The owner of Innerdal Lodge, Olav Innerdal, is an authorized guide and has made a series of 1st ascents and new routes.

THE LILLEDAL RANGES (map E27/28 Lesja): This is the mighty group of peaks which rises S of Sunndalsøra between Lilledalen and Haremsdalen. Every peak can be reached from the E by a scramble up Haremsdalen, but the Lilledalen side provides real sport. *Lille Kalken* is the northernmost peak. Its impressive N face which overlooks Sunndalsøra, was climbed in 1880 by Ole Håsen, a fine 1st asc which even today would rank very high. *Hårstadtoppen* stands immediately S of Lille Kalken, its S ridge connecting with *Hårstadnebba* (1640), the famous peak with Slingsby's "awful chimney of nearly 6000 ft". Alas, it is not a chimney but a wall, and the height is nearer 5000 ft than 6000 ft, and — worst of all — now is has been climbed! This wall has for many years been the dream of expert climbers from many countries, and it was made partly in 1959 by O Mork and O Nesje, and finally and completely in 1961 by R Høibakk and O Innerdal, a fine feat and an exposed route. The gully is very prominent from the Lilledal road and starts opposite of enjoyable diff climbing, descent by the W ridge. Its S ridge was climbed in 8/1957 by R Mason, A Rogers, R Thompson and N Williamson, descending by the W ridge. The same party also climbed *Røyskattfjell* (or Lamda), a minor peak on the W ridge of Fosstind. *Anderstind* (959) rises N of Fosstind. 1st asc 7/1957 by T J C Christie and P M Gerrard, following the ridge from Sukkertoppen, a delightful ridge, narrow and exposed in places, descent by the awkward S ridge to Foss col. Its W ridge will provide an easy route. *Sukkertoppen* or Larsgrunntind (3590 ft) is the most impressive peak on Arnøy. Its NE wall rises steeply from Tjyvdalen and is crowned by a ridge of 4 peaks and numerous pinnacles. 1st asc 1953 by V Aubert, up from the S saddle. Its NW ridge was climbed in 7/1957 by T J C Christie and P M Gerrard, descent by the S ridge to Anderstind. The SE ridge was climbed in 8/1957 by E H Hutton, L Noble and K C Treacher. They traversed the 4 summit peaks and descended by the NW ridge "against the grain of the overhangs".

Anderstind from Sukkertoppen — The main difficulty is a squat obstruction on the ridge, overhanging in the approach side. This is turned to L and surmounted by a 2-pitch rock climb (v diff). Belay under the overhang. Spectacular move round corner, followed by very steep and exposed climb hard v diff), up a mossy crack to convenient belay. The 2nd pitch has a few v diff moves, but less steep and less sustained than the first. Avoid the next obstacle, the Vulture Pinnacle, which appears very rotten, by descending into Black Coire a little way, crossing the base of pinnacle and cutting steps up steep and unpleasant groove of water-ice for about 200 ft, regaining ridge which is followed to top. Descent to Foss col by awkward S ridge. (T J C Christie).

Sukkertoppen by SE Ridge — Start from col between Sukkertoppen and Tågtind, then dip to waterfall heading for Tjyvdalen, where route defines itself into narrow ridge. The final 400 ft are more of a face climb than a sharp arete and one v diff pitch is required. Fine situations and views. The last section is fairly steep and care is required with loose stones and rock. Traverse 4 summit peaks and descend via NW ridge. Gaining the 2nd peak from the summit on the descent offers climbers a difficult moment. (M C Treacher).

The Arnøy W Group (maps 1635/3 Karlsøy & 1635/2 Arnøy) comprises the peaks W of Lang fjord and up the W coast to Nord-Rekvik. *Trolltind* (845) is situated W of Akkarvik. It is a good viewpoint for Lyngen and is often climbed by the locals. *Sotnestind* (842) rises out of the ocean, NW of Trolltind. Its W side is formidable. 1st asc 8/1957 by R Mason, A Rogers, R Thompson and N Williamson, up by the S ridge. From the E it offers a steep scree walk. *Trolldalstind* (906) is a fine looking mountain N of Trolltind. 1st asc 8/1957 by E H Hutton and K C Treacher, up by the E ridge, which affords a delightful climb. They proceeded by the superb NW ridge and cairned the little peak at its termination, but progress was then stopped by the formidable S wall fo *Breidskardtind* (880), which is a dangerous peak. Its E side is sensational, whilst the W side sweeps right into

Aerial view of the Kvenangstinder with the Arnøy mountains in the background
(Photo: Widerøe)

the ocean. The S wall offers the rock tiger a grand prospect on very loose rock. 1st asc 8/1957 by P Adams, R Bambridge, E H Hutton and L Noble, from the N col via an obvious rock tower. The route is loose and very exposed. Descent by the same way. A new route was made in the same month by E H Hutton, R Mason, A Rogers and K C Treacher, up by the NW arete. *Raudbergtind* (840) is a mountain of reddish rock, N of Breidskardtind. Two monoliths decorate the summit. It has an elongated N ridge leading to a subsidiary summit. 1st asc 1953 by V Aubert. The SE face was climbed in 8/1957 by P Adams, E H Hutton, L Noble and K C Treacher, a long and very good climb, which involves 500 ft in a narrow, loose and dangerous gully.

Breidskardtind from N Col — The low N col offers a feasible way of avoiding the lower E face by granting a way to an obvious rock tower. The col takes 2½ hrs from Akkarvik. The tower is gained by a crack on L (20 ft), then a traverse R (30 ft). Scramble to point high up on steep, loose and overhanging face on E side. An ascending traverse L (2 v diff pitches) takes one to a grass ledge going R, leading to summit ridge. Continue to top. The route is loose and very exposed. Descent via the same route. (K C Treacher).

Breidskardtind by NW Arete — Gain the same col but drop down the seaward side, then contour to base of obvious arete. The first few pitches require care on loose rock, but there are belays. After 300 ft of climbing, the first part is completed. Then follows a descent into deep gap of 70 ft before superb and exposed pitches are encountered for another 400 ft. A steep wall finishes the arete but it can be turned on easier ground to R. The party took it direct and then to top. Diff. (K C Treacher).

Raudbergtind by SE Face — From col between mountain and low flat-topped hill, standing by a high level tarn, the E side offers a fine looking buttress, a deep high gully, then a wide snow and scree shoot with a second steep buttress. The climb takes the narrow gully for 500 ft and then moves onto the rib of first buttress, terminating at a deep gap 560 ft above gully, and slightly to L of it. Over the gap, the summit ridge is taken for another 200 ft. A long and good climb, although the gully is loose and rather dangerous. Climb out of it and L wall. Belay. (K C Treacher).

The peaks between Akkarvik valley and Lang fjord afford a few climbs. *Sandnestind* (571) is the southernmost peak, crowned by a surveyors' cairn. Then follows *Lappeguden* (787), *Kistefjell* (748) and *Dalbakktind* (898). The latter was cairned in 7/1957 by M C Prestige and D Rhodes, up by the N ridge from Høgtind, easy descent to the W. *Høgtind* (924) rises on the same ridge. Its NE ridge was climbed by the same party. This ridge steepens at the top, overlooking the precipitous E face. A tower forms the summit and gives moderate climbing. *Svarttind* (645) is a saw-backed ridge in the centre of the island, NE of Høgtind. It was climbed in 7/1957 by I C Fowler. Its SW arete was climbed in 8/1957 by L Noble, R Thompson and K C Treacher and offers 450 ft of pleasant diff climbing before traversing the summit pinnacles. The 1st N-S traverse from Høgtind to Sandnestind was made in 8/1957 by L Noble and R Thompson in 13 hrs from Akkarvik and back.

Høgtind-Sandnestind N-S Traverse — Ascend Dalbakktind from Trolldalen, followed by an ascent of Høgtind. Retracing steps, difficulty is found S of Dalbakktind at the huge drop into the col that leads to Kistefjell. This is turned on W, because an abseil is unfeasable, but it is a dangerous turn because of loose rock. Lappeguden is a delightful peak to traverse and offers no difficulty. A descent from Sandnestind can be made on W, where a long rake offers an obvious and steep route. Care by the gully. Full traverse of ridge from Akkarvik and back, 13 hrs. (K C Treacher).

On the NW sector between S and N Rekvik stands *Klovsteinfjell* (856) or Platåtoppen which is a flat-topped peak E of Sør-Rekvik. Its NE ridge from Dalbakktind was climbed in 7/1957 by M C Prestige and D Rhodes. They traversed to *Kjeiletind* (677), which rises out of the ocean. *Storfjellet* (752) is another flat-topped mountain which is situated above Årviksand. It was climbed from the SE in 7/1957 by D Rhodes.

THE KÅGØY ISLAND (map 1635/2 Arnøy) lies S of Arnøy and SW of Skjervøy, reached by motorboat from Skjervøy in half an hour. *Store Vågtind* (1163) should offer interesting routes up the N and E faces. The usual route is up by the W side. Some of the peaks on the S side of the island may also afford scope for good climbs. (Sverre Dyrnes of Skjervøy).

THE VANNØY ISLAND (map 1635/3 Karlsøy) is reached in 2 hrs by boat W of Arnøy, an excellent climbing area with a huge range of peaks and at least one small glacier. Only 2 unnamed and uncairned peaks were climbed in 8/1957 by P Adams, R Thompson and K C Treacher during 30 hrs stay in bad weather. They landed at Vannvåg, which was a mistake, as Burøysund or Vannahamre would provide better starting points. There are good shops both at Vannvåg and Vannahamre.

THE FUGLØY ISLAND (map 1635/3 Karlsøy) lies 15 miles NW of Arnøy. A few empty cottages are situated at Gamvik. The island is little more than a high plateau of over 2500 ft with superb cliffs, but not so much for rock climbs as for ornithological and botanical purposes. It can be reached by fishing boat from Akkarvik on Arnøy island.

KVENANGEN (maps E 145 Bergsfjord and 1734/4 Nordreisa) is a peninsula which is reached in 1½ hours by local steamer from Skjervøy. A complicated system of sharp ridges rises gradually from the SW side of the peninsula and falls steeply into the sea on the NE side. The *Kvenangstinder* (1100) are the sharpest peaks. Very loose rocks. 1st asc of Store Kvenangstind in 1914 by C and J Lysholm, ascending by the W face. Its N wall has never been climbed. The *Kvenangspigger* are the pinnacles on the main ridge. *Presten* and *Highest Kvenangspigg* were cairned in 1914 by F and L Schjelderup, and the 5 remaining pinnacles were climbed in 8/1926 by E Fjeld and S Sigvang.

THE ØKSFJORD REGION

Øksfjord is a small fishing village in Finnmark, reached by coastal express steamer from Bergen in 4 nights. There is no direct road connection, but motorists may drive up the Arctic Highway to Alteid and then take a branch road to Storvik, perhaps also to Gamvik, whence there is a boat journey of 2 hrs to Øksfjord.

THE ØKSFJORD GLACIER (maps E 145 Bergsfjord and E 996 Øksfjord) is situated on the large peninsula SW of Øksfjord village. It can also be reached by boat from Alteid on the Arctic Highway, W of Alta. The glacier covers an area of 37 sq km and is said to be the only glacier in Europe that calves into the sea. The Jøkel fjord is rather narrow, and whenever a huge chunk of ice breaks loose and tumbles into the fjord, it is dangerous to come near it. The 1st asc of the glacier plateau (1166) was made in 8/1898 by G Hastings and E Hogrenning. The 1st traverse from Jøkel fjord to Øks fjord was made on skis in 6/1904 by J Thoner. *Brettentind* (1025) is a long and narrow ridge N of the glacier and E of Nuvs fjord. 1st asc 1897 by O Baur, making a complete S-N traverse.
The "Oxford Øksfjord Expedition" explored the mountains around the glacier in 8/1956. The party consisted of L Lewis, G Murray, T Norrish and W Roberts. "The

mountains were well up to expectations. In height they were not very impressive, the highest being only 3820 ft, but the rock is mostly gabbro and the general character is very like that of the Cuillin. We soon found that the mountains could become very hard if tackled from the wrong side, but nearly all of them had a fairly easy side. There are any number of fine rock faces, pinnacular ridges and tempting buttresses, but shortness of time made us go for the easiest route in almost every case" (G Murray in Oxford Mountaineering 1956). It appears from the press that R Davis, P J Hodgkiss and H Morris made several new ascents in this area in 8/1956. "And the weather? Exceptionally hot! The thermometer often showed 70 degrees F. The only rain they saw was on the last day as they waited for the boat" (Western Mail, Cardiff).

An Austrian expedition consisting of M Baldauf, R Schinnerl and K Spreng made the 1st asc in 7/1958 of unnamed peaks 530−750−850−940−720 which lie E of Øksfjord glacier, reached from Langstrand and Arnenes in Øks fjord. These heights were based on their "special maps dated 1907"!

Langfjord Glacier is situated on the same peninsula, W of Øksfjord glacier, and it appears from the map that the surrounding peaks might afford several good climbs, but there are no reports.

STJERNØY ISLAND (maps E 996 Øksfjord and E 885 Sørøy) lies N of Øksfjord village and SW of Hammerfest, reached by local steamer from either port, to Pollen fjord. Store Kvalfjorddal is the most suitable camping area for climbs on the S peaks, and the head of Smal fjord for the N peaks. Stjernøy supports no permanent ice. The S mountains are massive in form, but on the N side of the island are several long narrow ridges, not unlike the Black Cuillins on the Isle of Skye. There is also one outstanding peak, Stubben, which is precipitous on all sides. An expedition from Oxford and Cambridge visited Stjernøy in 1956. The party consisted of M J Bayley, D C Ford, B E Swift and B A G Weston. These notes are based on an interesting report from Derek C Ford.

Stjernøy S Group (map E 996 Øksfjord): *Rottenhaller* (907) is a fine ridge on the S half of the island. Its S and W sides offer easy routes. Its very fine N and E faces offer nearly 2000 ft of sustained climbing. The two are separated by the narrow NE ridge which was climbed in 7/1956 by M J Bayley, D C Ford and B E Swift in 3 hrs from Pollen fjord to top. The N face might give very severe ascents on its western flank. The E face is divided into two buttresses by a huge snow gully. The N buttress was climbed in 7/1956 by the whole party. Started direct, the ridge gives 200 ft of steep and v diff climbing. Then steep scrambling to a pleasantly rickety arete, which somehow sustains itself to the summit. Time, 3 hrs. The S buttress is probably more difficult. *Rottenhallerhorn* lies beyond the S buttress and is partially detached from the parent peak to form a minor peak. Climbed from Rottenhaller in 7/1956 by M J Bayley, D C Ford and B E Swift. Descend 200 ft of broken rock to a col, then 100 ft ascent. Easy. The N face of this peak is very steep and long and might make an excellent climb.

Stjernøy N Group (map E 885 Sørøy): *Stubben* (829) is a fine steep peak at the head of Smal fjord. It has 2 main ridges to E and W, a pleasant S face and a steep N face which is sustained from ocean to top. Its E ridge was climbed in 7/1956 by the Oxford/Cambridge party, up 600 ft of short faces and overhangs. V diff. The summit was uncairned. Descent via buttress on S face. Standing out from the W ridge about 300 ft below the summit is a slender 100 ft high rock tower with near vertical sides of very clean rock. The W-E traverse of Stubben, taking in this tower, might make a very pleasant excursion. *Smalfjordfjell* (886) rises on the ridge between Smal fjord and Lille Kjerring fjord. The 1st asc was made in 7/1956 by the same party, traversing the ridge from pt 849 on Kjerringfjell. Parts of the ridge overhang the E face, which contains some really fantastic pinnacles. *Kjerringfjordfjell* (849) is narrow and broken 5 km long ridge between Lille and Store Kjerring fjord. It was partly traversed from S to N by the same party in 7/1956. They reached the highest point (uncairned), but could not proceed further owing to thick mist.

SEILAND ISLAND (maps E 885 Sørøy and E 340 Hammerfest) lies N of Stjernøy and SW of Hammerfest. It can be reached by local boat from Øksfjord or Hammerfest in a few hours. The best camp site is Gyfjorddal for the W mountains and Bekkarfjord for the E parts. Apart from the two glaciers mentioned below, good rock routes could be made on the cliffs flanking the valley S of Skrei fjord, on the N face of Bårdveggen (859) and on the very steep flanks of the Haratinder in the W group. A party from Oxford and Cambridge visited Seiland in 1956. The party consisted of M J Bayley, D C Ford, B E Swift and B A G Weston. These notes are based on the report from Derek C Ford.

Seiland W Group (map E 885 Sørøy): *Nordmanns-fjord Glacier* (1075) is the highest point on the island, covering an area of 24 sq km. It can be ascended easily from Skrei fjord or Bard fjord on its N and W flanks, and also from col at head of Gyfjord valley. Harder routes are availlable on the E face, which is between 1200 and 1700 ft in height and 2 miles in length. It can be divided into these major cliffs: (1) S *Buttress* — lacks the interest of the other buttresses, but a pleasant arete ascent is

The " ConesButtress" on the E face
of Nordmannsfjord glacier
(Photo: Derek C Ford)

possible. (2) *Cones Buttress* — this central buttress is of peculiar form and is the outstanding feature of the E face. The direct ascent would probably make a fine climb with superb positions. (3) N *Buttress* — the principal face is excessively steep and made very dangerous by possible rock falls. Safer routes might be made on the adjacent faces. (4) *CB Icefall* lies between Cones and N buttresses and offers an "all-ice" route to the summit. The main fall is about 800 ft high and has 2 major zones of fracture, culminating in a short ice-cliff. Above this, a glacier and then smooth ice leads to the top. Ascended in 7/1956 by D C Ford and B E Swift. (5) *Red Buttress* lies N of the N buttress and is distinguished by its red colour. There is very good gabbro in places. Attractive routes abound. "Pinnacle Arete" stands out, climbed in 7/1956 by M J Bayley, D C Ford and B A G Weston, avoiding the last pinnacle. Diff. (6) The *Amphitheatre* is a glacial cirque lying between the N and Red buttresses. Several attractive gullies and very steep faces. In 6/1956 the Oxford/Cambridge party made a route up a buttress just to the N of the centre, traversed a broad gully and followed a narrower one to the plateau above. Mod diff.

Seiland E Group (maps E 885 Sørøy and E 340 Hammer-fest): The *Seiland Glacier* (981) is the northernmost icefield in Norway, covering an area of 35 sq km. It can be ascended easily from all sides. The 1st asc was made in 1826 by Robert Everest and B M Keilhau.

THE FINNMARK
MOUNTAIN PLATEAU

This is the very heart of the Lapp Country. There are probably not more than 32.000 Lapps altogether. Of these, some 21.000 live in Norway, 7.000 in Sweden, 2.000 in Finland and 2.000 in Russia. Lapps and reindeer herds can be seen at a number of places in north Norway, but the main centres are the Lapp villages of Karasjok and Kautokeino. Travel by coastal express steamer from Bergen to Hammerfest in 5 nights, and then by bus to Karasjok in 9 hrs, to Kautokeino in 11 hrs. By air from Oslo to Alta or Lakselv, then by bus from Alta to Kautokeino in 4 hrs, or from Lakselv to Karasjok in 2 hrs. These villages can also be reached by car by the Arctic Highway from Oslo.

The Finnmark mountain plateau is the only district in Arctic Norway where there is a network of tourist huts and youth hostels. The "fjellstuer" are built and owned by the State, and they provide simple but clean accommodation for wayfarers. Every fjellstue is also affiliated to the Norwegian YHA. The most popular walking tour in this area is the tour from Kautokeino to Karasjok, a fine walk of 4 days, spending the nights at Mieronjavre Lappoluobbal, Sjusjavre and Karasjok. Any walking tour in Finmark should be combined with a river trip on the Tana — Norway's largest salmon water, where 60-pounders are caught every season. The Tana covers a distance of 402 miles and is one of the most fascinating inland waterways in the whole of Europe. It is navigable by flat-bottomed canoes with an outboard engine, handled by a Lapp helmsman. Passengers sit in a rather cramped position on the floorboards. It takes 2 days from Karasjok to Skipagurra or vice versa, the intervening night being spent at Levajok Fjellstue. There are two series of rapids on the way down — first the Aile rapids at Øvre Storfoss, which are bypassed on foot on the Finnish side of the river, a distance of about 3 miles, and then the Nedre Storfoss rapids, where passengers are conveyed by lorry over a distance of about 5 miles on the Norwegian side. The boats are perfectly safe — although uncomfortable — and they are handled by expert boatmen. Motorists arriving at Karasjok or Skipagurra may have their cars transferred to the other end by experienced and reliable drivers.

THE NORTH CAPE REGION

An adventurous Viking named Ottar rounded the northern-most point of Norway in his Viking ship in 880, bound for the White Sea. Later he was sent to England as an emissary from King Harold the Fairhaired (860—940). Ottar met King Alfred the Great (871—901) and recounted the strange experiences from his journey "beyond the known world", and King Alfred wrote the historical account which is in the British Museum today. A British expedition in search of the NE passage to China landed at the top of Norway in 1553, and Stephen Burrows named it North Cape. This name has stuck ever since. In Norwegian it is called Nordkapp. In 1873, King Oscar II unveiled the monument which can be seen today on the summit plateau of North Cape. This event created the fame of North Cape as a tourist attraction.

The coastal express steamers do not normally call at North Cape, but they sail around it during the tourist season. They do call at Honningsvåg (5 nights from Bergen), and then you can travel 22 miles by bus to the very top of the North Cape summit plateau. When travelling by car from Oslo by the Arctic Highway, the distance is 1257 miles, including 5 ferry journeys. The whole disc of the Midnight Sun is visible at North Cape from May 14 to July 30, but it is never really dark at night long before and after these dates.

NORTH CAPE (map E 660 Nordkapp) rises 963 ft out of the ocean, a black cliff which is more famous for its location than for its climbing potentialities. An ascent by its SW side was made in 1820 by Sir Arthur de Capell Brooke. Robert Everest scrambled up the SE side from Hornvika in 1827, now the usual tourist route, aided by some hundreds wooden steps. Its N side provides the "most northerly climb in Europe", made in 1899 by K Bing and Per Grande. They also climbed *Nordkapphorn* by its E side. This is the peculiar pinnacle which struts out from the N face of the Cape.

FINNKJERKA (297) (map E 865 Sværholt) is said to be Norway's "most elegant sea cliff", situated at the entrance to Kjølle fjord, a branch of Lakse fjord. It rises like a magnificent cathedral with steep walls, graceful spires and solid towers. It was considered utterly inaccessible, and even A R Heen — Norway's best expert of Himalaya fame — had to give up his attempts in 1937. Finally, the 1st asc was made in 1955 by O Augestad and P Skavang. Somewhat further away lies another attraction — *Kapellet* — which is still unclimbed.

BJØRNØYA (BEAR ISLAND)

Bjørnøya or the Bear Island lies in the Arctic Ocean between Norway and Svalbard, covering an area of 178 sq km. It is only about 20 km long and 15 km wide with a great profusion of lakes — over 700 in all. The N sector consists of lowlands with shallow lakes. The SE sector is characterized by *Miseryfjell*, a large rock plateau with 3 peaks, of which the highest is only 1800 ft. The SW sector consists of rugged mountain country with no peak higher than 900 ft. The climate is unhospitable, cold and usually foggy throughout the summer, but not always; with luck, Bjørnøya is a fascinating sight.

The island is entirely uninhabited but for the crew operating the radio and meteorological station. There are no regular steamer connections, but the ms "Lyngen" will call when necessary, on her way between Tromsø and Svalbard. Such requests should be made in advance to Troms Steamship Company of Tromsø.

Bjørnøya's South Cape is distinguished by high cliffs lifting straight out of the sea, the home of millions of auks, guillomots and types of gulls. It is possible, while viewing this remarkable sight, to fish for cod with a hand line, and it is not at all uncommon to catch 50 lbs of fish in an hour, for here lie the famous Bjørnøya fishing banks. The bays and shores of Bjørnøya are strewn with fascinating remnants from its past — a coal mine, a rusted narrow-gauge railroad, walrus carcases and whale skeletons, all destroyed but preserved by the cold; monuments to the power of nature and the feebleness of man in this wild region. (Fred Baldwin).

JAN MAYEN

The Arctic island of Jan Mayen is Norwegian territory, situated between Iceland and Svalbard. It is 55 km long, up to 15 km wide, covering an area of 383 sq km. Jan Mayen is of volcanic origin, rising from the ocean depth of about 3000 metres, with peaks of over 2000 metres, the highest being *Beerenberg* (2545), an extinct volcano. The climate is notoriously bad, and the island is highly inaccessible. There are no regular shipping services, but a seal catcher, especially chartered for the purpose, calls once a year (around July 1) in order to bring new staff and provisions to the radio station and take back those who have completed a year's service. The relief ship is chartered by the meteorological institute in Tromsø, and enquiries should be directed to Vervarslinga for Nord-Norge, Tromsø.

the quarry. The main obstacle in the first part of the climb is a 15 ft high waterfall about 250 ft above the road. The rock is smooth, presenting no cracks for pitons and is slippery and overhanging. *Lillenebba* is the subsidiary peak of Hårstadnebba, which overhangs the Lilledal. The 1st asc was made in 6/1953 by J H Høye and L Sjølsvik, up from Haremsdalen to Hårstadnebba, traversing the short and narrow ridge to Lillenebba. *Store Kalken* (1872) rises S of Hårstadnebba. Its W wall has never been climbed. It is not continuous, but consists of a lower and an upper part, separated by a shelf which widens southwardly so as to give room for a tarn. The upper face leans back at an easier angle and is not visible from the Lilledal road. A party from the Polytechnic Mountaineering Club explored .Store Kalken in 7/1958. The party consisted of J Barucki, M Boardman, G Doughty and A Stephens. They traversed the snow fields of the W face and they climbed the E and W ridges of the N face.

THE SUNNDAL RANGES (maps E27/28 Lesja & E25/26 Surnadal) are situated on the N side of Sunndalen and S of Innerdalen. *Hofsnebba* (1565) is a fine peak with huge precipices and a jagged crest, rising shoreless out of deep waters, overlooking Sunndalsøra, opposite Lille Kalken. The 1st asc was made in 7/1906 by Wm C Slingsby and J Sjølsvik, climbing the N ridge from Sandvikdal Skar, which is the col between Hofsnebba and Furunebba, the latter being an outlier of the Vinnufjell. It was climbed from Sunndalsøra direct in 1939 by J Sjølsvik. The climb starts at the foot of the face near Riise Pension. An alternative route can be made by taking a more northerly course. Two pinnacles on Hofsnebba are called Rebekka and Tande. *Furuveita Ghyl* is the fearsome-looking gorge over 3500 ft high from Furugrenda up to Furuveita Skar, which lies between Hofsnebba and Furunebba. It has never been climbed in its entire length, but is considered feasible under favourable conditions. Slingsby and Sjølsvik attempted it in 1906, but were halted by the 30 ft high waterfall just below the top. This is the crux of the climb, as success will depend on the size of the torrent.

Vinnufjell (1823) rises between Hofsnebba and Trolla, crowned by 2 peaks. The S and highest peak is called Store Vinnufjell (1823), the other is Nordre Vinnufjell (1765) or Dronningens Krone (Queen's Crown). The best approach is from Dalsbø in Wirumdalen on the road to Innerdal. "There is an air of mystery and romance ebout the Vinnufjell and its great snowfields", Slingsby wrote in 1907, and his words still hold good, for this group is still far from explored. The 1st asc of both summits was made in 7/1906 by Wm C Slingsby and J Sjølsvik, ascending N Vinnufjell by the N face from Grasdal glacier, a route which involves very interesting ice work. They climbed Store Vinnufjell from Sunndalsøra and up via Tjustien ledge, which is highly sensational with a number of tricky obstacles and of a type which is rarely met with. It opens access to Sandvikdal Skar and on to Furuveita Skar and so to the main summit. The Polytechnic party from London also explored Vinnufjell in 1958 and made various routes up Store Vinnufjell. A new route to the Queen's Crown via the Queen's Veil was made in 1960 by Ø Dahle and N Faarlund. They also climbed Kongens Krone via Kongens Kappe. The 1st asc of *Austre Hesten* which stands N of Vinnufjell, was made in 1911 by P Nerdal.

Hoåsnebba (1609) rises abruptly from Sunndalen, 6 miles E of Sunndalsøra and connects northwards with the Trolla ridge (described under the Innerdalen ranges). Its impressive S face which overlooks Sunndalen, has never been climbed, although it may afford some first-rate climbing. The rock appears firm but overhanging. Any route up this face would be of high standard. The 1st asc was made in 1911 by O Bjerknes and H Tønsberg, from Hoås farm and up by the W face in 5 hrs. *Såtbakkollen* (1850) stands NE of Hoåsnebba. The asc by the S ridge is merely a scramble. The 1st winter asc was made in Easter 1939 by H Berg and O Innerdal, up by the NW ridge from Tårnfjell. A route up the NE ridge from the outlier towards Tårnnebba was made in 1950 by O Innerdal and L L Rødseth. Its E neighbour is *Navvarkollen* (1700), which terminates in a sharp peak called *Navvarnebbet*. Its N face has never been climbed, but it is believed it can be made. The 1st asc of Navvarnebbet was made in 1911 by C and J Lysholm. *Smørklumpen* (1663) is a massive mountain S of Navvarkollen. 1st winter asc 1956 by O Holm, B Ottesen and N G Skarland. *Storsalen* (1808) stands E of Navvarkollen. Its N wall has never been climbed.

THE INNERDAL RANGES (map E 25/26 Surnadal): *Grøvelnebba* (1390) is an Alpine peak between Sunndal fjord and Innerdalen, W of Innerdal Lodge. Its W side rises sheer out of the fjord. Its S face has never been climbed. The 1st asc was made in 1895 by E Bjørbæk,

N Johannessen, O Ottesen and L Pedersen, up by the N face. *Skarfjell* (1741) is one of the most interesting peaks in Nordmøre, situated SW of Innerdal Lodge between Grasdal and Giklingdal valleys. The 1st asc was made in 1850 by H Halthaug and J Holten, up by the W ridge from Grasdalen, which is the usual route. Time from Innerdal Lodge and back, 6 hrs. Its SE gully was climbed in 1921 by R Ødegaard and G N Sabro, a severe route which is suitable for experts only. The NE wall was climbed in 1927 by E Fjeld and J Innerdal, a strenuous route which requires great experience. The SE ridge was climbed in 8/1955 by L Arentz-Hansen and O Innerdal. The 1st winter asc was made in 1956 by O Innerdal, S Lid, O R Nesje, A Næss and A Wenaas. A new route by the E wall via the E ridge was made in 1958 by R Lapierre and P Vigerust. Two new routes were made in 1959 by R Høibakk, F Hørtnagl and A Mayr — Skarfjell by Fugleggen (E ridge) and by Olavsveggen (E wall). Even more new routes were made in 1960: Skarfjell was climbed by Giklingveggen (E wall of the SE foretop) by R Høibakk and A Næss; Skarfjell via Dørstokken by O Innerdal and S Ivarson, and finally Skarfjell's SE ridge (winter asc) by R Høibakk and P Vigerust.

Jutulene are the pinnacles on the N ridge of Skarfjell. It takes only a couple of hours from Innerdal Lodge to get to them. The first pinnacle is *Jutulhytta* with a fine chimney and *Jutulbladet*. The 1st asc of the latter was made in 1937 by A I Hoem. Very good sport. Then follows *Hammerhodet* resembling a giant hammer which is just about to knock down the Jutulnålen pinnacle. 1st asc 1911 by C and J Lysholm. *Jutulgubben* is a 200 ft high rock tower with slippery walls on all sides. The 1st asc was made in 1926 by O Broch and E Fjeld, up by the W face. The 1st winter asc was made by the W face in Easter 1949 by H Berg, O Innerdal and P Sylow. Its S face was climbed in 1952 by T Bersås and O Simenstad. Severe and airy. A new route via Kjellerhullet and Keisersnittet was made in 1960 by R Høibakk and S Ivarson. *Jutulnålen* is the sharpest pinnacle, a fine needle. 1st asc 1912 by H Tønsberg. A narrow crack leads from foot to top , but the usual route lies to the right of it, up by narrow ledges. The 1st winter asc was made in 1959 by G Hestad, R Høibakk and A Næss. *Jutulen* and *Tassen* were cairned in 1912 by H Tønsberg. The former is a long narrow ridge, about perpendicular, formed by square blocks. The latter is a small pinnacle near the precipice facing the valley. Two unnamed pinnacles on the N wall proper were cairned in 1950 by R Holth, O Innerdal and P Sylow.

Skarfjell by SE Gully — Up on snowdrifts in bottom of gorge, keeping R almost to top. Continue up on grass tufts, turn R, past ridge, up 1 easy pitch, then L to same ridge, which is followed for 3-4 rope lengths, the last one under overhanging buttress, to large shelf. Belay. Then (a) either straight up a buttress and 2 rope lengths up to new grass patches, or (b) by an airy traverse to L towards gorge. Belay. Continue into bottom of gorge, easier angle, 2 rope lengths up to more grass patches. The final pitch terminates in a short chimney. Time from Innerdal Lodge to top, 7 hrs.

Skarfjell by NE Wall — This route leads via an 80 ft high unclimbed pinnacle which can be reached from W and E. (a) The W route starts from Gikling-dalen, up a loose gully to uppermost pinnacle. (b) The E route starts a 100 ft to R of skar between Skarfjell and its N outlier. 1 rope length up, into crack which is jammed halfway up by large boulder. Creep under it and climb up to large ledge. Walk R. Difficult climb up to small 7 ft pinnacle. Up around corner and continue up first gully. Steep, but good holds, up to up-permost pinnacle. (c) Half a rope length straight up. Traverse L for 2 rope lengths, up to 3 small cirques with 35 ft high sheer walls. Follow good ledge at bottom of cirque to waterfall from glacier. Up on R or L side of waterfall to glacier and so to top. Severe. Time from Innerdal Lodge to top, 6 hrs by W route, 7 by E route.

Skarfjell by SE Ridge — Up 2 rope lengths from grass shelf at foot of ridge to foot of 30 ft high pinnacle. Up on wall to large plateau. 1 rope length straight up depression in centre of ridge until somewhat below chimney. Exposed but easy traverse out on wall to L. Up 1 rope length along steep crack. Safety belay at foot. Small cave midway. Then 7 difficult ft to plat-form. Up wide chimney to foot of long unclimbable crag. Bypass to R by abseiling to ledge. Continue up blocks to corner of long crag. Exposed trav-erse upwards to L, to platform above crag. Up on slab to good ledge. Follow crack towards L, then towards R and follow blocks to top. Time from Innerdal Lodge to top, 8 hrs. 120 ft rope. 5-6 safety belays.

Skarfjell by Fugleggen (E Ridge) — From cairn at foot of ridge climb up 1 rope length towards L to another cairn. Straight up until level with 30 ft high pinnacle, continue towards R to good belay in cave. Cairn. Up narrow gully, towards L to another gully leading to large shelf. Up slightly over-hanging gully, towards R and L to plateau beneath large open gully. Up to large plateau with 50 ft high slightly overhanging buttress. Follow rift in centre of buttress up to spacious shelf. Up overhanging gully to good shelf. Steep up to open crack, up it and up rift to fine plateau. Straight up ridge to overhang, traverse L, difficult ascent to shelf, up into overhanging gully, turn R and climb 18 ft up to good shelf. Diff pitch to R and up gully near ridge to shelf. Up 2 rope lengths over blocks in gullies near ridge to top. Time from foot to top, 4 hrs. 15 safety belays.

Skarfjell by Olavsveggen (E Wall) — Up on right-hand side of narrow gorge which cuts through the N sector of Skarfjell's two E walls. Up loose gullies to large shelf on right. Up gully on L towards bottom of gorge. 1 rope length up to overhang in gorge. Steep up on R side to overhanging crack which follow, then traverse to R around corner, up 120 ft along perpendicular gully to small shelf on R. Difficult traverse towards L, up gully near gorge, into new overhanging gully which is followed to shelf in bottom of gorge. Up 2 cracks to large horizontal band across wall almost halfway up. 1 rope length along band towards R to cairn. Another rope length along rifts to-wards R to belay under large overhang. Up to L of overhang to slanting ledge, up rifts to small shelf above overhang. Traverse 90 ft to R on grass shelf and 90 ft in gullies slanting L. Climb 15 ft towards R to perpendicular gully, 15 ft up it, then traverse R to shelf. Turn R, into steep gully until it overhangs, traverse L across smooth slab with loose block into overhanging gully which follow to shelf. Traverse 50 ft R on grass shelves, 10 ft down to R, behind large loose block. Up gully to R, on to NE ridge which is reached about 150 ft below top. Time from foot to top, 10 hrs. 35-40 belays.

Skarfjell by Dørstokken — This is a variation about 50 m to R of route by SE Gully. Start from big shelf at bottom of (and to R of) gorge and up to large slanting ledge with glacier under lowest part of Skarfjell's E front. Up from L of cubical block ("pulpit") and R of black buttress. Straight up 5 m, then slantwise to L and straight up to good ledge. Then somewhat R and up to hollow with crack and overhang. Over to L and up to balcony platform (exposed). Straight up steep wall, 1 rope length to good shelf below black buttress. Up buttress in wet gully, first very steep and with few holds, then less steep but with small holds. Then an easy half rope length up to large slanting shelf, where the route by SE Gully is joined. Mainly good and solid rock, but some loose blocks here and there. Severe. (O Inner-dal, S Ivarson).

Trolla, famous ridge in the Innerdal (Photo: NTK)

Skarfjell by Giklingveggen (or Søre Østvegg) — Start somewhat L of centre of wall and climb up 25 m steep gully with crack in L wall. Straight up to next large horizontal layer. Traverse L and slantwise up wall, 2 rope lengths towards R. Traverse 1 rope length to L, first over grass ledge, then under roof overhang to shelf, 15 m below depression in L section of wall. Up gully to shelf below depression. From its R end, up steep slab with one crack, towards R into perpendicular gully, which is climbed. To R and up by gully which eventually overhangs, up towards L and traverse back towards R above overhang and up to continuation of gully. Or travers around corner to R and then up. Continue up and then a long way to R over grass ledges and up to upper horizontal layer, where this peters out in slanting slabs. 40 m to L and up a steep and slightly overhanging pitch of 15 m, slightly towards L and up deep chimney-like gully. Continue straight up and then towards L to top. The wall is 350 m high, 40 m rope, 7—8 pitons, time 5 hrs. Very severe. (R Høibakk and A Næss).

Trolla (1840) is a famous ridge with 3 distinct peaks between Hoåsnebba in Sunndalen and Skarfjell in Inner-dalen, flanked by Grasdalen to the W and Giklingdalen to the E. *Søre Trolla* (1735) is separated from Hoåsnebba by the deep Pinnakel Skar. The 1st asc of Søre Trolla was made in 1921 by F Lorentzen, R Ødegaard and G N Sabro, up by a snow gully from Giklingdalen to the N ridge, which is followed mainly by its W side to top. This route was also used in the 1st winter asc in 1958 by G Hestad, T Johansen and A Næss. Its S ridge from Pinnakel Skar was climbed in 7/1950 by H Hagen, A I Hoem and O Innerdal, a really good climb and an exposed route. Time from Innerdal Lodge to top, 10 hrs. The 1st asc of *Stortrolla* (1840) was made in 8/1895 by K S Klingen-berg and the Meisterlin brothers, up from Giklingdalen by the E side, which is the usual route. Its W side from Grasdalen was climbed in 7/1912 by O Bjerknes, H Tøns-berg and J Sjølsvik. The S ridge from Søre Trolla was climbed in 1921 by F Lorentzen, R Ødegaard and G N Sabro. The only obstacle is a 35 ft gap with high over-hangs on its S side. It is turned either by abseiling or by climbing out on to the E side. The N ridge from Grasdalen was climbed in 1927 by E Fjeld and J Innerdal. This ridge is fearsome-looking with several vertical crags. The 1st winter asc was made in 3/1951 by L Arentz-Hansen, K Eide and O Simenstad, up by the usual route. *Nordre Trolla* (1733) is separated from Skarfjell by Snø Skar, which is the lowest gap on the ridge, reached from Grasdalen as well as from Giklingdalen. However, the latter route involves a steep glacier. The 1st asc of Nordre Trolla was made in 7/1911 by O Bjerknes and H Tønsberg, from Snø Skar and out on to the Giklingdal face, thereby bypassing obstacles on the E ridge. This is now the usual route. Time from Innerdal Lodge and back, 11 hrs. A traverse from Skarfjell via Snø Skar and Trollporten was made in 7/1912 by O Bjerknes, H Tønsberg and J Sjølsvik, bypassing all difficulties by turning E or W. Trollporten is a peculiar rock formation caused by giant rocks which have fallen down in an arch over a steep gap. Its N ridge proper from Snø Skar was climbed in 7/1950 by H Hagen and A I Hoem. This ridge is long, narrow and steep with good holds and fine climbing. The 1st winter asc of N Trolla was made in 1957 by A Bækkelund, I Hostad, N Husby, O Innerdal, A Næss, N G Skarland and B Ugelvik. The 1st traverse and the 1st winter asc of the whole Trolla ridge was made in 1960 by R Høibakk and P Vigerust. They returned, however, from S Trolla to the usual route between Søre and Stortrolla.

Stortrolla by E Side (usual route) — From Innerdal Lodge, walk up Giklingdalen to foot of Stortrolla. A distinct snow gully leads towards top. Its upper part terminates in a number of loose gullies of which the northernmost is best. Then turn L and follow inclining ledge to ridge which is reached L of top. Time from Innerdal Lodge and back, 8 hrs. Ice axe.

Stortrolla by W Side from Grasdal — Up on glacier and on to ridge between Nordre and Stortrolla. Follow ridge to top apart from steep section which is bypassed to E. Descend by usual route to Giklingdal. Time from Innerdal Lodge and back, 10 hrs. Ice axe.

Dalatårnet (1394) is the local "Matterhorn", overlooking Innerdal Lodge. It is a twin-peaked pyramid, the smaller tower being Lilletårnet, but both summits are usually included in most expeditions. The 1st asc of *Dalatårnet* was made in 7/1889 by E Holsen, J Nerdahl, G J Nygaard and A O Roseth, up by the W gully from Giklingdalen, the usual route. The 1st winter asc was made in Easter 1949 by H Berg, O Innerdal and P Sylow by the usual route. Its W ridge was climbed in 1952 by T Bersås and O Simenstad. It was climbed by the S ridge in 8/1954 by G Bolsønes, O Innerdal and B Lindgren by the sharp ridge from the skar between Tårnfjell and Dalatårnet.

Its NW ridge was climbed in 1959 by R Høibakk, F Hørtnagl and A Mayr, and a winter asc of the SW ridge was made by D Dawes, R Høibakk and P Vigerust. The impressive N wall which has haunted climbers for years, was conquered in 1960 by R Høibakk and A Næss. They also climbed the W wall. The SW wall was climbed in 1960 by J Hattestad, H G Nebell and S Serck-Hanssen. But the E wall of Dalatårnet is still unclimbed.

The first British climbing course in Norway.
Dalatårnet in the background (Photo: NTK)

The 1st asc of *Lilletårnet* was made in 1911 by C and J Lysholm, up by the W gully from Giklingdalen, now the usual route. Time from Innerdal Lodge and back, 5 hrs. The 1st winter asc was made in Easter 1950 by E Arentz-Hansen, H Berg, O Innerdal and P Sylow by the usual route. The E gully from Innerdalen was climbed in 1951 by H Berg, P Harvold, A I Hoem, Å Stavran and F Waldvogel. Time from Innerdal Lodge and back, 5 hrs. Its N wall was climbed in 1953 by O Simenstad and party.

Tårnfjell (1460) is a flat-topped peak, separated from Dalatårnet by a steep and narrow gap. The 1st asc was made in 1896 by G P Meisterlin and party, up from Mangebekkdalen via the skar, now the usual route. Its N face was climbed in 1939 by A I Hoem and D Thorstensen. The 1st winter asc was made in Easter 1949 by H Berg and O Innerdal by the usual route. They then traversed to Såtbakkollen.

Dalatårnet by W Gully from Giklingdal (usual route) — The track starts from NE corner of lake, up grassy tongue between two gullies, and later takes to main gully formed by junction of these two. At this junction also is the divergence left for Lilletårnet. (B J Banner). Time from Innerdal Lodge and back, 6 hrs. No rope.

Dalatårnet by W Ridge — Follow usual route to small snow glacier from which ridge rises. Up 5-6 rope lengths to large buttress. Up L for belay. The climb commences 15 ft to R, up small gully to overhang which is bypassed to R. 1 rope length up to shelf. Up steep gully with overhang. 1 rope length to large shelf. Up small buttress, then 3 rope lengths of easier angle to wall facing Lilletårnet. Up by gully towards R to good shelf and so to top. Time from Innerdal Lodge to top, 6 hrs.

Dalatårnet by NW Ridge — From skar between both towers, climb 1 rope length slightly to R, then turn L, back to ridge. Straight up to small shelf, and on to poor belay under large overhang. Follow 2 parallel and perpendicular cracks towards L side of overhang, up to shelf under overhanging gully. Up gully with slight traverse to L, up again and return to gully which is followed to shelf. 2 easier rope lengths on ridge proper to top. Time from skar to top, 2½ hrs. 7-8 belays.

Dalatårnet by SW Wall — 1 rope length up 2 steep crags between E ridge and the ridge which lies W of usual route. From cairn, climb 15 m up slanting gully to L. Traverse R. Up and to R of small projecting crag. Traverse R on shelf, around flake and up crack. Straddle across boulder, up over grass ledge. Up 10 m to R over slab. Up towards L to shelf, which follow L. Up through chimney to another shelf. Cairn. 6 m straight up, to L of crag. Straight up to grass shelf, then easy to top. (J Hattestad, H G Nebell and S Serck-Hanssen).

Dalatårnet by N Wall — From col between Lille and Store, climb 10 ft up ridge, traverse towards L to shelf below loose flakes. Leftwards and up across flakes. Up slightly overhanging rock to L, traverse L to shelf, which lies R of distinct gully. From shelf, up overhang, past nasty looking block to small shelf, straight up slab with crack, traverse L past blocks, descend 6 ft and traverse L into bottom of 22 ft high chimney, which is climbed. Traverse R and up to belay. Follow grass shelf 25 ft to L, then straight up, around ridge to L, steep up on pinnacled block to R. Straight up faintly overhanging gully to slanting shelf. Continue L, up small overhang and then easier towards R to top. The wall is about 600 ft high. 40 m rope. 6—7 pitons. Time 3½ hrs. Very severe. (R Høibakk and A Næss).

Dalatårnet by W Wall — From below gap between Lille and Store, traverse out on to W wall on large grass shelf. From this point one can see a gully-shaped incline, slanting towards top. Start up ridge to L of extension of this incline, first towards L in steep gullies, then short traverse to R and up small gully to shelf. Across shelf to L and steep up to another shelf. From its R end, follow steep cracks towards L to shelf, which is level with great incline. Traverse R over slab until the incline is visible. Straight up and across ridge to L, then follow steep gullies, into main gully to R, up and back to L and up on shelf. Across a couple of shelves to L and up steep gully towards top. Where gully overhangs, traverse 6 ft to R and up small gully with loose block at bottom. Up overhang, slightly to R and up through hole to belay behind block. Then easy to top. The wall is about 600 ft high. 40 m rope. 6—7 pitons. Time 3 hrs. Severe. (R Høibakk and A Næss).

Snøfjell (1468) rises NW of Innerdal Lodge, separated from Skjeringsfjell by Bjørås Skar. Some climbing may be had on the E face from the skar, but the usual route is up by the W face. The 1st winter asc was made in 1952 by O Innerdal, Å Stavrem and P Sylow, on skis up the W side. The E ridge as well as the NE ridge were climbed in 1954 by S Lid, A Næss and B Ugelvik. *Skjeringsfjell* (1415) can be reached by a scramble. It was traversed in 1948 by Th Volckmar and party. *Renndalskammen* (1195) rises E of Innerdal Lodge, opposite Dalatårnet. A new route by the SW chimney was made in 1960 by R Høibakk and A Opdal.

Renndalskammen by SW Chimney — Up 1 rope length in gully to bottom of chimney. Up chimney to overhang below top, out to R and follow ridge to top of Neglen (loose flake). Slantwise L to perpendicular chimney, which follow to large grass shelf, then up steep wall with good holds to another grass ledge. Up to overhang below cracky crag. Traverse L over slippery slab, up gully with cracks, terminating in small overhang. Up past pyramid-shaped block to R. Easy up to large shelf with birch trees below final buttress. Up gully, which ends in small roof overhang, to L below overhang, up crack, slightly towards L and up past large roof overhang to L, then easier up to summit ridge. Total height 200 m, good rock, 6—7 pitons, time 3 hrs. Severe. (R Høibakk and A Opdal).

The dome of Snøhetta dominates the Dovre mountain plateau (Photo: Mittet)

THE DOVRE RANGES

The Dovre railway between Oslo and Trondheim runs right across the Dovre mountain plateau, where the glistening white snow dome of Snøhetta is the main attraction. Travel by train from Oslo to Hjerkinn in 6—7 hrs and next morning walk to Reinheim Lodge in 6 hrs. The new Reinheim Lodge, built in 1962, is an ideal starting point for walks and climbs. Although the Dovre peaks reach a considerable height, the terrain is very easy and provides great opportunity for a series of fine mountain scrambles.

Fokstumyren which lies along the Dovre railway between Fokstua and Vålåsjø is a famous centre for bird watching and mountain flora, with more species of animal and plant life than is found anywhere alse. Kongsvoll railway station boasts a fine botanical garden with unusual mountain flora. (Map D145 Dovrefjell).

THE REINHEIM RANGES (map J470 Snøhetta): *Snøhetta* (2286) is a huge rock massif, a grand S-shaped ridge with 4 distinct peaks. *Stortoppen* (2286) is the highest point on the ridge towards E. 1st recorded asc 1796 by surveyor J Esmark and party. Its S face is a steep precipice. Cairned footpath from Reinheim up the E face. Time from Reinheim and back, 3—4 hrs. No guide required in good weather, but keep away from the S face. Stortoppen's W ridge sets off pt 2278 which can be reached without difficulty. *Midttoppen* (2262) is the only peak which affords real climbing on all sides. 1st asc probably by foreigners in 1923; 1st recorded

asc 1924 by A Moen; 1st winter asc 4/1954 by A R Heen
and O Skiri, from the NW. *Vesttoppen* (2249) is the SW
peak, separated from Midttoppen by a deep gap called
Vest Skar. Easy ascent from Reinheim via tarn 1632
and Hettpynten and up by the SE ridge, a scramble
of 3 hrs. The 1st traverse of the Snøhetta ridge was made
in 7/1941 by B and M Lyche and O Ottesen. The only
difficulty is the descent from Midttoppen into Vest Skar.

Larstind (2106) is a peculiar peak, W of Snøhetta, looking
like a giant anvil. 1st recorded asc 1932 by B Bommen,
up by the N ridge. The distinct gully which leads up
to the N ridge affords one obstacle — a steep pitch
which involves a climb through the waterfall inside the
gully. In one place it is also necessary to make a short
traverse on to the E face. The S ridge was climbed in
4/1954 (1st winter asc) by A R Heen and S Byrkjeland.

Langvasstind (2056) is situated SW of Larstind. Its highest
points is *Store Langvasstind* (2056). 1st recorded asc 1929
by H Giverholt and C J Koren, up by the W ridge. The
descent is either by the same way or by the SW ridge. The
SW ridge can also be climbed via pt 1971 up to the W
ridge which is then followed to the top. The SE ridge was
climbed in 8/1945 by N A Sørensen and wife, an interesting and greatly varied climb. A gap on Langvasstind's
S ridge separates it from *Svånåtindan* (2215), which is a
long ridge with several peaks and subsidiary ridges and
glaciers.

RONDANE

Rondane is different from any other mountain range in
Norway. The scenery gives a peculiar impression of pre-
historic times, and the spooky peaks and cirques create
images of long forgotten troll strongholds, rising in grand
solitude amidst peaceful surroundings. Geologists and
naturalists flock to Rondane every year, because there
is probably no other part of Norway which can tell
scientists more about pre-glacial times than Rondane.
The Rondane cirques are of particular beauty, and you
need no scientific background in order to enjoy them.
Perhaps the most outstanding cirque is Styggebotn below
Rondeslottet. It is hard to get into and it is seldom visited.
A unique phenomenon can be seen in the Uldal between
Sel and Mysu, where there are numerous earth-pyramids
called Kvitskriuprestinn. They consist of white moraine,
void of clay and chalk.

The Rondane ranges are well served by mountain lodges and tourist huts
(Photo: Mittet)

Rondane lies E of the Dovre railway and W of the Røros railway. Travel by train from Oslo to Sel in 7 hours and then by hotel car to Høvringen in less than 1 hour. Next morning walk via the Peer Gynt hut to Rondvassbu Lodge (5 hrs), which is situated almost in the centre of the Rondane ranges. Or by train from Oslo to Atna in the Østerdal valley in 7 hours, then with connecting bus to Straumbu Lodge in 3 hours. Next morning walk to Rondvassbu Lodge in 5 hours.

Many interesting walking tours can be made in Rondane, and the whole area is well served by mountain lodges and tourist huts. There are no really difficult rock climbs, and a rope is seldom called for, but the type of climbs encountered is unusual. Although the rock is very rotten and the amount of boulders is appalling, most rock faces consist of large square blocks, seldom met with in other areas. Several cirques will provide delightful glacier work.

The Rondvassbu Ranges (map J 440 Rondane): *Storronden* (2142) is the second-highest peak in Rondane, situated just NE of Rondvassbu. There is a cairned footpath right up the W face. Time from Rondvassbu and back, 3 hrs up, 3 down. *Rondeslottet* (2183) is the highest peak in Rondane, a splendid viewpoint N of Rondvassbu. 1st asc 1875 by C Nielsen. Cairned footpath via pt 2042 up the S ridge with sheer precipices into cirques on either side. Time from Rondvassbu and back, 7 hrs. *Digerronden* (2020) is a fine cone halfway between Rondvassbu and Dørål Lodge. Can be climbed from almost any angle. *Midtronden* (2043) is an easy peak between Digerronden and *Høgronden* (2114). The latter looks like a splendid pyramid when seen from the E. The usual route leads up by the SE ridge and down by the NE ridge.

Veslesmeden (2016) is situated NW of Rondvassbu. Cairned footpath via pt 1869, then up by the SE ridge. Time from Rondvassbu, 4 hrs each way. A descent by the SW ridge was made in 8/1901 by J Thoner, who also made the 1st traverse of *Storsmeden* (2017) from Veslesmeden, continuing by the N ridge of Storsmeden to pt 1902. Storsmeden comprises several grand cirques and has 4 distinct ridges. *Steet* (1992) stands SW of Storsmeden with 4 sharp ridges, each of which holds a fine cirque. 1st asc 8/1901 by J Thoner, who also cairned *Sagtindan* (2020), a long and jagged ridge which he traversed from Steet. It can also be climbed by the N ridge or the W face, but i ts E face presents a steep precipice into Langholet.

Sølnkletten (1826) is a group of 3 peaks somewhat E of Rondane, near Brei-sjø seter. Its highest point is Storsøln (1826), which can be climbed in 3 hrs from Breisjø. (Not to be confused with Storsøln near lake Femund).

ØSTERDAL — LAKE FEMUND

Lake Femund lies between the Røros railway and the Swedish frontier in a grand district whose main features are rounded hills and thick pine forests. There is fine trout fishing to be had nearly everywhere. Travel by train from Oslo to Hanestad in 7 hours and then 20 miles by bus to Undset, whence there is a walk of 3 hours to Misterheim Lodge with a fine view of Søln, the only rock massif in this area. It takes 7 hours to walk from Misterheim to Vesterheim Lodge, through Søln Skar, a fine pass which was known even in the Viking Age, when pilgrims went through it on their way to St Olav's shrine in Trondheim.

Søln (1751) (map D 590 Øvre Rendal): Its highest point is called Storsøln (1751), which can be climbed in 7 hrs from Misterheim and back. The usual route goes via tarn 1185 and pt 1680 and up by the ridge. Its NW face presents an impressive rock wall of over 2000 ft which rises out of Nordre Søln-hull cirque. This wall was climbed in 1935 by O H Furuseth and G N Sabro, a grand but exposed route. A variation of this route was made in 6/1938 by J H Høye and L Norberg, following a somewhat northerly course. Severe.

SYLENE

The Sylene district forms an integral part of the frontier between Norway and Sweden, SE of Trondheim. It is a grand area for walking tours and rock climbs, and there are good mountain lodges on either side of the frontier. The most interesting approach to Sylene is to go by train from Trondheim to Hell in 1 hour and then 47 miles by bus through Tydalen to Vektarstua, where a cairned footpath leads to Nedal Lodge in 3 hours. This is the best starting point for Sylene. There is also a bus service from Trondheim & Stugudal, 137 km, 4½ hrs.

Sylene (maps D 480 Stuesjø & D 175 Essandsjø): *Storsola* (1710) was considered inaccessible when the frontier was stipulated, and it was not until 1929 it was confirmed that its summit lies in Norway. The 1st asc was made in 1929 by over 20 stone masons, carrying stones for the frontier cairn. *Storsylen* (1867) is the highest peak, situated 200 yds W of frontier cairn No. 155 B. 1st asc 7/1885 by A Ravnø and P T Steensaas, up by the N ridge which is now the usual route. Time from Nedal and back, 12 hrs. Its S ridge via the E glacier was climbed in 8/1899 by H L Joseland and J Fjell-berg. *Lillesylen* (1704) lies in Sweden, N of Storsylen, but its SW and NE ridges lead into Norway. The ascent is easy.

North Norway

NORTH NORWAY
"LAND OF THE MIDNIGHT SUN"

North Norway is probably the most ideal playground in Europe for hiking, glacier walks and rock climbs. The scenery is indescribably grand, and the journey itself is full of scenic delight. There are peaks of all shapes and sizes, some are even unclimbed, and there are many rock walls and ridges which provide unfinished work. The climate is unsually warm and the Midnight Sun provides sunshine-around-the-clock.

In North Norway there are altogether 96 peaks higher than 1600 metres. Of these, 35 are over 1700 and 10 are over 1800. Only 4 peaks are higher than 1900 metres, namely Oksskolten (1915), Suliskongen (1913), Okshorn (1907) and Storsteinsfjell (1901), according to Mr K Gleditsch, director of the Norwegian Survey Dept (NGO). As there is continuous daylight during the summer season, you are of course never restricted in your movements, and you can set out on important expeditions at midnight or at noon, just as you please. The Midnight Sun never dips below the horizon as follows (but even long before and after these dates it is really never dark at night):

Svalbard (Spitsbergen)...	April 21 —	Aug 24
Bjørnøya (Bear Island) ..	May 3 —	« 11
North Cape	« 14 —	July 30
Hammerfest...........	« 17 —	« 28
Tromsø	« 21 —	« 23
Narvik	« 26 —	« 19
Svolvær, Lofoten isles ...	« 29 —	« 15
Bodø	June 5 —	« 9

Distances in Arctic Norway are enormous, and intending visitors would do well in planning ahead exactly how and where they will travel. There are four main routes:

By Air — from Oslo, Bergen or Trondheim to all principal towns in North Norway. Services by day and night during the summer.

By Sea — from Bergen or Trondheim by coastal express steamer past North Cape to Kirkenes on the Russian frontier. These steamers are modern and comfortable, but advance bookings are essential. When leaving Bergen in the evening (daily service all the year round), it takes 2 nights to Trondheim, 3 nights to Bodø, 4 nights to Narvik or Tromsø, 5 nights to Hammerfest and 6 nights to Kirkenes.

Trenstaven (right) is a spectacular rock fortress rising sheer out of the ocean
(Photo: Widerøe)

By Rail & Bus — from Oslo via Trondheim to Bodø in 26 hours by train, or by express bus northwards from Fauske (near Bodø) to Narvik in 1 day, to Tromsø or Sørkjosen on the second day, to Lakselv on the third day and to Kirkenes on the fourth day.

By Road — from Oslo by the Arctic Highway (road No. 50) to Trondheim 346 miles, Mosjøen 601, Bodø 815, Narvik 902, Tromsø 1051, Hammerfest 1280, North Cape 1400 and Kirkenes 1577 miles.

BELOW THE ARCTIC CIRCLE

When travelling by the coastal express steamer into the Land of the Midnight Sun, the mountainous landscape will give you an inkling of pleasures to come. Apart from the beauty and grandeur of the scenery, there is often an interesting story behind some of the sights you will see from the boat deck. Several mountains are closely linked with ancient legends and sagas dating back to the Viking period. There are trolls and gnomes, old witches and fair maidens, woven into strange fairy tales.

A Norwegian passenger will undoubtedly ask you to waive your hand towards a perky peak, the *Leka Maid* (Lekamøen (209), map E 370 Helgelandsflesa), when you sail past the Leka island, and he will tell you that she was once courted by a fiery lover, the *Horse Man* (Hestmannen (568), map E 560 Lurøy), which lies on the Arctic Circle. Her brother Torg came rushing to her aid, when the Horse Man shot his bow, and in terror the Leka Maid turned into a petrified mountain. The arrow, however, hit her brother, piercing his hat. He drowned, but his hat changed into solid rock, and you can still see the gaping hole in *Torg's Hat* (Torghatten (260), map E 975 Vega) on a little island off Brønnøysund. The hole is an enormous tunnel some 200 yds long and 15 to 20 yds wide with smooth walls and a jagged ceiling. The tunnel is easily traversable and it is also easy to reach the top of the mountain above, by following a ridge.

Near Sandnessjøen are the *Seven Sisters* (De Syv Søstre (1066), map E 595 Mosjøen), evenly spread out on a long ridge, almost like sparrows on a telegraph wire. This is where you are in for some leg-pulling. "Where is the greatest distance between any two sisters?", you will be asked. Perhaps you will reply it is between Nos 2 and 3, but then the local informant will laugh triumphantly: "Oh no, it is between Nos 1 and 7!"

90

Trena Island (map E 915 Trena) lies just below the Arctic Circle. *Tren-staven* (338) is an almost circular rock fortress which still offers scope for exploring. The 1st asc was made in 1877 by A Antonsen, up by the NW wall, which provides the one and only known route. The *Cathedral Cave* is a peculiar rock formation containing a giant cave, which was actually used as a church during the Middle Ages, a real find for archeologists who may here still discover hidden treasures right back from the Stone Age.

In the *Lurøy area* (map E 560 Lurøy) between Sandnessjøen and the Arctic Circle, there are several smaller mountain ranges which are worth visiting. The *Liatinder* (935) are situated in Aldersundet. The 1st asc of Høgste Lia-tind was made in 1940 by S Bratland and K Hugvik, up by the S face. *Okstind* (786) rises N of the Liatinder. Its E ridge was climbed by two local lads, and the N face was climbed in 1920 by N Backer Grøndahl, E Quale and F Schjelderup.

The proud profile of the *Red Island Lion* (Rødøyløven (440), map E 960 Valvær) can be seen for miles off the coast. It is situated on the Rødøy island, just beyond the Arctic Circle. An eagle's nest rests on the top. An ascent was made by three British explorers in 1833.

THE OKSTIND GLACIER

The remoteness and isolation of this range have an inde-finable charm, and there are many rock walls which will afford strenuous work even for expert climbers. The Okstind glacier covers an area of 76 sq km near the frontier with Sweden. Travel by train from Trondheim to Mosjøen in 10 hrs, then 41 miles by bus via Korgen to Leirskardalen, finally a walk of 8 miles to Kjennsvass Lodge, which lies N of the glacier. Map J 420 Okstindan covers the whole range.

THE OKSSKOLTEN GROUP (map J 420 Okstindan) rises on the E fringe of the glacier, capped by the highest peak in North Norway, *Oksskolten* (1915), a horse-shoe ridge, which contains a hanging glacier. 1st asc 9/1883 by P Stordal. Its W ridge was climbed in 7/1900 by K Bing, P K Fjelddal and K P Krokan in 5 hrs from Kjensvass Lodge, 4 hrs back. Its N face was climbed in 8/1960 by R D B Steward and J Bray. A snow pass, col 1775 or Ox Col, leads southwards to Okshorn (1907), previously called Keiser Wilhelmstind. The 1st recorded asc of Ox Col from the E was made in 8/1960 by R D B Steward and B Woods. *Okshorn's* (1907) NW ridge was climbed in 7/1900 by K Bing and A Bonta. In 9/1908, A Hoel and T Riis with P K Fjelddal and M J Rapliåsen climbed the W face, descending by the NW ridge. Its S ridge connects with *Svartfjell* (1868), earlier called Hekletind, which was traversed in 7/1946 by G Billing. The ascent from the W or SW is easy, but its E wall has never been climbed. Svartfjell's E ridge leads to *Austre Svartfjell* (1602), which was climbed in 8/1908 by A Hoel and party, up by the E ridge, down by the W ridge. *Stekvasstind* (1751) rises S of Svartfjell. 1st asc 8/1908 by A Hoel and party, up by the NW ridge, down by the sharp S ridge.

Oksskolten by N Face — The ridge bounding the E side of the N face glacier is followed to pt 1278, the glacier joined and ascended up the centre. Crampons will aid the ascent due to slippery dry ice at start. Halfway up the glacier a crevasse is leapt from broken snow bridge. Nearer the central cliffs, a great deal of traversing is necessary to avoid crevasses. After a bounding buttress on NW ridge, a snow couloir leads to large rectangular buttress, separated by snow and slab scree from an "hour glass" buttress to L. The rectangular buttress is reached below obvious gully fault on face. 30 ft of balance climbing leads to 50 ft chimney, one half being a rock wall on L, the other half an ice wall on R. Traverse L for 60 ft to overhang. 2 pitons are inserted here for pulley tactics. Traverse up and L on to scree between rectangular buttress and lower half of hour glass buttress, the latter being followed to top. Descent by NW ridge (scree) across glacier terminal moraine and down ridge of ascent. (R D B Stewart).

Ox Col from E — Foot of E glacier is reached from N. For 500 ft the S border of glacier is followed on steep moraine. Below 1st gendarme on E ridge of Okshorn (1907) is a barrier cliff which is best passed by traversing R on long gangway from near ridge crest, until one overlooks glacier and only a short chimney remains to be climbed. Then traverse L, on top of barrier cliff, to ridge crest. Step cutting, mainly on 30 degrees snow, with short steeper stretches, under crest of bergschrund lying under E ridge gendarmes and N face of Okshorn, lead in 1000 m to foot of 80 ft v diff pitch at col bergschrund. 2000 ft of step cutting required. Descent by same route. (R D B Stewart).

THE OKSKALVENE RIDGE (map J420 Okstindan)

is situated S of the Kjensvass Lodge and forms 3 distinct peaks. The 1st asc of *Nordre Okskalv* (1591) was made in 8/1908 by A Hoel and P K Fjelddal, ascending by the steep and craggy W face. Its NW ridge was climbed in 1957 by J F Beattie and P Broadhurst. Hoel's party of 1908 also made the 1st asc of *Midtre Okskalv* (1509), up by the W side. Its N wall is absolutely vertical. *Søre Okskalv* (1676) was climbed in 7/1883 by C Rabot and P K Krokan. A traverse from Midtre to Søre was made in 9/1908 by A Hoel and party.

THE CENTRAL GROUP (map J420 Okstindan):

Okstind (1804) rises solitarily in the centre of the glacier. 1st asc 1860 by A O Brygfjelldal and son. Its S face was climbed in 7/1875 by O A Corneliussen. The N face was climbed in 8/1908 by A Hoel and K P Krokan. The *Tvillingtinder* are situated S of Okstind. 1st asc of *Vestre Tvillingtind* (1830) in 9/1900 by V H Gatty with J Vigdal and E Hånde. It was traversed from E to W in 9/1908 by A Hoel, T Riis, P K Fjelddal and M J Rapliåsen. *Austre Tvillingtind* (1681) or Kvassnip was climbed in 9/1908 by the same party, traversing from Bessedørtind, descending towards the Vestre peak. *Vesttind* (1724), previously called Okshorn, rises SW of Tvillingtind. 1st asc 8/1900 by Gatty and party by a snow ridge on the E face. Its NW ridge was climbed in 9/1908 by Hoel and party, descending by snowdrifts towards the N.

THE SOUTHERN RANGES (map J420 Okstindan):

Oksfjelltuva (1522) is an easy peak on the SW fringe of the glacier. 1st asc 9/1908 by A Hoel and party, up by the

Svartisen glacier seen from the Holands fjord (Photo: Hellberg)

S face. *Peak* 1233 faces lake Oksfjell. 1st asc 9/1908 by
A Hoel, up by the E ridge. *Bessedørtind* (1562) rises on
the S edge of the glacier. 1st asc 9/1908 by A Hoel and
party, up by the SSE ridge, down by the N ridge.

THE SVARTISEN GLACIER

Svartisen — the Black Glacier — is the largest icefield in
Arctic Norway, covering an area of 489 sq km. The ice
is slowly receding, and smaller glaciers have disappeared
completely during the last 50 years.
The glacier region can be reached both by sea and
land. Travel by coastal express steamer from Bergen or
Trondheim to Ørnes (21 hours from Trondheim) and then
12 miles by connecting bus to Glomfjord, a center of
heavy industry and giant hydro-electric plants. An aerial
cablecar will take you right up into the mountains.
There are many interesting peaks around the little fjords
in this area, particularly in Tjongs fjord, Holands fjord
and Mel fjord. Glomfjord also affords access to the N and
W sectors of Svartisen. Or you may travel by train from
Trondheim to Mo i Rana (9—10 hours), and then by bus
to Røvassdal (18 miles), whence there is a motoring road to
Svartisdal Lodge and a walk of 2—3 hours to Blakkådal
Lodge. Both lodges are situated on the SE fringe of Svartisen, in terrain which is ideal for hiking and glacier walks
also visits to Grønli and Plurdal stalactite caves.

THE PLURDAL CAVES (map E 940 Umbukta) are
situated near Jordbu farm in Plurdal valley, 10 miles by
bus from Mo i Rana, on the road to Umbukta and Sweden.

The main tunnel is believed to be over 1.000 yds long, but only the first 400 yds have been explored. The average height in the tunnel varies from 25 to 45 ft. There are also several huge "cathedrals" and smaller caves. The entrance lies about 60 ft above ground level, in a steep rock wall, and there is also another entrance even higher up. The Plurdal caves were first discovered during World War II, and were only partly explored in 1940.

SVARTISEN W SECTOR (map E 855 Svartisen): *Strandtind* (1169) lies S of Mel fjord and was climbed in 1882 by C Rabot and surveyor Grimsgaard. *Høgtuva* (1291) is the highest point on Høgtuva glacier S of Mel fjord. Its long and flat top is a remnant of the peneplane which formed the surface of the whole country in pre-glacial times. 1st asc 1884 by C Rabot. *Burfjell* (1082) rises E of Mel fjord. 1st asc 8/1882 by C Rabot. Merely a scramble, but magnificent views. The *Skaviktinder* (1319) lie N of Mel fjord. 1st asc 7/1884 by C Rabot. Several fine peaks are found N of Mel fjord and immediately S of Tjongs fjord: *Blokktind* (1032) is likely to offer good sport and has almost certainly been climbed. *Kjettatind* (688) is a twin-peaked rock which was climbed 8/1919 by K Hanssen, R Ødegaard and F Schjelderup. The same party also climbed the connecting ridge of *Strømdalstind* (893), whence they proceeded to the top of *Reppaste* (913) by the "one and only route". The top is absolutely flat and commands a fine view of Svartisen. On the main glacier lie *Snetind* (1599), *Sniptind* (1591) and *Istind* (1577), which are the highest peaks in this area. They have all been climbed, but there are no reports.

SVARTISEN SE SECTOR (maps E 215 Dunderlands-dal): *Ørtfjell* (1442) is a group of peaks and glaciers E of Svartisen, near Dunderlandsdal railway station. 1st asc 1873 by C de Seue. *Tverråfjell* (1090) is another peak in the same range. 1st asc 1883 by C Rabot. The famous *Grønli stalactite caves* lie S of Svartisdal Lodge, reached by bus from Mo i Rana in half an hour. The rock consists of marble, and the hollows are created by sub-terranean rivers and waterfalls, now extinct. The tunnels are over a mile in length, with several "cathedrals", also a complete "maze", where a guide is required (available at Grønli farm). The sensation of walking through this maze of corridors, shafts and cathedrals is something unsual.

SVARTISEN NW SECTOR (map E 590 Meløy): Between Tjongs fjord and Holands fjord lies *Trolltind* (893). It can be reached from either fjord, but access is easier from Holands fjord. 1st asc 8/1919 by K Hanssen, R Ødegaard and F Schjelderup. Adjoining Trolltind are the *Reindalstinder* (889), whose westernmost peak was climbed in 1874 by O A Corneliussen. One peak is said to be unassailable. *Helgelandsbukken* (1454) rises E of Holands fjord. The ascent from Fonndal takes 6 hours and involves a great deal of ice work. 1st asc 7/1883 by C Rabot. The *Bjerangtinder* (1028) lie between Bjerang fjord and Glom fjord. One peak is said to be difficult. *Breistjerna* (673) rises near Noviken, N of Glom fjord. It was considered unassailable for many years, but was climbed from NE in 1956 by A R Heen and R Pedersen. *Smørtampen* (approx 650) rises near Breistjerna, but is not noted on the map. Said to be inaccessible.

ARCTIC HIGHWAY AREA (map E 130 Beiardal): *Høitind* (1405) lies W of Storjord on the Arctic Highway. 1st asc 1882 by C Rabot. Fine views. *Ramsgjeltind* (1237) rises E of the highway. Surveyors' cairn. Traces of ancient Lapp burial mounds can be seen near the foot of the mountain.

SULITJELMA

In 1864, a farmer found a little glimmering stone in the Sulitjelma rock massif. It proved to be copper ore, and since 1891 when the Sulitjelma mining company was founded, the desolate area along lake Langvatn has been turned into a bustling mining centre with a population of nearly 3.000. But the vast glaciers and the impressive peaks are still there to be enjoyed by anybody who cares to seek adventure and excitement in territory which even today is little or seldom touched by human footsteps. Sulitjelma is a huge area of glaciers and peaks, E of Bodø. Travel by train from Bodø to Finneid (40 miles) and then 2 hours by narrow-gauge mining railway to Furuland, which is the mining centre. Accommodation at Furulund Hotel. The local touring club owns a little tourist hut with 10 beds at Lake Låmi, S of Otertind.

There are 2 main glaciers — Blåmannen and Salajekna — the latter comprising most of the Sulitjelma peaks. The icefields extend into Sweden, with 40 sq km in Norway and 28 in Sweden. The highest peaks are in Norway.

The best season for expeditions into the icefields is in May and June, because the snow conditions are then most suitable for skiing and it is not too cold.

THE SAULO AREA (map E 445 Junkerdal): *Saulo* (1776) is a twin-peaked mountain on the frontier, 12 miles S of the Sulitjelma massif. 1st asc of Søre Saulo (1776) was made 7/1891 by O Aanderud and W Myhre, ascending by snowdrifts on the NE side and descending by the W side. Time from Fagerlund and back, 22 hrs. Nordre Saulo (1745) offers a number of short but attractive routes. Both peaks are also reached from W via the intervening saddle. South of Nordre Saulo and linked by a ridge, there is a small rocky crag of commanding aspect, resembling a miniature Matterhorn, but it is not known whether is has been climbed.

SULITJELMA W SECTOR (map E 755 Saltdal): *Blåmannen* (1571) is the highest ridge on the Blåmannen glacier. Its SW wall rises steeply 600 ft high. The ascent from Langvatn is strenuous. The easiest approach is via the S slope of Kobbertoppen up to the plateau and then straight towards Breporten. On the return journey, there is non-stop skiing for several miles. 1st asc 7/1891 by O Aanderud and W Myhre, ascending from Fonndal. Time from Furulund and back, 26 hrs.

SULITJELMA E SECTOR (map E 845 Sulitjelma): *Lairococka* (1004) is topped by "frontier cairn No 239". The ascent is merely a steep scramble, but the views are magnificent. The slopes abound with fossiles from pre-historic times. *Otertind* (1557) rises N of Låmivatn and has a surveyors' cairn. Its neighbour is *Vaknacocka* (1700) which was climbed in 1807 by G Wahlenberg. Further N lies *Vardetoppen* (1722) which was first climbed by surveyors. Its S wall has never been climbed. It is connected with Stortoppen by a long and razor-sharp arete with a sheer drop of 2.000 ft towards S and 1.500 ft towards N, and this fine ridge has never been traversed. *Stortoppen* (1830) has a fearsome-looking W wall which has never been climbed, although several attempts have been made. 1st asc 7/1889 by O Aanderud and W Myhre, ascending by the N ridge and returning by the same route. *Suliskongen* (1914) is situated 2 miles E of Stortoppen, flanked by 2 smaller peaks called *Dronninga* and *Knekten*. Suliskongen's S wall has never been climbed. 1st asc 8/1900 by V H Gatty, J Vigdal and E Hånde, believing they climbed the Swedish peak. Up by the E face, down by the N ridge.

The famous Saltstraum maelstrom and the Børvasstind peaks
Photo: Normann

THE BODØ REGION

Bodø is the capital of Nordland county, situated N of the Arctic Circle, reached by air or rail from Oslo or Trondheim direct. From Bergen by coastal express steamer in 3 nights. The scenery is beautiful and the terrain is suitable for all kinds of outdoor activities.

The main attraction is the famous Saltstraum maelstrom, where huge masses of tidal water forces its way 4 times a day through the narrow sound between Salta fjord and Skjerstad fjord, 13 miles by bus from Bodø. A local steamer will take you from Bodø to Beiarn in 3 hours, where you should see the Gråttådal grotto and climb the Beiartinder.

Solvågtind (1561) (map E 445 Junkerdal) is the highest point of Solvågfjell, which rises E of the Arctic Highway, where Junkerdal joins Saltdal. Its E side was climbed in 1943 by E Beuge and H Engelhardt.

Sandhorn (994) (map E 300 Gildeskål) rises sheer out of the ocean at Gildeskål, S of Bodø, and terminates in a snow-covered dome, which is easily ascended from N. Its S wall has never been climbed. Sandhorn was climbed in 1820 by Sir Arthur de Cappell Brooke and in 1827 by Robert Everest. Gildeskål is reached by local boat from Bodø in 3 hours.

The Gråttådal Grotto (map E 175 Bodø) in Beiardalen is an interesting natural phenomenon. The grotto lies about 300 ft above sea level, above a small lake with crystal-clear water, which is fed by a slow-moving sub-terranean stream, A boat is required to get into the grotto, but the owner, farmer S Løvstad, has built a small rowing boat, which is available to visitors. The grotto contains many stalactites and a series of fascinating rock formations with glorious color patterns.

The Beiartinder (1329) (map E 175 Bodø) are situated SW of Beiar fjord. The westernmost peak is called Stortind and the others are the Småtinder. Stortind (1329) is said to be difficult. 1st asc of Vestre Småtind (1120) was made in 1920 by N Backer Grøndahl, E Quale and F Schjelderup, by climbing up to the E gap and then to the top by a chimney and a very steep wall, which involved exposed climbing. The next day they climbed Midtre Småtind (1211) by a steep gully from the E gap. Afterwards they traversed to *A*ustre Småtind (1313).

The *Børvasstinder* (map E 175 Bodø) rising N of Beiarn consist of 2 distinct parallel ridges, called Falkflågtinder and Åselitinder. Some of the *Falk-flågtinder* (1155) were climbed in 1888 by O Aanderud. The 1st traverse was made in 1916 by W Morgenstierne, C W Rubenson and F Schjelderup, ascending *Rundtind* (1085) by S ridge, then across *Spisstind* (1155), the northernmost Falkflågtind and a lower peak between Rundtind and Spisstind. The rock consists of loose slate. The *Åselitinder* (1180) consist of 5 peaks on a long ridge. *Point 1048* was climbed by its E side in 1885 by O Aanderud. 1st asc of *Point 1069* was made 6/1930 by B Bommen, B Lyche and O Ottesen by a faint gully in the corner of the S face and the steep E wall. Its N wall is absolutely vertical. The same party also made the 1st asc of *Store Åselitind* (1180) by climbing an almost vertical gully on the E wall, descending by the W wall towards the gap facing Point 1114, followed by a glissade into the Åseli valley.

THE FOLLA REGION

Sørfolla and Nordfolla are two huge fjord basins beyond Bodø, comprising a network of fjords and mountain ranges. There are two sensational peaks — the "fantastic walls" of Strandåtind and the "terrible monolith" of Husbyviktind — also a number of ranges which provide good sport, and where much unfinished work is still waiting. Every little fjord in the Folla region is served by local steamers from Bodø, and the Arctic Highway between Bodø and Narvik also renders easy access.

THE SJUNK FJORD AREA (map E 475 Kjerringøy): *Strandåtind* (862) is the star item, a famous tourist attraction, seen from the coastal express steamer. It rises on Kjerringøy island, N of Bodø, a gigantic wall of solid granite, almost a mile long, flanked on both sides by almost vertical precipices of ice-polished rock, with an absence of cracks such as is never seen in the Alps. It affords more difficult sport than most of the Lofoten peaks. The 1st asc of *Vestre Strandåtind* (712) was made 8/1889 by C Hall and Matias Soggemoen, climbing the NW ridge. 1st asc of *Store Strandåtind* (862) 7/1912 by H Jentoft, C W Rubenson and F Schjelderup. There are 2 really difficult pitches. The NE ridge was climbed 8/1912 by the same party accompanied by Wm C Slingsby. A difficult 10 ft crag requires the shoulder of one climber. Its S face was climbed in 1936 by Else Hertzberg and A Næss. The first complete W-E traverse was made in 1924 by K Motzfeldt and F Schjelderup. This is probably one of the grandest rock climbs in Arctic Norway.

Låterfjell (815) adjoins Strandåtind and affords good sport, but there are no reports. *Eidetind* (1023) (or *Trolltind?*) rises NE of Låterfjell. 1st asc 8/1889 by C Hall and Matias, ascending from SW gap. *Skeistind* (975) is a grand peak which rises on the promontory between Nevels fjord and Sjunk fjord. 1st asc 1898 by T Norman, climbing the W side, which is furrowed by a distinct but dangerous gully. Its N ridge was climbed 8/1912 by H Jentoft, C W Rubenson, F Schjelderup and Wm C Slingsby. *Sjunkhatten* (1188) stands S of Skeistind. 1st asc 1909 by T Norman and E Rostrup, by NE ridge. Its W face was climbed in 1924 by F Lorentzen, K Motzfeldt and F Schjelderup. A ridge running westwards links Sjunkhatten with *Straumstind* (927). 1st asc 1889 by C Hall and Matias. Further S lies *Kjerringtind* (966). 1st asc 7/1915 by F and L Schjelderup, ascending from E from Sjunk fjord. Its western neighbour, *Kjeipen* (903), is said to be inaccessible. *Osantind* (1115) rises E of the head of Sjunk fjord. 1st asc 8/1912 by H Jentoft, C W Rubenson, F Schjelderup and Wm C Slingsby, via Drogvass Skar, which separates it from *Drogvasstind* (965). 1st asc 1915 by F and L Schjelderup.

THE RØSVIK AREA (map E 880 Sørfolla): *Vatsviktind* (1054) rises E of Sjunk fjord and 8 miles W of Røsvik, which is a ferry point on the Arctic Highway. 1st asc 1908 by surveyor Lund and party. It adjoins *Middagstind* (1131). 1st asc 1915 by F and L Schjelderup. A wide gap separates it from *Prekstoltind* (1071), which is said to be inaccessible from N and W. 1st asc 7/1915 by F and L Schjelderup, climbing the S face. Good rock and fine sport.

THE RØRSTAD AREA (map E 880 Sørfolla) lies between Sørfolla and Sag fjord, near Rørstad. *Midnattstind* (904) has a N face which has never been climbed. 1st asc 7/1921 by E Jensen, H Jentoft, C W Rubenson and H Tønsberg, from E gap and up by E ridge. The "terrible monolith" of *Husbyviktind* (806) rises NE of Rørstad. Its lower part is an almost perfect dome, and, perched curiously on top of this, the upper half is a sharp cone. Only one route is known, and this provides one of the most difficult climbs in the county of Nordland. 1st asc 7/1913 by W Eger, R Løchen, S Saxlund and H Tønsberg, climbing the W ridge. A variation of this route was made in 8/1921 by E Jensen, H Jentoft, C W Rubenson and H Tønsberg Sr and Jr. (Report by H P Spilsbury).

VEIKDALSISEN GLACIER (map E 880 Sørfolla) lies E of the Arctic Highway and NE of Leir fjord. It is an isolated territory, which is visited very seldom. *Gaskacocka* (1512) rises on the N fringe of the glacier. 1st asc 1920 by N Backer Grøndahl, E Quale and F Schjelderup, up by the NE ridge. The same party also traversed the ridge westwards and made the 1st asc of *Litletind* (1334).

Typical Folla scenery from the Arctic Highway

On the extreme N end of the map lies *Blåfjell* (1002), situated W of the Arctic Highway. The S and E sides consist of steep overlapping slabs, but routes look possible from W and N.

STEIGEN (map E 830 Steigen): *Hanekamtind* (542) rises above Steigen on Engeløy island. It is a peculiar ridge which resembles a cock's comb. 1st asc 1888 by a Prussian officer. *Sfinxen* is said to be an extraordinary rock needle at Steigen, but its location is unknown. The *Skotstinder* (747) are situated SW of Steigen. Its highest point is called *Skotstind* (747). 1st asc 8/1889 by C Hall and Matias.

NORDFOLLA (map E 655 Nordfolla): Just by looking at this map, you will realise the climbing potentialities of this district. *Hatten* (1031) is a steep and peculiar peak W of Ballkjos between Nordfolla and Sag fjord. 1st asc 7/1921 by E Jensen, H Jentoft, C W Rubenson and H Tønsberg, up from W col to top of Hatten, whence they traversed the whole ridge, including the *Høgtinder* (936). The westernmost point on the latter ridge, *Middagstind* (765) was first climbed by K L Rensvold. *Kråkmotind* (924) rises E of the Arctic Highway, above lake Femte-vatn. It presents smooth, sometimes overhanging walls on all sides except the SE, where there is a gentle, rocky slope.

A Britich expedition from Oxford University — R J Barber, J Cole and D C Witt — visited Nordfolla in 1957. They concentrated on Veggfjella, Stolotinder and Rein-oksfjella, and confirmed that there is still plenty of scope for good sport in this region. *Veggfjella* (1126) are several sharp peaks S of Sag fjord and NW of Tømmernes on the Arctic Highway. The party climbed all peaks over 1.000 metres in height. *Point* 1050 was a fairly sensational ridge walk. The complete E-W traverse of *Points* 1062 — 1072 — 1126 — 1227 was attempted. Enormous walls on the N side of 1126 (not noted on map) with top over-hanging. If it affords any route at all, it would be very hard. Descent from *Point* 1126 by the NE ridge. *Point* 1227 was climbed by its SW ridge, descent by the E ridge. Rocks in this area are fairly bad. The *Stolotinder* (1097) lie E of Tømmernes on the Arctic Highway. The party climbed *points* 1097 and 1051 by their S ridges, *Point* 1072 by its W ridge. Possibly a 1st asc. The NW ridge of *Point* 1097 may provide a fine route. There is some splendid rock climbing to be done in this range. The complete traverse of the remaining peaks was done in a fine 10-hour day. *Spisstind* (1151) was climbed by its S ridge after a dirty traverse on loose ledges across the W face. The ridge to *Point* 1137 is incredibly sharp and airy. Scrambling led to *Point* 1195 via *Point* 1137. Possibly 1st ascents. The ridge overhangs at its E end. Descent by steep snow gully on the N side. (Report from J Cole).

THE FRONTIER AREA (map E 375 Hellemobotn): *Reinoksfjella* (1455) or Kirkavarna are situated near the Swedish frontier, reached by a rough 12 mile walk from the Arctic Highway from Kråkmotind. Lodging at "Skogstue" at E end of lake Sjuendevatn. The Oxford party of 1957 also climbed this range, setting up camp at S shore of lake 640. *Point* 1306 was climbed by steep snow gully on its N side, then up good rocks to surveyors' cairn. Splendid glissade down same gully. Ascent of highest points made by traversing small glacier and kicking steps up to col between *points* 1344 and 1325. Scrambling and knife-edge ridge over *point* 1325 to *Point* 1445. Descent E down snow to col and up broken W ridge of *Point* 1455 to long, level summit ridge. Pro-bably 1st ascents. Down by snow slopes and glacier to N. Excellent day's expedition. The traverse was repeated some days later, when descent was made by a steep snow gully N of *point* 1445. Two days were spent on climbing the W ridges of *points* 1344 and 1306. Both gave excellent climbs on very good rock. "There is endless scope for rock climbs of all standards in the group. *Kirkefjellet* (1182) presen.s an incredibly steep and smooth wall to the SW, over 2.500 ft high. The W wall of Pt 1445 is impressive and steep, but rather loose and unpleasant." (J Cole).

THE TYS FJORD REGION

Here is truly a grand district, which still offers great scope for exploring. This is the narrow part of Arctic Norway between Bodø and Narvik, stretching from Hamarøy on the ocean — with the fantastic rock needle of Hamarøyskaftet — through Tys fjord with the magnificent Stetind pyramid, said to be the most remarkable natural obelisk in the whole world — via Frostisen icefield and the Storsteinsfjell rock massif to the frontier. This area is best reached from Bodø — by air or rail from Oslo or by sea from Bergen or Trondheim — and then by bus on the Arctic Highway to any suitable starting point. Camping is necessary almost anywhere. In 1957, the Oxford University Mountaineering Club organized an expedition to the Storsteinsfjell rock massif and adjacent areas, when they made a series of 1st ascents and new routes. The following notes are based largely upon a report from the President, Colin J Mortlock, who is acutely aware of the fact that opportunities for rock climbing in Norway are limitless. "The scope for new climbs of all standards of difficulty in this region is still considerable. Several outstanding problems of a high order remain: W face of Haugsbakktind, N pillar of Kuinarcocka, N Wall of Storstein and many others. These problems would only be solved by an extremely competent party." Some virgin peaks still remain.

THE HAMARØY GROUP (map E 335 Hamarøy): *Hamarøyskaftet* (613) is a "fantastic rock needle" which rises straight out of the ocean near Hamarøy, 8 miles off the Arctic Highway from Ulfsvåg. 1st asc 8/1888 by M H Ekroll with Angell Johannessen. The 1st asc of the highest *Hamarøytind* (896?) was made in 8/1888 by C Hall and Matias Soggemoen. *Jura* (460) is a high pinnacle W of Hamarøyskaftet. 1st asc 8/1939 by I Halmøy, M Rath and T Romsloe. The same party also made the 1st asc

Tilthorn seen from the sea

of *Kjerringa*, which is a pinnacle near Jura. *Tilthorn* (592) is an amazingly sharp needle on the N promontory of Hamarøy, 3 miles W of Tortenås on the Arctic Highway. The summit is a 300 ft long knife-edge, nowhere wider than a foot or so. Its highest point is so narrow that it affords space for only one climber at a time. 1st asc 8/1889 by C Hall with Matias, up by an ill-defined gully. In 6/1946 it was climbed from the S gap by H K Lorentzen and T Romsloe, mainly following Hall's route, with a variation to the L in the final pitch. *Vestre Skartind* (691) is the neighbour of Tilthorn, situated on the same ridge. 1st asc 6/1948 by I Hartviksen and T Romsloe, from the gap between both peaks towards the ridge of Skartind, then out on the N wall, over shelves and slabs to the top ridge just W of the summit.

THE STETIND GROUP (map E 930 Tysfjord): *Stetind* (1381) rises between Tys fjord and Ste fjord, a magnificent pyramid with unbroken slabs from top to bottom on all sides except the SE ridge. It is probably the most remarkable natural obelisk in the whole world, unique in appearance and considered unassailable for many years. It withstood every serious attempt from 1870 to 1910, when it was finally conquered. 1st asc 7/1910 by A B Bryn, C W Rubenson and F Schjelderup, climbing the SE ridge, which is now called Sydpillaren. There is no difficulty apart from the now famous hand traverse on the W face, which is severe. This is still the one and only route used by more conservative climbers, but several routes have been made with the aid of pitons by Else Hertzberg and A Næss in 1935 and 1936: Nordgalleriet direct from Ste fjord, Sydpillaren from SW and Stetind from Sydpillaren, Stetind by the SE wall, Stetind from Halls Fortopp via the SE wall, Halls Fortopp by the S face from Amfi, and Vestfortoppen from Nordgalleriet. A new route from saddle 931 was made in 6/1956 by J James, S Kaye and B Thompson of the Vibram Mountaineering Club.

Prestetind (1345) is separated from Stetind by the steep Preste Skar. The summit ridge of Prestetind is so narrow that you can sit astride it. 1st asc 1881 by O Holm, by the S ridge. A long vertical cliff forms its SW side and affords access to the summit ridge. An ascent from the SE saddle was made in 6/1956 by J Ramsden and J Thompson. *Kopptind* (1277) rises SE of Prestetind. 1st asc 6/1956 by Jesse James, Stuart Kaye, Jack Ramsden, Brian and Jean Thompson, from the W col and up snow shoulder.

Stetind — a magnificent pyramid with unbroken slabs from top to bottom

The *Tømmeråstinder* (920) lie NW of Stetind. The 1st asc of *Nordre Tømmeråstind* (814) was probably made by C Hall, and the 1st asc of *Highest Tømmeråstind* (920) was made in 8/1904 by W Carr, T G Ouston and H Priestman. The same party also made the 1st asc 8/1904 of *Straumtind* (1274), which lies S of Kopptind. It is a rotten ridge with tottering gendarmes.

THE SILDBOTN GROUP (map E 930 Tysfjord): The *Sildbotntinder* (819) are situated E of the Arctic Highway between the ferry points of Skarberget and Setran. 1st asc of *Peak* 819 in 7/1921 by C W Rubenson and H Tønsberg. A gap separates it from *Kuglhorn* (979). 1st asc 7/1921 by E Jensen, H Jentoft and H Tønsberg. The 1st W-E traverse of the whole range was made in 1936 by D Dekke and P W Zapffe. *Vestre Eidetind* (770) rises NW of Kuglhorn. 1st asc 7/1949 by I Hartviksen and T Romsloe, from the skar between Eidetind (846) and Vestre Eidetind, up on shelves facing Skrovkjosen, finally by distinct gully to the summit.

GICCECOCKA GLACIER (map E 930 Tysfjord): This huge icefield SE of Tys fjord seems to be almost unexplored, as there are no reports. In the *Fonntind* (1312) *Group*, the unnamed glacier between lake Fonnvatn and lake Baugevatn was explored in 6/1956 by J James, B and J Thompson They climbed *Peaks* 1300 and 1412 by the W ridge. Further N lies *Skårisen Glacier*, where *Peak* 1175 was climbed by its W side in 6/1956 by J James, S Kaye, J Ramsden, B and J Thompson.

FROSTISEN GLACIER — W SECTOR (map E 930 Tysfjord): There are few reports of ascents in this area. *Tverrfjell* (1364) is a range N of Frostisen, embracing a fine cirque. The 1st asc of *Tverrfjellspiggen* (1278) was made in 1947 by P Hohle and T Romsloe. *Klubbviktind* (1329) is a shapely sugar-loaf mountain NE of Tverr-fjell. It rises steeply on all sides, but the N ridge which is more broken, may offer some climbing on its several rock towers. 1st recorded asc 7/1954 by G R E Brooke, up from Klubbvik on the Skjom fjord via S shoulder. Time 5 hrs up, 3 down.

Three ranges near Kjøpsvik — Blåfjell, Botnelvtinder and Leirelvdalstinder — were climbed in 6/1911 by G Kunne and R Pøtsch, but their location is unknown.

FROSTISEN GLACIER — E SECTOR (map E 790 Skjomen) is situated S of Skjomen fjord, covering an area of 37 sq km. *Gangnesaksla* (1318) rises S of Frostisen, an easy peak which can be reached in 4 hrs from Skjom-botn. Fine views of the great icefield. Vester Skar sepa-rates Gangnesaksla from *Meraftastind* (1349) which is said to resemble the profile of King Karl XII. The im-pressive *Lappviktind* (1417) dominates the head of Skjomen fjord. Its upper section consists essentially of a long wedge-shaped ridge, whose E side is a tremenduous precipice some 2000 ft high. Its W slopes of scree and rock decline more gently. G R E Brooke climbed this route in 7/1953 in 5 hrs from Skjombotn. *Skjellingfjell* (1334) rises S of Lappviktind. Its W face is precipitous. There are 2 sharply defined summits. 1st asc 7/1953 by G R E Brooke, from Skjombotn across gap 1070 and up E side to 1334 in 5 hrs.

THE IPPOCOCKA GROUP (map E 790 Skjomen): The highest peak in this glacier and rock massif is *Ippococka* (1732). An asc by the NE ridge was made in 7/1953 by G R E Brooke in 9 hrs from Skjomdal to top, 7 hrs down. The N face was climbed in 7/1957 by D Duffield and C J Mortlock. This route is generally severe, with 3 pitches of very severe. The E face has an average angle of 70 degrees. The cliffs are mainly unbroken, apart from a steep and prominent snow gully bounding the right edge of the cliff, which should provide a good climb. A bergschrund runs below the whole length of the cliff. The SE face is a 700 ft cliff, uniformly steep on the E and becoming slabby to the S. The rock appears to be sound, and offers several routes on the southern end of the cliff. The W face is broken and slabby, probably of little interest. *Nordre*

Ippococka (1367) is probably still unclimbed. Its N face is steep and imposing, overhanging in the centre, but split by diagonal gullies at its western end. These gullies may offer good routes. Ascent from E, W or S would be easy. *Durmålstind* (1577) rises SE of Ippococka. Probable 1st asc 6/1956 by S Kaye and B Thompson, climbing the S ridge to 1524 and traversing to 1577, returning the same way. The N face cliffs are shattered, vegetatious and liable to rock fall, but appear to offer some interesting climbs. D Duffield and C J Mortlock climbed 600 ft of this face in 7/1957. The standard was very diff on dirty and loose rock. The E face consists of slab and scree. The icefield marked on the map does not exist. The W face is apparently loose and seamed by many gullies. It offers a variety of routes. *Tverrfjell* (1064) lies W of Durmålstind. It has little to offer.

Ippovarre (1665) is an imposing ridge, 2 km S of Ippococka. The main ridge runs W-E and comprises peaks 1569−1581−1665. The cliff faces appear very loose and cannot be recommended. The N face is swept by rockfall and avalanche in summer. Probably the 1st asc of this ridge was made in 6/1956 by J James and S Kaye, climbing 1569 by its S ridge, traversing to 1665, descending by the NE ridge and corrie to the S. Fine sporting ridge, but no real difficulty, though steep in parts. *Peak* 1210 rises S of Ippovarre and provided another probable 1st asc in 6/1956 for J James and J Ramsden, ascending the NW ridge and returning the same way. A parallel ridge but situated NE of the main ridge comprises *Peaks* 1579 and 1574. The 1st W-E traverse of both peaks was made in 6/1956 by B and J Thompson, starting from col 1439 and descending by the E ridge of 1574. Snow work, fine ridge, no real difficulty − and no cairns. A traverse in the opposite direction was made in 7/1957 by D Duffield and G K Richardson. The N face of 1579 could give a good route in suitable snow conditions. Another ridge SE of Ippovarre stretches N-S with *Peaks* 1700−1618−(1541, on map only, it is only a large boulder plateau). The map is quite in error in this area. The 1700 has a sharp arete descending to 1618. The relative height of the peaks is also probably inaccurate. The 1st asc of this ridge was made in 6/1956 by J James, S Kaye, J Ramsden, B and J Thompson, up by easy slopes from SSW to 1618, thence a narrow snow and rock ridge to 1700, descent by the N ridge and snow slopes to the W. J James and B Thompson also abseiled down the NE cliff of 1700 and climbed the upper part of the E arete of 1700. Steep, fine arete, not very difficult, but rather loose. This E ridge was climbed in 7/1957 by D Duffield and G K Richardson, a good route containing a knife-edge gap and several good mod diff pitches. The E face of 1700 is a 200 ft cliff of steep granite, and the W face is steep and well broken. *Peak* 1626 rises E of 1700. Its SE face has 600 ft of slabs, probably of high technical difficulty. 1st asc 7/1957 by P A Dawson and C Evans (followed a few days later by D Duffield and G K Richardson), ascending by way of plateaux 1373 and 1374 and up by the boulder-strewn E ridge, descent to col 1533. *Cainhavarre* (1383), not to be confused with another peak of the same name further SE, was climbed in 7/1957 by P A Dawson and C Evans. They built cairns on both summits and proceeded across plateaux 1373 and 1374 to 1626.

THE CAINHACOCKA GROUP (map E 790 Skjomen) lies SE of Ippovarre. The main ridge of *Cainhacocka* (1596−1593) runs W-E and has a S face which is broken up with some steep snow, affording good scrambling. Its N face is a steep cliff and holds a small ice sheet with a prominent bergschrund, liable to be corniced. 1st asc of 1596 in 6/1956 by J Ramsden, B and J Thompson, climbing the W ridge, descending by snow slopes on the N face. The 1st traverse of both peaks was made in 7/1957 by D Duffield and G K Richardson, ascending the E wall of the NE ridge, reaching the ridge where it steepens abruptly. Broad summit ridge of no difficulty. Descent by the N face on steep but easy snow. *Cainhavarre* (1596) rises E of Cainhacocka. The large glaciers shown on the map have shrunk to small ice sheets. Probable 1st asc 7/1957 by D Duffield and G K Richardson. Merely scrambles. *Stokkenjunjes* (1342−1442) is an unimpressive and easy rock ridge on the frontier, N of Cainhavarre. Probable 1st asc 7/1957 by J Farren and J R Setchell, traversing both peaks from N to S, descending by steep snow of the E face of 1442.

THE STORETIND GROUP (map E 790 Skjomen) is best defined as the triangle with Stortind as the S apex. The W side includes the Skjomen valley peaks, and the E side the main Stortind ridge. *Stortind* (1537) is the highest point. 1st asc 7/1957 by J Farren and J R Setchell, up by the E ridge which overlooks a small glacier, down by the SE ridge via col 1044 to Skjomdalen. Another asc was made a week later by P A Dawson and C Evans via col 976 and the SE ridge. The 1st asc of Stortind's subsidiary peaks 1450 and 1353 was made in 7/1957 by L G Hill and C J Mortlock, from Skjomdalen to the base of the prominent gully which cleaves the W face. To reach the gully base, an upward traverse to the left of 1000 ft was made up steep isolated snow patches and then 300 ft up mod diff slabs. The gully was then followed to the SW summit (1450). Descent by the W ridge to col 1162. The E face of 1450 is an 800 ft cliff rising very steeply above a small glacier. Several cracks offer routes of a high standard. On the N side of the central gully which cleaves the W face, the cliff is vertical for 1000 ft. Further N the angle decreases and should offer a few routes of a serious nature. The rock may be loose.

Tverrdalsfjell (1053 − 1247) forms the northernmost point of the main Stortind ridge. *Peak* 1053 was climbed in 8/1957 by J Farren and L G Hill from Skamdalsbakkan via 553 and 830 and across scree. Descent by the extremely steep snow gully on the N face. This face is steep, composed of sound granite with very few weaknesses, but some diagonal cracks might afford routes of great difficulty. The NE face is split by a steep gully which should give an easy route to the summit. The 1st asc of *Peak* 1247 was made in 8/1957 by L G Hill from lake by 1053 and up a buttress of 550 ft of mod diff scrambling to the summit, descent to col 1222 and down the E face which is steep and loose, to 830. Its W face is an attractive 1000 ft slabby pyramid split by a central gully which should yield a good route direct to the summit. Further S on this W face is a steep terraced wall with a trap dyke ladder 600 ft high. This face would give some good artificial climbs up prominent cracks.

Stortind's Main Ridge is 7 km long, continuously narrow, but rarely more than a walk. 1st traverse 8/1957 by D Duffield, L G Hill and C J Mortlock, from col and across summits 1432 − 1466 − 1426 − 1444 − 1514 to Stortind 1537. Superb views. The E face runs the whole length of the ridge and ranges from 1000 to 1700 ft in height. It is often extremely steep and any climbs would probably be of a high standard. In several places are feasible gullies. Near col 1263 there is an obvious gully, and from the steep gap N of 1466 a curious slanting ledge gives a possible route. The W face is very broken up and offers a variety of routes.

Gamnestind (1373) rises on Stortind's Skjomdal ridge. Probable 1st asc 7/1957 by L G Hill and C J Mortlock, easy scrambling up the NW ridge and a steep descent by the SE ridge. Its W face is an 800 ft high cliff with an average angle of 80 to 90 degrees, offering a few routes of a very high standard on clean rock. The W face below col 1275 has an obvious gully and chimney of 300 ft which should give routes of medium difficulty. *Haugbakktind* (1454) has a surveyor's cairn. It was climbed in 7/1957 by L G Hill and C J Mortlock via col 1215 and up the NE ridge to 1378 and easy scrambling to the top. Descent by the SE ridge to col 1275. Easy. Its W face is an extremely impressive cliff of 1000 ft with an average angle of 80 degrees, and in several places the summit ridge overhangs the base of the face. Two routes appear possible though probably artificial, but of a very high standard. A magnificent cliff. *Peak* 1337 is situated between Haugbakktind and Elvegårdstind, a small peak but with impressive W and E faces. 1st asc 7/1957 by L G Hill and C J Mortlock, up by the NW ridge, down by the SE ridge. *Elvegårdstind* (1299 — 1358 — 1434) consists of 3 distinct summits on a broad plateau. 1st asc probably in 7/1934 from Mølndalen via the N ridge. 1st recorded asc 7/1957 by L G Hill and C J Mortlock, up and down from lake 995. The W wall of 1299 was climbed from Skjomdalen direct in 7/1958 by W Andersen, B Halvorsen and T Romsloe, up by a distinct gully. The N face of 1358 which rises above a small corrie glacier, looks loose and dangerous. Both the E and N faces have steep corrie walls which could offer some diff rock climbs. *Sukkertoppen* (1430) is the E spur of Elvegårdstind. Its E face is an impressive cliff of 1000 ft and of high angle with few possible routes, if any. The N and S walls of this face also appear very impressive. The easiest route would appear to be from 1434, which would involve crossing a steep gap. The 1st and only asc was made in 9/1957 by B & T Romsloe, a varied and interesting climb.

Sukkertoppen from Tverrdalen — From Tverrdalen (781) via giant amphi up to deeper skar. Follow N side of ridge to foretop. Descent into small skar. Follow S side of ridge up to final top. Descent by the same route. (T Romsloe).

THE KUINARCOCKA GROUP (map E 790 Skjomen)

is bounded on the S by Norddalen, on the W by the Stortind ridge, on the E by the Storstein rock massif and on the N by Skamdalsbotn. *Lositind* (1044) which overlooks Norddalen, has small cliffs on its S side, but looks uninteresting. *Losifjell* (1213 — 1004 — 1012), probable 1st asc 7/1957 by J Farren and J R Setchell, up by the E ridge. *Losivarre* (1259 — 1161 — 1164 — 1170) is the long ridge N of Losivatn. It is an ideal centre for preparation for the longer faces and serious problems in this district. Probable 1st asc 7/1957 by L G Hill and G K Richardson along the main ridge, easy but arduous snow conditions. 800 ft of the 1000 ft high S face of 1170 was climbed in 7/1957 by L G Hill and C J Mortlock. The standard was very severe and gave delightful open climbing on good rock with the crux hard very severe on the final pitch. Retreat by abseil owing to accident. The N face of 1170 is 1500 ft high and consists of a very slabby face wall broken up. The centre of the face is less broken and was climbed in 8/1957 by C J Mortlock and G K Richardson, an enjoyable and interesting climb. *Nordre Losivarre* (1208) has a very impressive N face, some 1000 ft high at a very high angle. No obvious route.

Kuinarcocka (1796—1620) is perhaps the most serious mountain in the group. All faces offer good climbing, often of a very high standard. Descent is normally by 3 abseils off the SE ridge to a col and then by a steep ice gully to Jotunsdalen. The steep and grassy E face was climbed in 7/1938 by T Rydberg and G Santesson, a fine route of the rubber climb variety. A route up the centre of the slabby W wall of the SE ridge was made in 7/1956 by B and J Thompson. This face has 1500 ft of continuous steep rock. The SE ridge was gained high up, above its difficult part, but the party did not go to the summit. An asc by the S face direct was made in 8/1957 by C J Mortlock and G K Richardson. The climb starts at the bottom of the central mass of slabs, above some broken slabs and 200 ft to the left of a prominent 300 ft diedre. An excellent climb on the lower tier and sustained difficulty for 1500 ft. It is a serious climb with long runouts and poor protection. The SE gully (descended by Thompsons in 1956) was ascended in 7/1957 by D Duffield. No technical difficulty, but the left hand fork near the top is loose and unpleasant. The Black Edge Route was made in 7/1957 by J Farren and C J Mortlock. This climb takes a direct line up the edge of the right hand buttress overlooking the SE gully. A fine steep route of high standard. Very severe. The E glacier was ascended in 7/1957 by D Duffield. The centre has 3 ice walls which appear dangerous, but these can be avoided by an upward traverse left up deep snow to the SE col. The E ridge was climbed in 8/1957 by D Duffield. Steep and loose rock encountered between 1182 and 1434. From 1134 the E glacier was crossed to the col between 1796 and 1671, then down the W snow slope of col to Nikkivatn. The *North Pillar* is perhaps the most impressive rock face in the group, about 2000 ft high with an average angle of 80 degrees. It appears devoid of weaknesses and the only route appears to be up the right edge by way of a steep gully ending in overhangs. The NW face is 2000 ft high and is seamed by many gullies. These and the buttresses may yield good routes on sound rock.

Peak 1671 lies immediately N of Kuinarcocka. Its E face was climbed in 8/1957 by C J Mortlock and G K Richardson. They explored the S ridge and then descended the steep N ridge to a col above the glacier. The W face consists of steep and unpleasant scree. The 800 ft high SE face runs along the complete length of the N side of the glacier at an angle of 70 degrees. The N face has several very steep buttresses. *Peak* 1589 is an uninteresting triple-headed peak further N of Kuinarcocka, but it affords a good ridge walk with extensive views. 1st asc in winter 1950 by G Billing from the E. In 8/1957 it was climbed by C J Mortlock and G K Richardson by the shattered steep S ridge to the first summit and then over boulders and scree to the other points. The N faces look as though there were numerous routes of high standard. The NW face drops steeply for 1000 ft to Skamdalsbotn, mainly loose rock and scree.

Nikkitind (1539—1497—1328) is a knife-edge ridge 2 km W of Kuinarcocka. A traverse from col 1208 across 1539 and 1497 (probable 1st ascents) was made in 7/1956 by J James, S Kaye, J Ramsden, B and J Thompson. A wonderful arete with exposure of up to 2000 ft. Several towers and gaps. A direct asc by the S face was made in 8/1957 by D Duffield and L G Hill, a fine route with 1650 ft of climbing. The N face has several very steep buttresses and any route would probably be a serious proposition. *Peak* 1328 is the unclimbed W point on the ridge. It appears as a beautiful cone as seen from Skamdalsbakkan, but the slabby rock appears to be very loose. *Nikkitoppen* (1302—1243—1270—1107) rises 3 km NW of Kuinarcocka, uninteresting rounded peaks with steep scree and loose rock to N and E, easy angled to S, cliffs on N. Probable 1st ascents in 8/1957 by C J Mortlock and G K Richardson by an E-W traverse.

THE STORSTEINSFJELL ROCK MASSIF (map E 790 Skjomen) rises between Kuinarcocka and the frontier. *Macalacocka* (1630) is the S spur of the group. Probable 1st asc 7/1957 by J Farren and J Setchell, up by the S face on steep snow and a 50 ft rock wall. Cornice. *Hjørne-toppen* (1875) is the S pivot of 2 ridges stretching NW and

NE. The S ridge leads easily from col 1503 to the surveyors' cairn. The NW ridge starts from col 1489 along
an easy angled ridge which steepens abruptly beneath the
summit. The top is best reached by joining the first rib
of the W face. The 1st winter asc was made in 4/1950 by
G Billing and T Romsloe. The E face was climbed in
8/1957 by L G Hill and C J Mortlock, a short but enjoyable route, very diff, 1 pitch of 20 ft severe. *Kirken*
(1734) rises NW of Hjørnetoppen. 1st asc 4/1950 by
G Billing, A Erikson and T Romsloe. Its E face is an 800
ft high snow-ice face rising above Storstein glacier. Two
routes were made here in 8/1957 by the Oxford expedition: E Face by the Diagonal Route — D Duffield and
J Farren, start from the centre of the face and traverse
diagonally right beneath a steep ice wall which crosses
the face. This led to the N ridge, 300 ft below the summit.
E Face by the Central Route — D Duffield, L G Hill and
C J Mortlock, crossing the ice band at 200 ft and then
140 ft of hard snow at a very steep angle to the top. Its
NW ridge looks like easy scrambling. *Peak* 1725 rises on
the same ridge. It was climbed in 7/1956 by J Ramsden,
up by the glacier cwm on the SW side to col 1349, then
up the S ridge, descent to col 1349. Its SE ridge was
climbed in 8/1957 by D Duffield, from col 1560. *Peak*
1651 is the N point of Storsteinsfjell's NW ridge. Climbed
in 7/1956 by J James and J Ramsden, up by slopes
from glacier pass to the NW. *Peak* 1562 is the fine looking
S point of a subsidiary ridge SW from 1725. Its W face
was climbed in 7/1956 by J James. Its N arete was climbed
on the same day by J Ramsden, a fine rock edge which
required straddling at one section, descent by the S face.
Some loose rock. The SE ridge was climbed in 8/1957 by
D Duffield.
The NE ridge from Hjørnetoppen holds 3 fine peaks.
Stortoppen (1901) is the highest peak in the rock massif
and the fourth highest peak in Arctic Norway. The 1st
asc was made by a surveyor, up from Smaillerieppe. 1st
recorded asc in 1933 by Th S Gudjohnsen. 1st winter
asc 5/1945 by G Billing. Its E face was climbed in
8/1957 by L G Hill and C J Mortlock, directly up to the
summit up scree and easy slabs. The ridge traverse
1901 — 1875 gives at least 2 problems of a severe standard,
but these can be avoided by traversing on to the easy
S face. The N face forms the wall of the whole ridge from
1875 to 1715, a 1000 ft wall with the only break being
a steep gully between 1901 and 1875. This "Rotten Gully"
was climbed in 8/1957 by L G Hill and C J Mortlock,
a climb of 570 ft, very severe, but not recommended
when free of ice, as it is extremely dangerous on account

112

of the consistent bad rock. The 1st asc of *Dobbelttoppen* (1797) and *Nordtoppen* (1715) was made in 7/1938 by T Rydberg and G Santesson, traversing from Hjørne. toppen (1875) via 1901 — 1797 — 1715, a grand expedition- The descent from 1797 to col 1635 was tricky.

THE BASSECOCKA-SELKACOCKA RANGES (map E 790 Skjomen) are situated immediately N of the Storsteinsfjell rock massif. *Bassecocka* is a large horse-shoe ridge embracing a large glacier. *Helligtind* (1638) is an impressive rock summit, soaring grimly above Hellig-vatn on the N tip of the W arm of the indented snow and rock ridge. The easiest route is by the S ridge from the gap towards 1657. The NW ridge from 1428 was climbed in 9/1944 by I Hartviksen and T Romsloe. *Selkacocka* (1657) is a lofty rugged mountain further S. Points 1591 and 1657 were climbed in 8/1941 by L & I Hartviksen and T Tomsloe, from Skamdalen via 1285. Pt 1657 was climbed in 7/1955 by G R E Brooke via lake 974 and a steep ascent up the flanking ridge to pt 1285, then SE across the stony plateau to a spur leading up to the main ridge near pt 1465. From here, the ridge which is mostly a few feet wide and sheer on its E side, mounts gradually for nearly 1 km, over *Peak* 1591 to its final sharp rise to the summit of pt 1657. Descent by the same route. *Jerntind* (1504) is a remarkable tower of dark red rock. 1st asc 8/1951 by B & T Romsloe, from Helligvatn over the Helligvatn glacier and up by a gully on the N side. Descent by the same route. It was climbed in 7/1956 by J James, S Kaye, J Ramsden, B and J Thompson, from the SE col. This is a superb jagged ridge with many towers and pinnacles — ,,a far better peak than the map suggests, and one of the nicest aretes that I have traversed" (Jack Ramsden). *Våmbtind* (1497) is a shapely peak N of Helligvatn. Its N aspect reveals a spade-shaped crest with 2 curving aretes en-closing a shallow snow-filled corrie. Its NW arete, which consists of sound rock and rises at a deceptively mild angle, provides 1000 ft of easy climbing to the summit, ascended in 7/1933 by B & T Romsloe. 1st winter asc by the same route in 5/1951 by P Groth and T Romsloe. The *Selkacocka* group lies E of Bassecocka. *Peak* 1654 was climbed in 7/1956 by B and J Thompson by the W face of the N pinnecle. This is a fine face route with several hundred feet of diff or severe standard. Descent by the W corrie. Another route by the N pinnacle by the N buttress was made on the same day by S Kaye and J Ramsden.

THE LOFOTEN ISLES

Sir James Bryce, late president of the Alpine Club, once said that "if the ocean rose to the foot of the Chamonix Aiguilles, one would get a characteristic view of the Lofoten peaks!" This group of islands, situated over 1200 miles N of London, still offers scope for exploring. The Lofoten peaks are often of fantastic shape and extremely wild-loking. They are ice-polished up to 2000 ft and the rock consists of gabbro, gneiss and granite. Many rock faces are unclimbable owing to the immense glacier-worn smooth slabs which are void of hand or foot holds. The usual routes are afforded by ridges or occasional gullies. The risk of avalanches is negligible. There are no paths or cairned routes. Many peaks have only been climbed once or only a few times, and climbing expeditions are few and far between. In short, it is a district as yet unspoiled, unique in situation and unsurpassed in all the elements of beauty.

Generally, ascent and descent are made by the same route. Climbers will here find ample confirmation of the dictum that "peaks with only one way up are always interesting!" It is often helpful to make two-stone cairns on the way up — but please remember to knock them down on the return journey! We want it that way. More than one peak can be climbed in one day, firstly because there is no long trudge to reach the foot of the peak, and secondly because one can climb in perpetual daylight during the period of the Midnight Sun.

Travel by air from Oslo via Bodø to Svolvær on Aust-vågøy. From Bergen by coastal express steamer to Stamsund on Vestvågøy or to Svolvær in 3 nights. From Oslo by train to Bodø in 26 hrs and then by coastal express steamer to Stamsund in 5 hrs or to Svolvær in 7 hrs. The road network on the islands has been greatly extended during recent years, now covering a distance of about 600 km.

MOSKENESØY ISLAND

MOSKENESØY ISLAND (maps E 545 Lofotodden and E 600 Moskenesøy) is truly one of the gems of the Lofotens with scores of graceful spires and a vast complex of sharp ridges. Several peaks have slabs over a thousand feet high, excessively steep and without crack or place where even a bird could find footing. The island is highly indented with fjords and studded with lakes. There are few trees. Vegetation is limited almost entirely to grassy pastures and a rich growth of moss and tall ferns. Usually there is no scree at the base of the cliffs which often rise sheer out of the fjords. Reine is the usual starting point, reached by local boat from Stamsund in 3 hrs. Sørvågen is another little village S of Reine, reached by boat from Stamsund in 4 hrs. Pensions in both villages.

THE ERTENHELLTIND RANGES (map E 545 Lofotodden): Very little is known about the southernmost peaks on Moskenesøy, but they look very attractive. The elegant *Gjertind* (837) which rises W of lake Å)pronounced Awe), was cairned in 7/1920 by N Backer Grøndahl, E Quale and F Schjelderup, up from lake Å via the SE ridge and a steep snow gully. Further N stands *Ertenhelltind* (942) which is a remarkable peak, rising precipitously out of the ocean. Its weirdly indented E ridge provides the only known route. 1st asc 8/1903 by J N Collie, D Northall-Laurie, Wm and Will Slingsby. Its E ridge continues to *Støvla* (824), whose smooth glaciated slopes may provide good sport. Its E ridge was climbed via the E peak in 5/1956 by S Kaye and J Ramsden, descent by the easy N slope, good sport and rather steep rock. A horse-shoe ridge encircling lake Krok, runs from Ertenhelltind to *Hermandalstind* (1034), the highest peak on the island, a real mountain which affords first-rate sport. The Ertenhell-Hermansdal ridge has never been climbed, altough attempts have been made. This traverse would probably take a good 24 hours, but it would make a memorable expedition. Surveyors climbed Hermandalstind (1034) in 1900 from Fors fjord via pts 450−539 and up by the SE ridge, time 3 hrs from the fjord. Its N ridge was climbed in 7/1903 by J N Collie, D Northall-Laurie, Wm and Will Slingsby from Fors fjord via pt 808 and E of pt 877 via the spectacular gap on the N ridge to Hermandalstind, time 4 hrs from the fjord. The 1st asc of *Middagstind* (877) or N Hermandalstind which overshadows the Hermansdal, was made in 8/1904 by E C C Baly, J N Collie, Wm and Morris and Will Slingsby and H Woolley, up by the N face. *Vestre Hermandalstind* (669) which consists of magnificent crags, was climbed from Hermansdal in 8/1904 by A M and Wm C Slingsby and H Woolley. The ridge W of Bunes fjord forms a sharp needle which resembles the Dru, called *Biskopshuen* (601) or the Mitre, which was cairned in 8/1904 by E C C Baly, J N Collie and Wm-Will-Morris Slingsby, climbing from Vindstad via the S col and S ridge. A subsidiary peak of Biskopshuen, *Trollhodet*, was cairned in 1926 by O J Broch, E Fjeld and S Sigvang,

Reinebringen forms a giant crescent (Photo: Mittet)

up by a fine chimney. The ridge terminates in an elegant peak, *Skiven* (850) whose W wall is composed of giant slabs from ocean to top. Scope for interesting routes.

THE REINE RANGES (map E 545 Lofotodden): Overlooking Reine village, *Reinebringen* (615) is a peculiar horse-shoe ridge with steep precipices, forming a giant crescent around lake Reine. Both outliers fall away in almost vertical slabs. It was cairned in 1906 by K S Klingenberg and party, ascending from Reine by the outlier which lies S of the lake. *Navern* (703) is separated from Reinebringen by a fantastic rift which makes Reinebringen overhang for 500 ft above a nasty gully which can be climbed by its NE face until magnificent ridge with loose rock. Its W side overhangs for about 40 ft and then sweeps down in face and then slabs. Climbed in 7/1956 by P Cocker and F Perlin. The E outlier from Navern forms a little pyramidal peak, *Hammerskaftet* (355) which overlooks Reine harbour. 1st asc 1906 by L M Hollander. Its E ridge was climbed in 1910 by A B Bryn and F Schjelderup in 2½ hrs from Reine. A fine ridge broken by a steep gap leads to *Veinestind* (729), cairned 1906 by K S Klingenberg and party. The ridge terminates northwards in a fine conical peak, *Tennestind* (700) which looks difficult, particularly when seen from Reine. However, the usual route up by grassy slopes on the W side is easy. A traverse from Tennestind to Veinestind was made in 7/1937 by H P Spilsbury and party. No difficulty, apart from one gendarme which is turned on the W side by a loose chimney and then a ledge. From Veinestind, a fine ridge runs southwards to Djup fjord. Its highest

116

point, N *Munken* (805), is a natural monolith, a fine rock tooth very similar to the Bhasteir Tooth in Skye. Its E side falls sheer and overhangs at top. 1st asc 7/1903 by J N Collie, D Northall-Laurie, Wm and Will Slingsby, up by the N ridge which can be reached by various routes from Fors fjord or Veines or via Veinestind. A good climb, though exposed. N Munken can also be climbed by its SE ridge from Djup fjord, but this is a nerve-racking climb over rotten rock. It includes the ascent of S *Munken* (701) by its SW face. 1st asc 1913 by C and J Lysholm, when they also cairned the *Prekstol* pinnacle. In 1930 the Lysholm brothers also cairned *Midtre Munken*, up by the SW face. An unidentified group of 4 peaks near Munken, named *Krokvasstind*, was cairned in 1926 by O J Broch, E Fjeld and S Sigvang (confused with Krok-hammertind?)

THE KLOKKETIND RANGES (map E 545 Lofot-odden): The promontory between Kirke fjord and Vor fjord, N of Reine, is capped by a conspicuous ridge with a series of interesting peaks. Its southernmost point, *Olstind* (680) boats a fine S face which has never been climbed. It consists principally of one gigantic slab, capped by grassy crags. Across this slab is one ledge, steep in some parts but inclining only gently upwards in others, towars E. A steep chimney with at least 2 bad pitches descends from the W end of this ledge. This sporting route was attempted in vain in 8/1904 by E C C Baly, J N Collie, Wm-Morris-Will Slingsby and H Woolley. Instead, they reached the top by the SW face which provides an interesting climb. The Olstind ridge continues across *Rostadtind* (773). 1st asc 8/1961 by G Bremnes and A R Heen, up from S across 2 steep gaps. The ridge continues across the *Klokketinder* (866), a magnificent group which is essentially for experts only. The precipices of the fearsome-looking Klokketind ridge are "as straight as a beggar can spit". Between Vestre (855) and Store (866) Klokketind there are 2 smaller peaks, the Tretinder, but these are separated from Store Klokketind by an awe-inspiring gap which is called Rubicon Skar. Although it is hardly more than 50 ft deep, it provides a highly sensational climb, which requires great physical strength. The *Tretinder* were cairned in 8/1904 by E C C Baly, J N Collie and Wm-Morris-Will Slingsby, up by the N face and W ridge. By traversing along two wide ledges on the N face, it is possible to climb the easternmost of 3 gullies up to the W ridge which is followed to the top. *Store Klokketind* (866) was cairned in 8/1910 by A B Bryn and F Schjelderup, from Tretind via Rubicon Skar. V

severe. The 1st asc of *Austre Klokketind* (849) was made in 7/1913 by W Eger, R Løchen, S Saxlund and H Tønsberg, up by the S ridge. A descent by the S wall from Rubicon Skar was made in 1930 by two Norwegians, but the leader commented that this was without doubt the first and last descent by this route! *Vestre Klokketind* (855) was conquered in 7/1953 by E A Goode and P Russel, climbing the W ridge. There is still more interesting work to be found among the Klokketinder. *Segltind* (741) rises NW of Klokketind, a majestic peak which is seldom climbed. An ascent by its E face was made in 7/1953 by E A Goode, D J and E R Munns and P Russell. Descent by the N ridge.

Vestre Klokketind (855) by W Ridge — From E shore of Kirke fjord to lake Farsan (319). A ridge running ENE from pt 731 joins it to Vestre Klokketind. The lowest point of this ridge is reached by a large gully which slants to L on northern slopes of pt 731, starting a few hundred feet above and and SE of lake Farsan. The gully consists mainly of loose rock and vegetation. Climb gully until it fades out after about 400 ft, halfway up towards ridge. The upper 100 ft are climbed on rocky rib to L of gully. This leads on to grassy saddle where the rib abutts against the rock face. Some scrambling up grass is followed by delightful grassy traverse to L. This is the key to the route. The whole traverse is several hundred ft long, but for about 100 ft the ledge is horizontal and narrow, under one foot wide at one place. Halfway along there is a rock for belay. Good belay at each end. From the far end, a shallow gully leads up to ridge at a point just above and to R of its lowest point. Turning to L, a rather awkward step down is made on to a little "knife-edge" which is very exposed. Beyond this section the ridge ascends again and is followed to top. It consists of a series of steep rocky steps with grassy platforms in between. There are 3 difficult places: A little slab lacking in holds; a 20 ft wall with grooves up it, and an overhanging wall, turned by a traverse to R, followed by a move up a slab and through a narrow gap which leads to a shelf from which the top of the wall is reached. From this point, there is easy scrambling to top. Descent by the same route. (Paul Russell).

The northern portal to the Reine harbour is formed by *Festheltind* (389), situated E of Vor fjord. It provides a jolly climb via its N gap and up by the N ridge. Cairned in 8/1910 by A B Bryn and F Schjelderup. The ridge runs northwards across *Bukskinntind* (771) and *Målhøgtind* (744), which were cairned in 8/1961 by G Bremnes and A R Heen.

THE KIRKE FJORD W RANGES (map E 545 Lofotodden): The promontory W of Kirke fjord affords a fine ridge which includes *Helvedestind* (606), a sharp peak with giant slabs from ocean to summit. It has been climbed, buth there are no reports. Its N ridge forms the crescent-shaped ridge of *Stamprevtind* (759) which yields good sport. Pt 759 was cairned by E Rostrup and party. Pt 480 on its SE outlier was cairned in 1938 by G Santesson and H Tjerneld. *Kvanndalstind* (705) is a twin-topped and unnamed peak on the ridge N of Stamprevtind. Its S top (705) was cairned in 7/1956 by P Cocker and F Merlin, up by easy gully on the W face between the twin peaks, then up by the N ridge which is smooth, narrow, steep and very difficult. 3 hrs up, 2 down.

THE N MOSKENESØY RANGES (map E 600 Moske-
nesøy): *Breiflogtind* (761) rises on the westernmost ridge
N of Kirke fjord and N of Kvanndalstind. Its N wall is
absolutely perpendicular and consists of slabs which are
practically void of cracks — except in the lowest section.
1st asc 1913 by C and J Lysholm, ascending by the Kirke
fjord face to a small gap. Its N ridge sets off 3 distinct
peaks called *Kamman* (503) and 2 subsidiary peaks called
Kniplingene, not named on the map. There are also 2
pinnacles which have never been climbed. The 1st
complete traverse of Kamman and Kniplingene was
made in 1960 by N Faarlund, A Schei and H Wortmann.
The ridge terminates with *Smeden* (544) which overlooks
Horseid. In 1913, R Løchen and H Tønsberg made a
traverse from Horseid via Smeden, Kniplingene and
Kamman.

(1)   (2) (3)   (4) (5)

*View from the Klokketind: (1) Breiflogtind 761; (2) Krokhammertind 758; (3)
Manntind 564; (4) Brasråstind 848 and (5) peak 862 (Photo: Magnar Pettersen)*

On the central ridge rises *Manntind* (564), see map E 545
Lofotodden. It overlooks the head of Kirke fjord and
was climbed in 7/1956 by P Cocker and F Perlin, by
slabs on the S face, followed by a traverse to the left and
up by short rock pitches and grass slopes to the top.
Krokhammertind (738) rises N of Manntind, above Snø
Skar. Its E face which consists of one immense smooth
slab from foot to top, was climbed in 7/1913 by W Eger,
R Løchen, S Saxlund and H Tønbserg, This is the only
known route, but Spilsbury believes it may be possible
to get up by the S ridge, which has been descended but
never ascended. Not noted on the map, *Madslitind*
(703) is a steep peak with loose rock, situated W of Krokhammertind and separated from it by Snø Skar. Its S
and W walls have never been climbed. The 1st asc was
made in 7/1913 by W Eger, R Løchen, S Saxlund and
H Tønsberg, climbing the W ridge from Horseid Skar.
Beyond the N col of Krokhammertind follows the fantas-

119

tic summit ridge of *Brasråstind* (862). Its southernmost peak (600) is reached easily via the pass above lake Fagerå, climbed in 7/1956 by P Cocker and F Perlin The W face of Brasråstind 862 consists of one colossal smooth slab from ocean to summit — one of the biggest sea cliffs in Europe and a rock face which has never been climbed. Spilsbury has descended it and believes it can be climbed as well. There is a narrow terrace on the W face, formed by a fault between two immense boiler plates, the key to an easy descent to Horseid. Facing east, there are tremendous walls of rock, but the only known route leads up by the E side and SE ridge, the route of the 1st asc in 8/1903 by H S Mundahl and T G Ouston. A protracted gap leads from Brasråstind to the third highest peak on the island, *Hjellbergstind* (911). 1st asc 7/1953 by E A Goode, D J and E R Munns and P Russell, climbing the SW ridge. Its NE ridge was climbed from Sel fjord in 5/1956 by S Kaye and J Ramsden, and by the S ridge in 7/1956 by P Cocker and F Merlin. *Kitind* (763) is separated from Hjellbergstind by a hanging valley. 1st recorded asc 7/1903 by G T Glover, H S Mundahl, T G Ouston and H Scott-Jones, up by the E side. Its NE ridge was climbed in 5/1956 by S Kaye and J Ramsden and its S ridge in 7/1956 by K Blackwood and A C White. *Kjerringa* (625) rises N of Kitind. 1st asc 7/1956 by A R Heen and P Langås, traversing the long ridge from Kitind to Kjerringa.

Hjellbergstind by SW Ridge — From Stokmarkpollen to obvious col at 1300 ft, then a further 800 ft of scrambling up S slopes to a point where these slopes taper into narrow ridge, from which vertical cliffs fall on R almost to sea level. The ridge ascends in a series of steep little rocky walls, alternating with easy mossy sections. The only pitch of much interest is about 2/3 up the ridge and consists of a 30 ft wall with large chimney up its centre. On the ascent, the party divided, some making a move round to R, whilst the others took a less exposed but not very pleasant route on L up steep mossy rocks. (On the descent everyone used the chimney, which was also subsequently ascended by one member of the party). The ridge continues almost to top, which was finally reached by balancing along sharp edge of huge flake of rock which bridges the top of great gully on E side of peak. From far end of this flake, a short pull up on steep firm rock leads to top. Descent by the same route. (Paul Russell).

FLAKSTAD ISLAND

FLAKSTAD ISLAND (map E 984 Vestvågøy) is wedged in between Moskenesøy and Vestvågøy, a narrow sound intervening on either side. Travel by bus from Stamsund to Ballstad (17 miles) and then by local boat to Nuss fjord or Napp. A road runs from Napp across the island to Ramberg. No accommodation, so camping is a necessity. A fine ridge runs across the middle of the island. *Stjernhodet* (932) provides an easy climb by the W face from Kvalvik. *Stjerntind* (937) is the highest

peak on the island. The 1st asc was made in 6/1930 by
A R Heen, S Martnes and A Sildsandvik, from Stjernhodet and up by the very steep N face, a short climb but
first-rate sport. V severe. Further N the ridge forms the
Storurtind (783) and *Stortind* (870). The NE side of the
latter is considered inaccessible. *Moltind* (703) is the
northernmost point on the ridge. Its E wall is practically
vertical and is said to be unclimbable. The traverse from
pt 779 to Moltind is an interesting expedition with magnificent views. From Kvalvik, ascend diagonally to pt 779
and then traverse along the highly indented ridge.
Descend by the W side of pt 703 to Ramberg. Time 10
hrs, standard moderate.

VESTVÅG ISLAND

THE VESTVÅGØY (map E 984 Vestvågøy) is different
from the other islands. There is a large area of arable
land with many farmsteads and several roads with bus
services. Stamsund is the main village, port of call for
the coastal express steamer service. Hotel accommodation.

THE BALLSTAD RANGES (map E 984 Vestvågøy):
Ballstad village which lies sheltered behind the Skottind
ranges on the southernmost promontory, is reached by
bus from Stamsund in a short hour. Boarding house.
Skottind (675) rises NW of Ballstad village, a conspicuous
peak which can be reached easily by its NW face. Its E
side was climbed in 1930 by A R Heen and W B Jensen.
Its S ridge is very jagged and narrow with many pinnacles, including *Tommelen*. This ridge is called *Skjeringene*.
A traverse from Skottind via Tommelen and Skjeringene
was made in 1930 by A R Heen and A Sildsandvik.

THE HIMMELTIND RANGES (map E 984 Vest-
vågøy): A bus journey of 2 hrs from Stamsund to Hauk-
land leads to the foothills of the *Himmeltinder* (965),
which form a huge rock massif. *Midtre Himmeltind* (934)
was cairned in 8/1902 by H S Mundahl and T G Ouston,
from lake Mørkedal to col and then to top by the S ridge.
The 1st asc of *Store Himmeltind* (965) was made in 1890 by
E Jacobsen and J Pedersen. The 1st asc of NE *Himmeltind* (870) was made in 1930 by A R Heen and S Martnes,
up by the W ridge, descent by ice gully on the NE side.
Ristind (867) rises E of the Himmeltinder. Its N face is
an almost vertical precipice. It was climbed in 8/1902
by H S Mundahl and T G Ouston from Rise via the S
col and up by the S ridge. A R Heen and S Martnes

traversed from Ristind to pt 729 in 1931, and A R Heen made the 1st winter asc of Ristind in Easter 1932, climbing the S ridge. In 1944 M Pettersen climbed pt 613 from NW and traversed to Ristind.

A bus journey of 3 hrs from Stamsund to Unstad, leads towards *Skolmen* (602) on the NW promontory of Vestvågøy, a jagged ridge which rises sheer out of the fjord. The asc from the NW is easy. It was climbed from the E in 1956 by E Olsen and M Pettersen.

GIMSØY ISLAND

THE GIMSØY (maps E 984 Vestvågøy and E 860 Svolvær) lies between Vestvågøy and Austvågøy, reached by bus and ferry from Stamsund or Svolvær in 2—3 hrs. No accommodation. The *Barstrandtinder* (762) form a long ridge facing Gimsøy sound. There are no reports, but it is believed that all peaks have been climbed.

AUSTVÅG ISLAND

THE AUSTVÅGØY (maps E 860 Svolvær & E 320 Hadsel): Climbers have compared the Austvågsøy aiguilles with those of Chamonix, and they certainly offer good sport. The island is a true paradise for climbers. The Troll fjord in the N is perhaps the outstanding attraction, a fjord which cuts into the island from the narrow Raftsund with numerous peaks and "trolls". Climbers could spend several busy weeks here without once retracing their steps. Svolvær is the best starting point, a port of call for the coastal express steamers from Bergen and Bodø. Hotel accommodation.

THE KABELVÅG RANGES (map E 960 Svolvær): Kabelvåg is a fishing village 6 miles SW of Svolvær. Frequent bus services. Local accommodation. Travelling 3 miles westwards by bus from Kabelvåg will take you to Kalle at the foot of *Vågekallen* (942), a famous complex of ridges and peaks. "Strip the Dent Blanche of its ice, double the number of its aretes, making them more jagged, cut off all but the upper 3000 ft, plant it by the seashore, and a fair idea will be had of Vågekallen!" There is first-rate sport and still scope for exploring. Though it is less in height than Scafell Pike, there is probably more rock climbing of the highest class upon it than could be found in the whole of the English Lake District. The main peak is said to resemble Aiguille

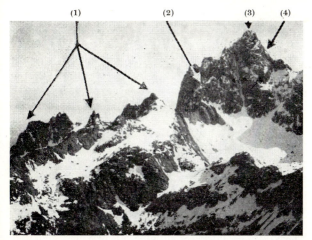

Vågekallen, a famous complex of ridges and peaks: (1) Småkallan; (2) N. ridge (3) Vågekallen. (4) W. wall (Photo: Magnar Pettersen)

Verte in Mt Blanc. The 1st asc was made in 1889 by M H Ekroll and A Johannessen, up by the S face which is now the usual route. The 1st winter asc was made in 1/1934 by A R Heen and J Jacobsen, from the S and up by a big snow gully which leads to the E ridge, then leftwards on to the S side and up to the top. This route has never been climbed in summer. Time 9 hrs from foot to top. Its N ridge was climbed in 6/1939 by A R Heen and L Hansen, up by the Småkallen ridge and then by the N ridge to top. The same party climbed the E ridge in 6/1940, following the ridge mainly by its left-hand side. The "Cambridge Route" by the N face was made in 6/1950 by J M Nedderman and J F West, a climb of very high class. The route leads by the N face up to the saddle on the E ridge, which is then followed to the top. The N wall proper is probably unassailable. *Småkallan* are the smaller peaks on the N ridge of Vågekallen. The 1st asc was made in 1932 by A R and E Heen. A peculiar 6 ft high pillar is encountered on the sharp ridge near the gap facing the highest Småkallan. A flat rock block is placed on top of it. *Kvanndalstind* (832) stands SW of Vågekallen. It was cairned in 8/1903 by H S Mundahl and T G Ouston, up by a 1000 ft high gully on the E face. The 1st winter asc was made in 3/1937 by M Furuli and A R Heen, ascending from the SE.

Vågekallen by S Face (usual route) — Land S of peak and climb up valley between Kvanndalstind and Vågekallen, then turn R towards prominent isolated square-cut pinnacle on middle of W ridge. Follow ridge to R, to knife-edge which is crossed by sitting astride it. This point can also be reached from W from lake Djupfjord. Ridge impracticable beyond. Turn slightly R and up well-marked ledge towards S face, which is very broken here. Follow easiest line to top. Time, 3½ hrs up, 2 down. Standard mod. (Arne Randers Heen).

The Cambridge Route (Vågekallen by N Face) — Start from corrie above lake and ascend to R of gully between peak and steep buttress nearer the sea. Up snowfield and across snow bridge to sloping terrace. Traverse L under rushing waterfall for 20 ft, then across easy rocks and grass ledges for 70 ft. Higher up are obstacles of broad vertical bands of rock, separated by stretches of grass slopes. The 2nd one necessitates the jamming of an ice axe in small crack and climbing up it. A higher band involves a tunnel which goes some 6 ft into the mountain. As a general rule, the ascent of each band of rock takes the climber from the waterfall further to R, away from gully, until wide terrace is reached. Then a long traverse to L, a short distance below gap between peaks, leads to easier rocks. Time from foot to top, 8 hrs. Very severe. (J F West).

Vågekallen by E Ridge — From foot of E ridge, start well to L of centre line of lower buttress. Soon angled up to L via diagonal cleft fault before one is able to climb more directly over short walls to top of this buttress. An attempt to follow the ridge proper, soon found us turning towers on R and then L flanks. This L flank helps with a grassy ledge traversing across immense boiler plates. Then upward progress on this face with much traversing eventually leads to ridge crest of lower summit. The descent into gap beyond involves climbing down a 40 ft overhanging chimney. Thence the L flank of final tower leads to summit. The climbing at several points is v diff. Time up, just over 4 hrs. (Jack Ramsden).

The *Småtinder* (752) are situated NE of Vågekallen and NW of Kabelvåg. Stortind or Store Småtind is the highest point. The 1st asc of Daletind or Austre Småtind was made in 9/1907 by A Pallin and a guide, from the W gap. A complete traverse of the Småtinder from tarn 324 to Breifjell was made in 7/1957 by S A Obrien and T Clinton. *Kongstind* (613) is a rugged triple-peaked ridge N of Kabelvåg. There is a legend that a Viking king once climbed it. The ancient moss-covered cairn looks centuries old, and Slingsby believes that this "King's Peak" was named after Olav Tryggvasson (995—1000). The ridge itself is of no climbing interest, but the highest point called *Løva* affords a short climb of about 150 ft. Its S wall has never been climbed and is considered unassailable. There is a gully on the extreme E side of the S wall, and this gully was climbed in 1943 by L Hansen, H K Lorentzen and M Pettersen.

THE SVOLVÆR RANGES (map E 860 Svolvær): Svolvær is the largest village in Lofoten, port of call for the coastal express steamer service. Hotel accommodation. *Fløya* (569) is a horse-shoe ridge above Svolvær, providing an interesting 1st day's outing. Its S wall is rather airy, rising steeply out of the sea. The famous *Svolvær-geita* (600) pinnacle struts out from the face overlooking Svolvær. It is a grand rock needle, crowned by two horns. Usually called Geita, but also known as De To Elskende (The Two Lovers). It struts out about 1800 ft up on the front of Fløya and measures only 150 ft from its inner base to the top. The base is reached in half an hour from Svolvær and is not difficult, but the climbing is exposed — and overlooks the cemetery deep down below! The highest horn is about 16 ft high and is called Storhorn; the other is Litlehorn. The distance between them is

"Geita" — *grand rock needle towering above the Lofoten fishing village of Svolvær*

only 2 ft, but owing to the difference in height, the famous leap from Storhorn to Litlehorn measures about 5 ft across space. But the jump is easy. The 1st asc of Svolværgeita was made in 8/1910 by A B Bryn, C W Rubenson and F Schjelderup, ascending the E wall from the shoulder. This is now the usual route up to the shoulder, an exceptionally fine and partly difficult route. From the gap between Fløya and Geita, climb up a chimney, past an awkwardly sloping slab, through a chimney hole to Geita's shoulder, a large platform on the right, about halfway up the climb, with large block for belay. Steps retraced down chimney for about 18 ft below the shoulder, then traverse to the left, out on the N wall. Up the nearly vertical face below horns to their base on the E wall. Climb Storhorn by its NE side facing Fløya. Time from gap to top, 1½ hrs. A slight variation of this route was made in 1938 by G Santesson and E Tjerneld. The new line is from the platform about 30 ft below the shoulder, and 6 ft to the right of the usual route. The W wall from the shoulder was climbed in 1928 by B Bommen and B Lyche. The first 6 ft above the shoulder are difficult, the leader hoisting himself by both arms up to two cracks in the W wall which are followed up to the horns. Very exposed. At the base of the horns, the route converges with the route by the E wall. Time from gap to top, 2 hrs. The 1st winter asc was made in 3/1937 by A R Heen and A Pedersen, up by the usual route. A new route by the W wall direct was made in 1947 by W Høyer and A Krane. This impressive and highly exposed route commences on the W wall at a point about 250 ft below the top. Up by very steep slabs for about 120 ft up to a spacious platform. Here, a crack leads diagonally from left to right up to the shoulder, whence the climb con-

tinues by the usual route. This airy route is most unin-
spiring, because climbers have to perform right above the
cemetery! Very severe.

The peaks N of Fløya are not of much interest, apart
from *Kvittind* (590), which was cairned in 1932 by C
and J Lysholm.

THE RULTEN RANGES (map E 860 Svolvær) are
situated on the peninsula NE of Svolvær, bounded to the
N by lake Rørhop. Reknes or Kveitvik on the E side are
the usual starting points. *Rulten* (1062) consists of 2
major peaks, separated by a deep gap. The 1st asc of
Vestre Rulten (1035) was made in 8/1903 by J N Collie,
Wm and Will Slingsby, climbing the W side from Reknes.
A variation up by the S gully was made in 1941 by L
Hansen, M Heggedal, E Olsen and M Pettersen. A new
route from the E was made in 1955 by W Høier, E Olsen
and M Pettersen. *Austre Rulten* (1062) is the third highest
summit in Lofoten. Its E ridge affords one of the finest
rock climbs in the whole of Lofoten, a splendid 1st asc
made in 8/1903 by J N Collie, H S Mundahl, D Northall-
Laurie and Wm C Slingsby. Small cairns are found at
each turning point. The same party also tried the SW
ridge but reached only a little above pt 820. They were
unable to find a way up by the N side from Snø Skar,
and they also prospected the ridge which leads straight up
from the pass to the summit. Finally they also attempted
the S face. These routes have never been made. *Lille
Rulten* is a subsidiary peak between Rulten and Reknes,
climbed by its NE side in 1950 by J M Nedderman and
J F West.

Beyond Rulten rises the *Langstrandtind* ridge (932), a
great maze of pinnacles which afford good sport. Some
peaks and pinnacles are said to be still unclimbed.
Kveitviktind is a conical needle behind Kveitvik farm,
climbed in 1950 by L Hansen and M Pettersen. Old
reports of 1st ascents and new routes are very confusing,
and here is a summary: (1) A northern peak was cairned
in 1886 by a German. (2) Midtre Langstrandtind climbed
by SE side in 8/1897 by G Hastings, H Priestman and
H Woolley. (3) Two peaks climbed in 8/1901 by J N
Collie and H Woolley. (4) Vestre from Midtre Langstrandtind in 8/1903 by J P Somers, S Spencer and Chr Jossi.
(5) Midtre Langstrandtind by N face in 8/1903 by J N
Collie, D Northall-Laurie, Wm and Will Slingsby. (6)
Store Langstrandtind by NW face in 7/1904 by E C C
Baly, J N Collie, J Collier, Wm Slingsby and H Woolley.
(7) "Several" Langstrandtinder in 1907 by O Schuster
with Austrian guide. (8) Nørdste Langstrandtind by N

ridge in 1930 by G F Abercrombie and Ness Walker. (9) Two northern Langstrandtinder by E face in 7/1938 by A M Binnie, H Herbert and L Letts. *Kjernadalsnebbet* (same as Kveitviktind?) is said to be a remarkably fine aiguille forming the N portal of Trangedal which is a small valley rising NE from Kveitvik. An attempt was made in 1904 to climb it from the deep gap on its NW side, but after a traverse on the SSW, the attempt was halted about 150 ft below the summit. The climbing is said to be of the very best Chamonix aiguille type. The 1st asc was made in 8/1904 by E C C Baly, J N Collie, Wm and Morris Slingsby, up by the E side.

The *Rørhoptind* ridge (941) comprises 7 splendid peaks, all of which can be climbed from E or W. Old reports are very confusing, mainly because the highest Rørhoptind has often been called Trakta, which is another peak N of lake Rørhop. One Rørhoptind was cairned in 1907 by O Schuster with an Austrian guide. Lille Rørhoptind which is a little needle towards the Langstrandtinder, was cairned in 1930 by C and J Lysholm, up by the S face. Store Rørhoptind 941 was conquered in 7/1930 by B Bommen and O Ottesen, climbing the E ridge. Its N ridge was climbed in 7/1939 by A M Binnie and H Herbert. Nordaustre Rørhoptind was climbed in 7/1950 by R A Brown and R Hardman. The same party also made a descent by the S wall of Sydligste Rørhoptind. The 1st complete traverse of the Rørhoptinder was made in 1960 by N Faarlund and P Vigerust.

THE TROLL FJORD RANGES (map E 320 Hadsel): The Troll fjord peninsula is bounded to the W by Higraf fjord and to the E by the narrow Raftsund. Camps can be made at the fishing hamlets of Liland, Higraf, Korsnes, Brakset or Svartsund, all of which can be reached by local boat from Svolvær. Rising sheer out of lake Trollfjord, the *Trolltinder* (1045) form a fantastically jagged ridge. The lake is a glorious sheet of water, 2 miles long, in a most romantic setting, S of Troll fjord, which is one of the principal tourist attractions on the voyage to North Cape. The long ridge between Store Trolltind and Higraftind comprises 9 distinct peaks and several pinnacles. Local climbers usually refer to them by number, each peak being called Trolltindmuren No. 1 and 2 and 3 (TM/1 — TM/2 etc). *Store Trolltind* (1045) falls abruptly into the S side of lake Trollfjord in magnificent slabs. Attempts have been made to climb this (N) face direct, but vertical rocks below the summit have proved impassable. Spilsbury believes a route can be found when snow conditions are favourable, but Magnar Pettersen

The Trolltind range seen from the Raftsund

is sceptical, because the uppermost 800 ft are practically
vertical. The 1st asc of Store Trolltind was made in
6/1890 by May Jeffrey with 2 porters, climbing the E
face. Its W face was climbed in 8/1897 by G Hastings,
H Priestman and H Woolley.

TM/4 (pt 994 Trollsadel) was cairned in 8/1897 by G
Hastings, H Priestman and H Woolley, climbing the S
face. TM/7 (pt 990) was cairned in 1907 by O Schuster
with an Austrian guide, up by the SW face. TM/4 and
TM/5 were climbed from Kjerna glacier in 1922 by N
Backer Grøndahl, K S Hanssen, E Quale and F Schjelderup. Two more Trolltinder were cairned in 1930 by B
Bommen and O Ottesen. A traverse from TM/4 to TM/7
was made in 7/1950 by R A Brown and P Wilkinson.
Among the Trolltind pinnacles, *Glassberget* and *Trolljenta* were cairned in 7/1948 by L Hansen, M Pettersen
and T Romsloe. Glassberget which was climbed by the
W ridge, stands on the col between Store Trolltind and
Korsnestind, previously called Prinsessa. Trolljenta was
climbed by its S ridge. It rises on the western outlier
from the short ridge on the N face of Store Trolltind.
Trollgutten was cairned in 7/1948 by W Høyer, A Krane
and E Olsen. This is a rock needle on the E outlier from
the N face of Store Trolltind, probably the one and only
rock needle in Norway which cannot be climbed without
the aid of pitons. Attempts to reach it from the E have
failed.

Facing the narrow Raftsund, *Braksettind* (550) rises SE
of the Trolltind massif. Its highest point is Store Braksettind or Peter's Church Tower. 1st asc 7/1930 by B
Bommen and O Ottesen, up by the N wall. Its E wall
was climbed in 1941 by H K Lorentzen and M Pettersen.
Store Braksettind is flanked by a smaller tower on either
side. A steep scramble up its W side leads to *Lille Brakset-*

tind or Sukkertoppen. There are no reports about the E tower. *Korsnestind* (950) rises steeply out of Raftsund, adjoining the Trolltinder. In previous reports, this peak (also called Jomfrua) has been confused with Braksettind or Trollgutten. The 1st asc was made in 1922 by N Backer Grøndahl, K Hanssen, E Quale and F Schjelderup, by the W ridge, and its E face was climbed in 1944 by L Hansen, H K Lorentzen and M Pettersen. A traverse from Korsnes farm via Austre to Vestre Korsnestind was made in 7/1930 by B Bommen, B Lyche and O Ottesen.

Trakta (990) is a famous twin-peaked ridge S of the Trolltinder, adjoining Kjerna glacier (confused with Rørhoptind in old reports). A deep cleft between Vestre and

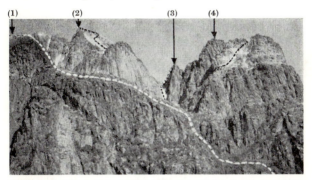

View from the S bank of lake Rørhop: (1) Trakta; (2) Store Trolltind; (3) Prinsessa pinnacle; (4) Store Korsnestind (Photo: Magnar Pettersen)

Austre Trakta is called Hakket or Djevel Skar. Avalanches have formed a bridge about 50 ft above the bottom of the skar. The 1st asc of *Vestre Trakta* was made in 8/1910 by A B Bryn, C W Rubenson and F Schjelderup. This is the highest and most difficult peak. They climbed its NW ridge. A traverse from Austre via Djevel Skar to Vestre Trakta was made in 1950 by E Olsen and M Pettersen. In spite of several attempts, its S ridge has never been climbed. It affords an entertaining variety of walls, aretes, slabs and letter boxes. Its S and N walls also remain unclimbed and are probably inaccessible, owing to exceedingly long slabs. *Austre Trakta* was cairned in 7/1930 by B Bommen, O H Furuseth, B Lyche and O Ottesen, up by the SE wall.

Geitgaljartind (1084) is a grand peak SW of the Trolltinder. The 1st asc was made in 8/1901 by J N Collie, G Hastings, H Priestman and H Woolley with E Hogrenning, up by the NE ridge. Its NW ridge was climbed in 1910 by A B Bryn, C W Rubenson and F Schjelderup. The SW ridge which proffers a sensational descent of over 1000 ft, is considered unassailable. One of its pinnacles was cairned in 1948 by W Høyer and E Olsen, a difficult and exposed ascent, but there are still 3 or 4 pinnacles, called Brudefølget, which have never been climbed. The *Lilandstinder* (696) are situated W of Geitgaljartind. A traverse W-E including the 1st asc of 2 peaks on the NE ridge was made in 6/1956 by K Blackwood and A C White.

Lilandstinder, W-E Traverse — From Lilandsdalen and up N rocks of most westerly Lilandstind. Walk along ridge to pt 696. Descend to cairned col, from which a ridge rises precipitously towards NE. The asc of this ridge to 1st summit offers grand sport on real knife-edge ridge. From cairned col, gain ridge on SE side by climbing up 20 ft and traversing on good rock to a belay point near bottom of vegetatious slabs. (90 ft diff). Follow up slabs to knife-edge crest of ridge. Keep to crest. Straddling tactics are used just before a sensational needle comes into view. The needle is turned by an 8 ft traverse of its SE side, a running belay on a spike on SW edge of needle will be spurned by few, in view of loose footholds and great exposure. Severe but short. Continue along ridge to 1st summit. Descend ridge until top of V-col is reached. Descend steep, vegetatious, loose rock face to col. No belays available. Severe. Climb up slabs of mossy but firmer rock to 2nd summit. Continue down ridge by ledge on N side to col, from which snow provides easy descent into snowfield of upper Lilandsdal. Cross over to N side and keep about 200 yds N of torrent, leading to steep but easy grass slopes, N of gorge and a fine waterfall, down to lower Lilandsdal. Time from Lilandsdal and back, 11 hrs. (A C White).

Higrafstind (1161) is the highest peak in the Lofotens, a fine ridge W of lake Trollfjord, adjoining Blåskavl glacier. This range still provides unfinished work. The 1st asc of *Store Higrafstind* (1161) was made in 8/1901 by J N Collie, G Hastings, H Priestman, H Woolley and E Hogrenning, up by the SW ridge which is now the usual route. However, a better route is to climb Store from Nordre Higraftind, as it involves more climbing and is more interesting. A descent by a long snow couloir on the NW face was made in 6/1956 by K Blackwood and A C White. The 1st asc of Nordre Higraftind (974) was made in 1871 by W S Green, probably from Laupstad and up by gully on the NW face. *Isvasstind* (933) rises between Higraftind and lake Trollfjord, a perfectly bell-shaped peak. The 1st asc was made in 8/1897 by G Hastings, H Priestman and H Woolley, up by the E face. An attempt has been made to descend by its NW face, but the party was stopped by a steep rock wall above lake 348. A subsidiary peak was cairned in 1907 by O Schuster with an Austrian guide.

Tverrdalstind (911), not named on the map, rises N of Troll fjord. The 1st asc was made in 1907 by O Schuster with an Austrian guide. The NW Tverrdalstind (882) can be reached easily either from E from Grund fjord or from W from Østpollen. It provides access to *Blåfjell* (998), a fine group of 5 distinct peaks between Østpollen and Grund fjord. Its main peak is *Svarttind*, a magnificent double-pointed tower, also known as the Black Needle. After several attempts by various parties, the 1st asc was made in 7/1922 by N Backer Grøndahl, K Hanssen, E Quale and F Schjelderup, up by the E ridge. Its lower peak was cairned in 1926 by E Fjeld and S Sigvang. *Austtind* which lies E of Svarttind, was climbed by its N face and E ridge in 8/1897 by G Hastings, H Priestman and H Woolley, and by the S face and E ridge in 8/1903 by H S Mundahl and T G Ouston. A traverse from NW Tverrdalstind (882) via Vesttind and Midttind to Nordtind was made in 1906 by O Schuster with an Austrian guide. Vesttind's E ridge was climbed in 7/1938 by A M Binnie and H Herbert. The *Meraftastinder* (977) stand N of Blåfjell. The highest peak was climbed in 1907 by O Schuster with an Austrian guide. On the E side of the Grunnfjord valley rises the twin-peaked ridge of the *Svartsundtinder* (1054). The 1st asc of *Store Svartsundtind* (1054) was made in 8/1897 by G Hastings, H Priestman and H Woolley, by the E ridge. Its NW face was climbed in 1907 by O Schuster with an Austrian guide. There should be scope for new routes, particularly up the NE and SE faces, which have never been climbed. *Vestre Svartsundtind* (873) is a sharp needle which affords one of the most severe and exposed climbs to be had on this island. Its E ridge was climbed in 1922 by N Backer Grøndahl, K S Hanssen, E Quale and F Schjelderup. This is the only known ascent of this peak. The long ridge between Svartsundtind and Olsanestind sets off several fine summits. *Peak* 938 was cairned in 8/1958 by L Clarke and J Ramsden, up by the SE corrie. They also climbed *Peak* 991 by the E ridge which joins the main ridge just N of the summit, descending the same way. The same party ascended from lake 453 and up by steep grass and outcrop face to the top of *Peak* 830, then traversed to *Peak* 860, returning by the same route. JUNE. 1956. J. RAMSDEN and J S KAYE .

Peak 938 by SE Corrie — The corrie is approached via the ravine ³/₄ mile S of Olsanes. From high up in corrie, the final ridge is gained by S face. The standard is moderate, but the mountain is quite steep and the route makes a complete spiral circuit, following the lines of least resistance. (Jack Ramsden).

The promontory between Mor fjord and Higraf fjord holds some peaks of interest. *Sautind* (635) is a conical peak, facing the head of Østnes fjord, climbed by the N ridge in 8/1902 by H S Mundahl and T G Ouston. The ridge connects with *Drågen* (1800 ft), a dominating rock tower, climbed in 7/1956 by K Blackwood and A C White, up steep slopes to the shoulder on the W side, then traverse across the S side and scramble to the top.

Memdra (Memorafjell 819) rises N of Drågen. The 1st asc was made in 8/1902 by H S Mundahl and T G Ouston, by the SW ridge. Its N ridge was climbed in 7/1938 by A M Binnie and L Letts. The jagged ridge between Memdra and Brettviktind was climbed in 1953 by M Pettersen. A broad gap separates Memdra from *Trolldalstind* (850), whose S face was climbed in 1914 by C and J Lysholm. This peak forms the focal point of a huge horse-shoe ridge; its NE outlier runs towards Brettviktind and its NW outlier towards Strøna. The S ridge of Brettviktind was climbed in 7/1937 by G A Deane and H P Spilsbury. The mountain ranges W of Mor fjord are probably of less interest. The only report is about *Matmora* (Madmoderen or Hamkorna 789) which rises NW on the island. The 1st asc was made in 8/1903 by G T Glover and H Scott-Jones.

MOLLA ISLANDS

MOLLA ISLANDS (map E 860 Svolvær): The little islands of Store and Lille Molla do not offer much climbing, but they make up for it in magnificent scenery. They lie E of Svolvær and are reached by local boat in 1 hr. No accommodation.
Lille Molla provides a complex of small ridges, capped by *Sprangtind* (535). The 1st asc of its W point was made in 7/1921 by E Jensen, H Jentoft, C W Rubenson and H Tønsberg Sr & Jr.
Store Molla has a twisting main ridge with several outliers and peaks including *Spånga* (534) and *Sukkertoppen* (707), but there are no reports of ascents, although all the peaks are believed to have been climbed.

HINNØY ISLAND

HINNØY ISLAND (maps E 570 Lødingen & E 505 Kvefjord) is Norway's largest island, comprising an area of 2.200 sq km, indented by numerous narrow fjords and crammed with a series of peaks and ridges of which there is only scant information. There is probably good scope for further exploring. The coastal express steamers call at Lødingen, Harstad and Sortland. The best access is by local boat from Svolvær to Lonkan on the W side of the island.

THE LONKAN FJORD RANGES (map E 570 Lødingen): *Møysalen* (1266) is Hinnøy's highest peak, situated NE of Lonkan fjord, a grand double-pointed mountain which affords magnificent views — including not less than 7 church spires. The usual route leads up by the W ridge. Its S ridge from Lille Møya was climbed in 1937 by G Brunner and M Butters. *Møyene* (1200) are two sharp peaks close to Møysalen. The 1st asc of *Store Møya* was made in 1910 by two Swiss guides, ascending by the E ridge. *Lille Møya* was cairned in 1930 by P Giglione and party, but no cairn was found when it was climbed in 8/1943 by L Hansen, M Pettersen and T Romsloe. The route leads up by the W and SE walls. Its N wall has never been climbed and is considered unassailable. Three peculiar peaks called *Tretind* (830) are situated W of Møysalen. The 1st asc of *Austre* and *Høgste Tretind* was made in 1945 by L Hansen and H K Lorentzen, climbing both peaks by their N walls. The N wall of Høgste Tretind is indented by several ledges, and the main difficulty is to find the only ledge which opens access to the summit. An ascent of Høgste Tretind from the W has been attempted but never made. Several peaks E of Møysalen may provide good sport, but there are no reports. Captain Angell reported in 1899 that some of the peaks are inaccessible.

THE INGELS FJORD RANGES (map E 570 Lødingen): *Durmålstind* (1017) which rises S of Møysalen and NE of Ingels fjord, is pierced by a fantastic hole near the top ridge. This peak has been ascended by climbers from Svolvær. Among the peaks S of Ingels fjord are *Høgfjell* (593), *Svartskartind* (893) and the *Viktinder* (807). These were climbed in 7/1961 by E Grann-Meyer, A R Heen and M Pettersen, but Heen reports that although they look tempting when seen from the coastal express steamer, they are not worth a visit.

THE FLESNES RANGES (map E 505 Kvefjord): Flesnes lies in Gulles fjord on the road between Harstad and Sortland. *Svarttind* (533) is a sharp ridge with several peaks on the promontory between God fjord and Gulles fjord, N of Flesnes. The ridge is said to be inaccessible and may still be unclimbed. The *Tretind* ridge (845) rises W of God fjord. Nothing is known about it. Its N ridge connects with *Totind* (834), a double-pointed peak which was climbed from the E in 1921 by C and J Lysholm. Its N neighbour *Skrivertind* (790) was climbed in 1921 by the same party, also from E from God fjord. *Foglan* (736) rises W of Totind and affords good sport. It was climbed in 1944 by L Hansen and H K Lorentzen, starting from Roksøydal, first by the SW ridge, then by a ledge across a slab to the NW ridge which was followed to the top.

Reka is said to be the most spectacular peak in Arctic Norway (Photo: Oppi)

LANGØY ISLAND

LANGØY ISLAND (map E 997 Øksnes) lies in Vester-
ålen, NW of Lofoten. Its is reached by coastal express
steamer from Svolvær to Sortland in 5 hrs. Hotel accommodation. An hour's bus journey to Bjørndal and an
hour's walk takes you to the foot of *Reka* (607), a spectacular conical peak shaped like a huge obelisk. The
summit is a 120 ft long knife-edge, only a few feet wide.
It resembles the Crib Goch, but the precipices on either
side are steeper, composed of clean rock with hardly any
loose stones. The 1st asc was made in 8/1902 by H S
Mundahl and T G Ouston, ascending by the W face.
Its NNW face was climbed in 1930 by A R Heen. Exposed and difficult. The NW face was climbed in 1946
by M Pettersen and T Romsloe. This is a fine route which
involves every variety of crag craft, including a chimney
which is almost an exact replica of the Slingsby Chimney
on Sca Fell Pinnacle. The SW ridge was climbed in 1956
by W Høier, E Olsen and M Pettersen, using technical
belays on the overhang.

THE NARVIK REGION

Narvik is a fine climbing centre on its own and also a
good starting point for expeditions into the interior
or to the islands. It is reached by air from Oslo to Bodø
and then by seaplane. By rail from Oslo to Fauske and
then by connecting bus on the Arctic Highway. By
coastal express steamer from Bergen to Svolvær in 3
nights and then by fjord steamer to Narvik in 9 hrs.

The best hunting ground for unfinished work in this area will undoubtedly be found on the Lavangen — Salangen peninsula.

NARVIK ENVIRONS (map E 620 Narvik): *Fagernes-fjell* (1270) which rises within the very town limits, can now be reached by an aerial cableway. Magnificent views. *Rombakstøtta* (1243) is Narvik's "Matterhorn", also called Tøtta, situated 4 miles E of Narvik. The usual route leads up Tøttadal via lake 830. The ascent can be made in 5 hrs from Narvik, 4 hrs down. The N wall was climbed in 7/1938 by T Rydberg and G Santesson, following a deep gully. *Beisfjordtøtta* (1448) rises S of Rombakstøtta. From Narvik via lake 657 and up by the N shoulder to the top in 5 hrs, 4 hrs down. 1st winter traverse in 1942 by L & I Hartviksen, from Fagernes-fjell via Jøden (1269) to Beisfjordtøtta, descending to the E via the gap between 1448 and 1436. *Kongsbak-tind* (1576) can be seen in full profile from Narvik's streets, also called the Sleeping Queen, because its sil-houette is said to resemble Queen Victoria when lying in state. The usual route is from lake Nedste at Håkvik, past Pepperhøgda to point between 1080 and 1576, then up the E side to the top ridge at the Queen's Eye, tra-verse to the Queen's Nose, which is the highest point. A traverse N — S was made in 7/1938 by T Rydberg and G Santesson. 1st winter traverse N — S in 1942 by L & I Hartviksen, across the Queen's Profile, abseiling the N wall from the Queen's Throat to the glacier. A direct asc by the N face up to the Queen's Brow was made in 8/1946 by O Bjørn and G Billing. A direct asc from W from Kongsbak village was made in 7/1952 by G R E Brooke. (For ,,Sukkertoppen'', see Elvegårdstind in the Tys fjord region, map E 790 Skjomen). *Blåisen* (1485) is a large glacier, capped by the flat-topped *Peak* 1485, situ-ated E of Narvik and 6 km S of Rombak fjord. It is readily accessible from Rombak station via 961 and up by the long NW ridge. *Detasjementstind* (1252) lies E of Blåisen, a slabby dome-shaped peak, reached in 3 hrs from Kątte-rat station (Hunnedalen on map). *Sildviktind* (1360) stands NE of Blåisen and can be reached from Katterat by the E or NE ridge in 3 hrs. When starting from Rom-bak station, follow the ridge from Sildvik Skar. *Revtind* (1208) is a boldly outlined ridge with 4 fine pinnacles called *Revørene* (Fox's Ears), situated in Ofoten, NW of Bjørkvik on the Arctic Highway. 1st asc of both W pinnacles 8/1942 by I Hartviksen and T Romsloe. 1st asc of central pinn-acle in 8/1936 by T Wartholm, B &T Romsloe. 1st asc of both E pinnacles in 7/1946 by P Hohle, B & T Romsloe.

Good sport and grand scenery. *Rivtind* (1458) rises SE of Gratangen (hotel) on the Arctic Highway, a jagged ridge with many pinnacles. 1st asc of highest pinnacle in 1932 by A Antonsen, B and T Romsloe.

OFOTEN DISTRICT (map E 685 Ofoten): *Niingen* (1074) rises 2 miles N of Bogen on the Narvik-Harstadroad. J Henriksen and T Vogt climbed it in 1913 by the E ridge, also from S from col 768. *Skidden-dalstind* (1306) is the

Rombakstøtta is Narvik's Matterhorn
(Photo: Per Prag)

highest peak in Ofoten, situated 3 miles NW of Niingen. Its E side was climbed in 1913 by the same party, descending by the S ridge which they also ascended. A glacier separates it from *Pungdalstind* (1262). 1st asc 7/1901 by surveyor Halle, H Langfjord and HPriestman, traversing via Slettfjell, Villdalsfjell and Grinddalsfjell and up by the SE ridge. *Novatind* is asharp peak on the Novafjell (1280) ridge. NE of Pungdalstind. 1st asc 7/1901 by surveyor Halle, H Langfjord and H Priestman, from Kjerringa (1016) and along the Novafjell ridge. It was climbed again in 8/1943 by P Michaelsen, B & T Romsloe, following the rift created by the great avalanche of 8/1936, which considerably reduced the height of the summit.

ANDØRJA ISLAND (map E 350 Harstad) lies E of Harstad, reached by steamer from Harstad in 3 hrs. A party from Cambridge and Durham universities visited the island in 1956 and "climbed by the easiest way all the mountains of interest and had a very pleasant time. We all enjoyed our stay in Norway very much, and were very well received by all the people we met. Wonderful scenery and wonderful people — what better combination for a holiday?" (Jack Tippett). *Åtind* (1097) rises on the NW promontory. 1st asc 7/1956 by G C Clark, F D Gill and J Tippett, up SW face from Å village, a 1000 ft climb on perfectly clean slabs, 3 hrs up, 2 down. A gully divides Åtind from *Kløfttind* (1097) (its E side on map E 750 Salangen), the 1st asc of which was made by the same party from col 768.

Kløfttind from Col 768 — Contour S face for 400 yds, losing a little height until wide gully is entered. Ascend this, keeping R, up grass and slabs. When gully curves to R, climb straight up until it is possible to descend into next gully to L. This is deep and narrow and divides pt 990 from Kløfttind. Ascend gully for 150 ft until it is possible to move L along ledge for 100 yds. Climb prominent twisting crack to its top and scramble to summit. Descend L ledge (looking down) of gully dividing Åtind from Kløfttind, avoiding cliffs as necessary. (J Tippett).

ANDØRJA ISLAND (map E 750 Salangen): *Restind* (1056) stands E of Kløfttind. 1st asc 7/1956 by F D Gill and J Tippett, up from col 768 via 851 and to the summit by the W ridge. *Snetind* (1215) lies further E. Its N ridge was climbed in 7/1956 by H Gibson, F D Gill and J Tippett in 4 hrs from fjord to top. *Trollan* (1244) is a group of "midget trolls" on the NE side of the island. It is a very impressive ridge with 500 ft cliffs on the N side for most of its length — with summit blocks of pinnacles overhanging in many cases. The 1st complete traverse was made in 1921 by C and J Lysholm, and a W-E traverse was made in 7/1956 by G C Clarke, H Gibson, F D Gill and J Tippett, a very fine expedition. *Vasskartind* (1143) is a fine peak adjoining Trollan, with very large N and E faces. The NE ridge would make a very fine though quite difficult expedition. Its W ridge was climbed in 7/1956 by G C Clarke, H Gibson, F D Gill and J Tippett.

Trollan, W-E Traverse — It is probably impossible not to make a detour if traversed E-W. The W-E traverse involves a 120 ft abseil. Ascend to pt 1150 in 3 hrs from fjord. Scramble along airy ridge to pt 1159. Two gaps are crossed between pts 1159 and 1193. One requires 40 ft abseil and a 60 ft slab pitch, avoidable 300 ft down on S side. 200 yds from pt 1193 is a deep gap (120 ft abseil) which turned the party back (avoided 1000 ft down on S side, climbed direct from there to Langlitind). From this gap is a pinnacle, avoidable on N side and then scrambling to pt 1244, then steep scrambling to another gap and easy ascent to Langlitind (1277). Descent from Langlitind easy to SW — aided by 1000 ft glissade. A very impressive ridge with 500 ft cliffs on N side for most of its length — with summit blocks of pinnacles overhanging in many cases. (J Tippett).

Vasskartind by W Ridge — Up through woods and large boulders to pt 800. The ridge becomes very steep in the form of a 200 ft tower. This may be turned on L or R. (1) *Left:* Traverse N face for 200 ft, then up slabs to top of ridge, or (2) *Right:* Traverse on SW face beneath steep wall for 300 ft, then climb up deep gully for 200 ft, traverse 50 ft L to second gully running up obliquely to R and climb 200 ft to top of ridge. Then easy to summit. Time, 4 hrs up, 2½ down. Mod diff. (J Tippett).

THE LAVANGEN—SALANGEN GROUP (map E 750 Salangen): This is the promontory between the fjords of Lavangen and Salangen, which lie W of the Arctic Highway between Gratangen and Bardu. *Reitetind* (1260) is the highest peak on the jagged Reitetind ridge. Its E ridge was climbed in 1957 by T Clinton and S A Obrien. Steep, dirty and dangerous. Its S ridge is still unclimbed and looks dangerous. The *Salangstind Ridge* is a long

S-shaped ridge which runs northwards from Reitetind. The 1st asc of *Peaks* 1247−1258−1028−1122−882− 1138 on the Salangstind ridge was made in 1957 by T Clinton and S A Obrien. This is a good traverse, but the ridge is gained easiest from 1236, which is more a plateau than a mountain. The E face of *Peak* 1138 rises sheer for about 2000 ft. It was attempted in 1957 by T Clinton and S A Obrien, but when 300 ft below the top, Clinton was swept from a belay by an avalanche. "If this climb is made, it should prove one of the best in Arctic Norway. The climbing is severe by any standard, and the exposure is terrible. This face is swept by avalanches throughout the summer, and the best period would be late autumn. Avoid the route which looks easiest − the gully on the left, as it is suicidal" (S A Obrien). The *Elveskartinder* (1241) run NW off the Salangstind ridge from 1258. Points 1241 and 1128 are 2 magnificent peaks, which have always been considered inaccessible, but the 1st asc of both was made in 1957 by T Clinton and S A Obrien. *Peak* 1241 was climbed by a chimney in the SW face, descending by the NE ridge which involved a 150 ft abseil. The N face is unclimbable. The NW ridge should go, if attacked by experts. This peak offers a number of good climbs of very high standard. *Peak* 1128 which looks like a chessman, has 2 razor-sharp ridges which can be climbed only by straddling. They climbed the SE ridge, and the last few feet were severe. The N ridge is still unclimbed.

Fakstind (1226) rises on the promontory NE of And-ørja. It looks difficult, but is said to have been climbed by a local schoolmaster. There are no reports on the adjacent peaks.

THE TROMSØ REGION

This is a grand and still partly unexplored region, which includes mainland and scores of islands of all sizes and shapes. Tromsø, the famous "Gateway to the Arctic", is reached by air from Oslo or by train from Oslo to Fauske in 21 hours and bus to Tromsø in 2 days, or by coastal express steamer from Bergen in 4 nights. The road distance from Oslo by the Arctic Highway (No. 50) is 1051 miles.

TROMSØ ENVIRONS (map E 910 Tromsø): The new bridge across Tromsø Sound now connects the island town with the mainland. An aerial cableway which starts

near the bridge, leads to the very top of Storstein mountain, affording a magnificent view of the surroundings.
Tromsdalstind (1238) rises SE of the town, an easy peak
which makes a fine 1st day climb. Time, 7 hrs from Tromsø and back. The 1st winter asc was made on skis in
1894 by P Sverdrup, the Arctic explorer. *Bentsjordtind*
(1169) is situated SW of Tromsø on the peninsula between
Malangen fjord and Bals fjord. 1st asc of Minste Bentsjordtind 1925 by P W Zapffe, up by steep glacier. There
are no reports about other peaks on this peninsula.

HAMPEROKKEN DISTRICT (map 1534/2 Ullsfjord)
is the large peninsula E of Tromsø and W of Ulls fjord,
reached by bus from Tromsø in an hour or two. *Hamperokken* (1359) is the highest point of the Bjørnskartinder.
It has 3 vertical walls. The usual route is up by the W
face, a steep ascent on fine slabs with good handholds.
This is the only known route. *Sommerbukttind* rises
opposite Holmbukt in Ulls fjord. 1st asc 8/1899 by C V
Rawlence with J and E Imboden, up by the E ridge,
traversing N to *Lalabaktind* and on to *Sjursnestind*.
The 1st asc of the latter had been made in 1895 by J
Caspari, by narrow snow couloir on the E face.

SIGNALDAL VALLEY (maps 1633/3 Signaldal & 1633/4
Storfjord): This magnificent mountain valley starts from
the head of Lyngen fjord at Kvesmenes, reached by bus
from Tromsø in 2—3 hours. *Otertind* (1320) is a perfect
pyramid, separated from a smaller pyramid by a steep
cleft called Hakket. It rises at the head of Lyngen fjord
at the entrance to the Signaldal, often called the "Arctic
Matterhorn". The 1st asc of *Store* (1360) and *Lille* (990)
Otertind was made in 8/1911 by K Endell and W Martin,
up from S from from Lopo Skar. Store Otertind was
climbed from Hakket in 1920 by E Jensen, C W Rubenson
and H Tønsberg. The 1st winter asc was made in 4/1939
by G Billing and G Santesson, up by snow gully to the
second gap on the N ridge. Abseil into Vesle Skar.
Piggsteinen is a peculiar rock formation on the main road
near Otertind. It is split in two, as if cut by a giant
sword, and offers magnificent resistance. One half was
climbed in 1924 and the other half in 1927 by P W
Zapffe. Lopo Skar is the col between Otertind and
Polvartind (1275). 1st asc 8/1911 by K Endell and W
Martin, ascending by the N ridge from Lopo Skar.
Mannfjell (1552) is a peculiar pinnacled ridge opposite
Polvartind in the Signaldal. 1st asc 1898 by J Caspari.
Very rotten rocks. *Hattetind* (1077) or Hatten is the peak
above Kvesmenes at the head of Lyngen fjord. The

Otertind, a perfect pyramid overlooking the Signaldal (Photo: Normann)

1st E-W traverse was made in 8/1920 by E Jensen, I Myklebust, C W Rubenson and H Tønsberg. Its N ridge leads to *Horsnestind* (1224) which is a giant fortress with spires and towers of rotten rocks. Søre Horsnestind was cairned in 1939 by E Thyholdt and P W Zapffe. *Addjet* (1263) or Agjek, stands E of Skibotn on the E side of Lyngen fjord. Its E wall has never been climbed. 1st asc 1909 by C B Heimbeck and party, up by the SE ridge. Magnificent views into Sweden and Finland.

SENJA ISLAND (map E 365 Hekkingen): Senja is Norway's second largest island, covering an area of 1590 sq km, situated SW of Tromsø, reached by fjord steamer in 3—4 hours. On the oceanside, a series of narrow fjords cut deeply into the island, surrounded by steep and rugged peaks and pinnacles. The rocks are generally rotten, with an appalling mass of detritus and large boulders, but some peaks do afford first-rate sport with definite scope for further exploring. Practically all known routes have been made on the promontory between Ers fjord and Me fjord. Ersfjord village is the best starting point. *Snøkollen* (700) is an attractive peak at Oksenes on the tip of the Ersfjord-Mefjord peninsula. A farmhouse is built at the foot of the peak, and the farmer can see the summit through his chimney! 1st asc 1926 by D Johansen and P W Zapffe. Its neighbour is *Okshorn* (506) which consists of a series of sharp pinnacles. 1st asc of highest pinnacle in 1926 by J Schancke, Theisen and P W Zapffe. *Staven* (535) rises SE of Okshorn, a strange-looking peak, which resembles a petrified eagle. Its N wall has never been climbed. 1st asc 1927 by O Lind and P W Zapffe, climbing its W ridge. *Presten* (755) was cairned in 1932 by J Schancke. *Mykkjetind* (609) rises on a subsidiary ridge at Mefjordvær. 1st asc 1926 by J Schancke and P W Zapffe. The 1st asc of peak 507 (or 582?) was made in 1926 by O Lind and P W Zapffe. *Roalden* (864) which stands S of Mykkjetind, looks like a sharp needle. 1st asc 1927 by P W Zapffe. *Breitind* (1010) at the head of Me fjord is the highest peak on the island. 1st asc 1927 by O Lind, J Pettersen and P W Zapffe.

KVALØY ISLAND (map E 720 Ringvassøy) lies W of Tromsø, reached by ferry and bus in 2 — 3 hours. The best climbing centres are S and N of Ers fjord. On the S side of Ers fjord stands *Middagstind* (1008) or Nonstind, 1st asc 1930 by J and L Pettersen and P W Zapffe. The same party plus H Birkeland also cairned *Skitntind* (1043). The horse-shoe ridge of the *Småtinder* (817) comprises a magnificent cirque. 1st asc of Søre Småtind (817?) in 1925 by K Tellander and P W Zapffe, up from the SW. Its NW ridge continues to *Stortind* (757), 1st asc 1930 by J Austad and P W Zapffe. *Skamtind* (883) rises N of Ers fjord. 1st asc 1928 by E Barlindhaug and P W Zapffe. Its NE neighbour is *Storstolpen* (981) which is a jagged ridge with numerous pinnacles, loose and rotten rocks. 1st asc 1927 by E and I and J Pettersen and P W Zapffe. Its ridge is linked to *Hollenderen* (1029), an interesting ridge with sharp pinnacles, separated by steep clefts. 1st traverse 1926 by M Mack and P W Zapffe. The network of ridges leads on to *Revbergtind* (968), 1st asc 1930 by J and L Pettersen and P W Zapffe. *Blåmannen* (1044) is the highest point on the island. Its N wall is a formidable precipice. 1st asc 1869 by surveyors. *Orvasstind* (985) or Ordalstind rises NW of Blåmannen. 1st asc 1926 by P W Zapffe. *Jorddalstind* (location unknown) was cairned in 1932 by E Barlindhaug and P W Zapffe.

RINGVASSØY ISLAND (maps E 720 Ringvassøy and 1534/1 Reinøy)lies N of Tromsø, reached by fjord steamer in 4 hrs, a rocky island but not much climbing. *Skull-gamstind* (824) rises N of Tromsøsund. 1st asc 7/1920 by E Jensen, I Myklebust, C W Rubenson and H Tønsberg, up from Hell's Valley. This peak comprises a grand cirque whose N wall may be of interest. The *Soltinder* are situated on the E side of the island. Store Soltind (Skalltind 907 on new map?) was cairned in 1927 by Capt Smith-Christiansen. Very loose rocks.

KARLSØY ISLAND (map 1635/3 Karlsøy) is situated NW of the Lyngen peninsula, reached by fjord steamer

The Lyngen peninsula is a remarkable region of peaks, ridges and glaciers
(Photo: Bolinder)

from Tromsø in 4 hrs. Its main peak is *Veidalstind*
(Peppartind on new map?) which was cairned in 1935
by E Hertzberg, A Næss and P W Zapffe.

THE LYNGEN PENINSULA

The Lyngen peninsula is a remarkable region of peaks,
ridges and glaciers, covering an area of 540 sq miles. It
lies E of Tromsø and is bounded by Ulls fjord and Lyngen
fjord, its S boundary being formed by the Arctic Highway. There is generally good rock — loose and rotten in
places, as can be expected on any mountain subjected to
alternating extremes of heat and frost — but on the whole
the Lyngen rocks compare well with Alpine rocks.
Most of the area is entirely uninhabited. Camping is
essential. Local guides are difficult to get hold of, and are
really not required. The locals are very little interested
in their mountains and are quite uncertain about their
names. There are local steamer services from Tromsø
to fishing hamlets all along the peninsula. Enquiries
regarding time tables should be directed to Troms
S/S Co, Tromsø.
The peninsula is divided into a southern and northern
region, separated by Kjosen fjord, which cuts deeply
into it, almost to Lyngseid on the Arctic Highway, a
village facing the Lyngen fjord. Lyngseid is reached by
bus from Tromsø in 4 hrs or from Narvik in 9 hrs. An
alternative route leads by bus from Tromsø to Brevikeid,
ferry across Ulls fjord to Svensby and bus to Lyngseid
in about 4—5 hrs. Accommodation at Lyngseid. For

larger expeditions, a base camp may be established at Lyngseid in Solhov Ungdomsskole (30 bunks).

Nordkjosbotn on the Arctic Highway at the head of Bals fjord is the starting point for climbs in the southernmost ranges. Nordkjosbotn is reached by bus from Tromsø in 2 hrs, from Narvik in 6 hrs. Local accommodation. A new road runs from Seljelvnes on the Tromsø—Nord-kjosbotn road right up to Lakselvbukt on the Ulls fjord. The excellent new maps which now cover the Lyngen area, are most welcome to climbers. As many names on the new maps differ greatly from those used in previous reports, it would be appreciated if climbers will notify us of any errors or mix-ups in the notes below.

THE PIGGTIND RANGES (maps 1533/2 Tamokdal & 1533/1 Balsfjord): This is the southernmost group, situated N of Nordkjosbotn on the Arctic Highway. A walk northwards from Nordkjosbotn leads to *Storvasstind* (1377) or Rassevarcocka, which is the local Matterhorn, a giant 3-peaked pyramid. In 1911, K Endell and W Martin made a W-E traverse, descending from the E peak by its S wall. An attempt has been made to climb it from Pigg Skar on the N side, but the party was halted by an ice couloir below the summit. Pigg Skar separates Storvasstind from *Piggtind* (1505), which affords good sport. Its twin summits are divided by a steep gap called Snø Skar. Both summits were climbed in 1920 by E Jensen, C W Rubenson and H Tønsberg, ascending from Pigg Skar by the S face. Piggtind's W and E walls have never been climbed, and nobody has ever reached either summit from Snø Skar.

Tverrfjell (1319) rises NE of Piggtind, embracing a huge glacier on its NE slopes. It forms the top of Rypedal valley, which runs in a northerly direction until it joins the Langedal valley. This group still offers scope for exploring. One of the highest points, *Rieosatvaggegaissa* (1257), which is really the extreme W peak of Biello-gaissa, was climbed by its W ridge in 1953 by A R Brown, P B Cook and P R Falkner. *Biellogaissa* (1356) rises NE of Tverrfjell glacier, a sprawling mountain mass with at least 4 summits and one or two inviting crags. Not much climbing, but magnificent views of Piggtind. *Durmåls-tind* (1257) or Spinnegaissa rises N of Biellogaissa between Rypedal and Langdal, both valleys converging into the Lakselvdal. The gap between Durmålstind and Langdals-tind is called Langdal Skar. An ascent of Durmålstind by its N face was made in 1953 by R A Brown, P B Cook and P R Falkner, descending by the long E ridge.

THE BALSFJORD — LAKSELVDAL GROUP (map 1533/1 Balsfjord): This is the area between Bals fjord and Sør fjord, bounded to the S and E by the Lakselvdal. Very little is known about the peaks in this sector. *Piggtind* or Saggecocka or Spisstind is a sharp cone on the main ridge, climbed by its W side in 1898 by Elizabeth Main (alias Mrs Aubrey Le Blond) with J and E Imboden. Steep and loose rocks.

THE LANGDAL — ELLENDAL RANGES (maps 1533/1 Balsfjord & 1633/4 Storfjord): This is a huge complex of peaks and glaciers between Langdalen and Ellendalen, not yet fully explored. The main *Langdalstind* ridge runs W-E, with 3 great spurs descending S from the summit. Its highest point is *Gukkesgaisa* (1554), whose easterly spur was climbed from Langdal Skar in 1953 by T Panther and R G Pettigrew, ascending over 2 subsidiary peaks. A few days later, the central spur was climbed by R A Brown, P B Cook and P R Falkner, by a route which leads directly to the summit.

The Ellendal runs SW into the Lakselvdal between the Langdalstinder and Lakselvtinder. *Ann Skar* is a pass which leads from Ellendalen between Anntind and Sfinxen and on to the unexplored Steindal glacier behind both peaks. *Anntind* was climbed by its W face (1st asc) in 1953 by P Jackson and G A Leaver, and by its E ridge in 1954 by D A Christoffel and A G Troughton. The latter ridge is long but straightforward, a little loose in places. An unnamed peak with 2 summits rises S of Anntind and is joined to it by a short ridge. It has never been climbed.

Anntind by W Face — From the little lake in upper Ellendal, proceed up the moraine on the dying remains of a glacier directly above the lake. From the glacier the couloir leads to Anntind. The Anntind couloir branches after 700 ft; the L branch leads towards the summit over loose rubble; the R branch leads to steepening snow towards the ridge joining Anntind and the "horn" to the S. (G A Leaver).

Sfinxen is the remarkably steep peak N of Anntind. It joins the Lakselvtinder, Njalavarre, Anntind and Gukkesgaissa peaks by connecting ridges. After a vain attempt of its W face, Elizabeth Main with the Imbodens climbed it by its S ridge in 1899. Very loose rocks. Its NE ridge was climbed by L Clark and J Ramsden in 1958.

Sfinxen by NE Ridge — Approach foot of NE ridge via a snow corrie above upper Andersdal and easy slabby rock. Easily up rocky lower ridge. About 800 ft of pleasant scrambling. The 500 ft above this forms the harder part of the climb. Here it steepens into a steep buttress, but a more or less direct line is taken up it, with a tendency L for the first 2 pitches. This section is at first extremely loose, but better rock is reached, and the final pitches are on good gabbro in fine situations. V diff. (Jack Ramsden).

The steep col N of Sfinxen is called *Sfinxen Skar*. It leads from Ellendal on to the great snow basin, and can be used instead of Anntind Skar. At the head of Ellendal, below Ellendal Skar, is a small lake, a few feet away from which is a large boulder which provides an excellent bivouac, reached in 7 hrs from Holmbukt via *Ellendal Skar*, which is a pass between Sfinxen and Austre Lakselvtind. When walking from Holmbukt through Andersdal Skar, continue from the second lake towards Sfinxen Skar, until below the lowest point in the ridge between Sfinxen and Austre Lakselvtind. When ascending to Ellendal Skar, avoid the ice wall on the left. This skar leads to Ellendal. *Andersdal Skar* is a pass between Holmbukt in Ulls fjord and Dalen in Lyngen fjord. From Holmbukt, the Andersdal (Goverdalen on new map) continues up through the narrows between the rounded E ridge of Titind and the SW end of the beautiful "Choux Fleur" face of Balgesvarrenebba, past 2 lakes, and then bends NE, rising to Andersdal Skar between Njalavarrenebba and Balgesvarre.

Njalavarre forms the N boundary of the snow basin which embraces Anntind and Sfinxen to the W. When seen from Andersdalen, it looks like a shapely pointed peak. Mrs Elizabeth Main with the Imbodens climbed it in 1899 by the S ridge, which rises from Andersdal Skar. Follow the S ridge, except where driven on to the E face. Descent from northernmost end of summit ridge, straight down steep rocks and snow couloirs to the upper plateau of Njalavarre glacier. Loose rocks.

The large snow basin E of Sfinxen and S of Njalavarre is about 2—3 miles in diameter. It feeds an icefall which leads to a valley S of Moskorieppe. The icefall is about ½ mile across and is guarded by 2 prominent peaks — Vakttind and Dinotind. *Vakttind* was cairned in 1954 by D A Christoffel, M T Howells, R S Knight and A G Troughton. Up from col E of Njalavarre, across snow basin to ridge bounding it on the S and thence around to the summit. *Dinotind* projects from the E ridge of Njalavarre. This ridge is serrated and appears like the back of a dinosaur when seen from Andersdalen. The summit overlooking the icefall is at the end of a short subsidiary ridge. Dinotind was cairned in 1954 by D A Christoffel, M T Howells, R S Knight and A G Troughton, up from the col E of Njalavarre, reached from Andersdalen. Easy scramble to the top. The main ridge was traversed to a low col and then ascended to a rather higher flat-topped peak, which presents a steep 3000 ft high face to the

Andersdal. Bad weather prevented completion of the traverse to Moskorieppe.

THE LAKSELVTINDER (map 1533/1 Balsfjord): This is a magnificent complex of sharp peaks, jagged ridges and glistening glaciers, situated E of Lakselvbukt and W of Andersdal (Goverdal on new map). Holmbukt in Ulls fjord is the usual starting point, reached by local steamer from Tromsø in 10 hrs. There is now a motoring road to Lakselvbukt, branching off from the Tromsø – Nordkjosbotn road at Seljelvnes, 5 miles NW of Nordkjosbotn. There are no shops at Holmbukt, only a few fishermen's houses, and supplies have to be obtained from shop at Lakselvbukt, which lies 5 miles further S, but milk can be obtained from Hundberg on the S side of Andersdal river. No accommodation. Holmbukt is situated at the foot of Andersdalen, which gives access right into the interior – to Lyngen fjord via Andersdal Skar, to Lyngseid via Lyngsdal Skar, to a great unexplored glacier via Sfinxen Skar, and to the Ellendal peaks over Ellendal Skar. It is difficult to cross the Andersdal river between Holmbukt and Lakselvbukt without a boat, but the valley widens 2 miles up from Holmbukt at the end of the tree line, and here the river may be crossed easily. There are a number of good camp sites below the great N face of Titind. There is a fine pass across the main ridge on either side of Store Lakselvtind – *Tomas Skar* on the S side and *Lakselv Skar* on the N side. The Lakselvtinder embrace 4 great glaciers – *Lakselv Glacier* flows towards Andersdal, E of Anderstind, N of Store Lakselvtind and W of Platåtoppen; *Austre Lakselv Glacier* also flows into Andersdal, E of Platåtoppen and W of Austre Lakselvtind; *Imboden Glacier* flows from Imbodentind, easterly into Ellendal; *Tomastind Glacier* lies between Imbodentind and Tomastind. It can be reached from Lakselvbukt by way of Tomas Skar, which lies between Store Lakselvtind and Tomastind. It appears to be impossible to descend from this glacier into Ellendalen (or vice versa), as the icefall terminates abruptly over a great rock wall. The main plan of the Lakselvtinder is L-shaped, the main limb pointing about N. A traverse of the southern sector was made in 1946 by G Billing, O Bjørn and H Hammarsten, when they made several 1st ascents. The first complete N-S traverse of the main ridge from Anderstind to Tomastind was made in 1951 by P R Falkner and S G Moore. It was a very fine expedition, 23 hrs from Holmbukt and back. The peaks below are described from N to S and then W to E (notes from G A Leaver):

Titind (Hundebjergtind in old guide) is the northernmost peak. The ridge is remarkably level throughout its length. Where it terminates on the great 5000 ft buttress overlooking Andersdalen, the edge overhangs on the E side. If a climb is attempted by the E face, snow conditions would have to be favourable. Its W face was climbed in 1899 by Mrs Elizabeth Main with J and E Imboden, starting from Holmbukt. The NW ridge was climbed in 1951 by K Clarke, S G Moore and H Pretty. This ridge is extremely sharp with a succession of small towers, notches and corniced aretes. Diff. Its N face which is the most impressive rock face in this area — a great 3000 ft buttress overlooking Andersdalen — was climbed in 1953 by G A Leaver, R Scott and J D J Wildridge. The final wall is very exposed.

Titind by N Face — From Andersdal, strike up scree to foot of gully in centre of crag (reddish coloured rock). Climb up L side of gully, up fairly easy firm rock slabs until bounded on R by a higher series of red coloured steeper slabs. Traverse on to slabs, which give good but somewhat diff climbing on beautifully sound rock. The final section of these red slabs is very hard and exposed, but can be avoided on broken rocks to R (inferior route). These slabs terminate in broken rock, which is traversed upward and L to a gully which is crossed and its L wall climbed. The traverse upward and L is continued until another gully is reached, whose L wall forms the start of the imposing top buttress. The wall is ascended to an open groove which is followed until it becomes very steep. Avoid the groove by traversing L (diff) on a very exposed slab to foot of narrow crack (not the broken crack in corner). This will prove hard. Ascend to a slab which is traversed to foot of chimney. This is climbed, leading to fairly easy rocks which eventually lead to summit. The climb is mostly on sound rock and the top buttress is hard and very exposed. Descent by a descending traverse of E face to moraine of glacier. This is not the easiest route and the rock is loose and at times dangerous. Time from Andersdal to top, 10 hrs. From Holmbukt and back, 16-18 hrs. (G A Leaver and J D J Wildridge).

Tommelen is the sharp tower which forms a very distinct feature of the Lakselvtind range. It was cairned in 1946 by G Billing and H Hammarsten, probably from Anderstind, reclimbed in 1953 by R A Brown, T Panther and R G Pettigrew, a very fine climb but distressingly short.

Tommelen from Anderstind — Traverse to neck on S side of pinnacle. From here 100 ft up deep chimney-cleft on W side to big platform with belays. Drop on E side of ridge sensational. Up L side of face above ledge, by a very awkward groove — outward tilt to all holds — to small shelf, and then up to R across easy slabs to foot of steep crack with cut-away base. Running belay. Up crack, hand jams strenuous. Across L to tiny ledge on L edge of W face. Pito_n_ belay. Small overhang above, short man needs shoulder. Precarious and very exposed. One move only, and then a few feet of easy rock to top. Time from S gap to top, 1½ hrs. Actual height above gap perhaps 120 ft, but route goes round as well as up. This seems the only way up. Abseil off, 150 ft rope at least. (Richard A Brown).

Anderstind or Nordre Lakselvtind is a beautiful peak seen from any angle. Its N ridge which connects with Titind, is a fine sharp and level ridge. A 50 ft high pinnacle on this ridge is still unclimbed. Anderstind was climbed by the NW ridge from Tommelen in 1946 by G Billing, O Bjørn and H Hammarsten. The gap between Anderstind and Taggtoppen is very difficult and involves an abseil. _Taggtoppen_ is the sharp peak S of Anderstind, cairned in 1946 by the Swedish party, probably ascending by the N ridge and descending by the S ridge. The two small western foretops were climbed in 1953 by P B Cook and P R Falkner. *Platåtoppen* is the flat top between Taggtoppen and Store Lakselvtind, climbed in 1946 by the Swedish party, probably by following the main ridge. *Store Lakselvtind* (1617) was climbed by its SE side in 1899 by C V and L C Rawlence. From Holmbukt via Tomas Skar, they went up by the narrow and steep couloir on the SE side and thence over 100 ft of good rock to the summit. Its N ridge from Platåtoppen was climbed in 1946 by the Swedish party. *Tomastind* is the second highest point, a fine peak S of Store Lakselvtind. It was climbed from Holmbukt via Tomas Skar in 1899 by Mrs Main and the Imbodens. Its SW ridge was climbed in 1946 by the Swedish party, combined with the 1st asc of one peak and 5 pinnacles.

Imbodentind is a fine peak on the E side of Lakselv glacier, overlooking Andersdalen. Its summit is supported to the N by a vertical and unbroken wall of a sensational character. Running northwards are 2 very fine unclimbed peaks, though not very high. The northernmost resembles a shark's fin, very narrow and jagged. The one nearer to Imbodentind is a flat-topped tower. Imbodentind was climbed from Tomas Skar across the glacier in 1899 by Mrs Elizabeth Main with Joseph Imboden and his son Emil, two Swiss guides. Its N face was climbed in 1956 by P R Falkner, W J Cartwright and L Pratt. This is a direct route from Andersdalen, with a more serious alpine feel about it than most of the routes in Lyngen.

Imbodentind by N Face — From Andersdal, ascend scree slopes to big glacial basin below Imbodentind. Crevassed glacier. The best route is found by keeping well to R at first, fairly close to Anderstind, later working across to L. At foot of the N face proper, a bergschrund has to be crossed. A direct line to the summit is then taken, first up steep rock, then up steep ice and finally snow. This last section, though short, gives quite concentrated and interesting climbing. (P R Falkner).

Austre Lakselvtind is the small outlier of Imbodentind towards the SE, climbed by its N side in 1899 by Mrs Main and the Imbodens, descending by the N ridge and E face to the glacier.

THE BALGESVARRE RANGES (maps 1533/1 Balsfjord & 1633/4 Storfjord): *Balgesvarre* (1523) is a snow and ice dome, throwing off several glaciers and hanging icefalls. It lies inside a circle formed by Andersdal—Andersdal Skar—Lyngsdal—Lyngsdal Skar. The latter pass leads up Sløkedalen (side valley to Andersdalen) between Balgesvarre and Jiekkevarri. It leads on to

Lyngsdalen and affords some of the finest scenery in Norway. Andersdalen and Lyngsdalen provide a popular passage from Holmbukt in Ulls fjord to Dalen in Lyngen fjord. Dalen consists of a cluster of farmhouses, but no hotel accommodation.

When seen from Lyngsdal glacier, Balgesvarre's dome-like nature is not at all apparent, since a short ridge projects forward over the upper glacier and gives the impression of a fine sharp rock tower. The end of this ridge overhangs for nearly 500 ft, and on its E side drops down to the glacier in a smooth slab, nearly 2000 ft high. The NW spur which projects from the ice cap, is called Balgesvarrenebba. Its S face is very steep. Its N side was climbed in 1899 by Mrs Elizabeth Main with the Imbodens. The N face of Balgesvarre was climbed in 1951 by R A Brown, K Clarke and H Pretty. Its N summit was climbed in 1958 by L Clark, J S Kaye and J Ramsden. The NE face was climbed in 1959 by H Brunton, G Hendry and G Lee.

Balgesvarre by N Face of Balgesvarrenebba — Up through Andersdal towards Lyngsdal Skar, until glacier between Balgesvarre and Nebba. Proceed up this glacier to the rocks by which ridge is gained between Nebba and Balgesvarre. (Richard A Brown).

Balgesvarre by N Face — From Lyngsdal Skar, the ascent is a steep scramble beside the upper ice of Balgesvarre glacier, which drops westwards on the Andersdal side of the col. (Richard A Brown).

Balgesvarre by NE Face — The large snow couloir containing a small hanging glacier, to L of main rock buttress of Balgesvarre, is little more than a long (nearly 2000 ft) steep snow walk, with the icefall providing interest. From the bottom bergschrund keep R all the way up. Negotiate the icefall at R edge and cross the upper bergschrund at a debris cone. Keep to R branch of upper couloir. Finally make towards the centre for an easy exit via a snow ridge above rocks rather than via a large cornice. Time, 5 hrs. (J Clarkson).

Klokketårn is a summit on the short ridge which branches off northwards from the main E ridge of Balgesvarre. It presents a wonderful N face with a tower-like summit to Lyngsdal glacier. An attempt to climb the N face was made in 1951 by P R Falkner and S G Moore. They were forced to abseil off pitons and traversed across the face, halfway up, to the bounding gully on L, from where they reached the L skyline ridge of the final tower. Here they encountered overhangs which drove them down to the glacier again. But the same party did climb Klokketårn by its SE face, up from the southern tributary ice-stream of Lyngsdal glacier. Mod Diff. In 1953, the NE ridge was climbed by H Barber, M Fraser and J Heap, a very fine and exposed climb. The best way on to the NE ridge is up Lyngsdal glacier and up the gully on L side of N face.

Jaytind is a rock peak on the ridge between Klokketårn and Laurettatind. From the N it rises steeply from the ridge, but on its S side it slopes gently to the main ridge. Its N face was climbed in 1953 by H Barber and M Fraser. This is the most interesting route, where an 80 ft open chimney leads to just below the summit block. The rock is good everywhere, but there is an absence of holds near the top of the pitch. The grading of the chimney is Easy Severe.

Laurettatind rises E of Klokketårn. Its N ridge was climbed in 1953 by H Barber and M Fraser. A descent by the SW ridge and steep snow from skar to Lyngsdal glacier was made in 1956 by R M Middleton, J G G Stephenson and R J Wathen. The SW ridge will probably also afford a route up. The NW face was climbed in 1959 by H Brunton, J Clarkson, G Hendry and G Lee.

Laurettatind by N Ridge — E of pt 38 there is a 200 ft scramble down to the ridge leading to the NE corner of Laurettatind. The quarter mile ridge in itself presents few technical difficulties, but it is very shattered and exposed. The outstanding pitch is the traverse of 40 ft of 50 degrees angle slabs below a sensational knife-edge, blocked at its far end by a large and very precarious-looking block. The ridge ends below easy slabs leading upwards for about 250 ft to summit of N face. The route is indefinite and is open to variations. Time from pt 38 to top, 3½ hrs. The whole route is graded Alpine grade 3. (H Barber).

Laurettatind by NW Face — Face rises above L branch of Lyngsdal glacier. A snowy couloir descends to glacier from lowest col on N ridge, and a clean square-cut buttress of slabby yellow rock lies immediately R. Climb first wall by line of crack in steep shallow corner (severe), then move L and up to second wall. Turn this by L traverse and steep chimney, to ledge with poor belays. Then back to crest, by steep slabs on R (severe). Continue by easier rocks to crest of N ridge. Thence by this ridge to summit (Barber-Fraser's route, 1953). The buttress makes an excellent climb on perfect rock almost throughout. Time, 2 hrs. (J Clarkson).

THE JIEKKEVARRI GROUP (maps 1533/1 Balsfjord, 1633/4 Storfjord, 1534/2 Ullsfjord & 1634/3 Lyngen): *Jiekkevarri* (1833) is the "Mont Blanc of the North", a huge rock massif with black ice-capped precipices, flanked by several glaciers. Its S face is said to be as big as the Brenva Face of Mont Blanc and incredibly fine. Jiekkevarri rises E of Holmbukt in Sør fjord, a branch of Ulls fjord. The ice-cap is topped by Store Jiekkevarri (1833), and the other peaks are reached by a walk over hard snow — to Søre in 40 minutes, Vestre in 30 and Austre in a good hour. The 1st asc was made in 8/1897 by George Hastings alone, reaching Jiekkevarri from Austre Jiekkevarri. The impressive avalanche scenes in the film "We Die Alone" were filmed on the Jiekkevarri. Mr K Gleditsch, director of NGO, suggests in his interesting book, ,,De høyeste fjellene i Nord-Norge" that the 3 domes of Jiekkevarri should be called Stortoppen (1833), Kveita (1725), (previously called Lille Jiekkevarri), and Nordtoppen (1705). These names will be adopted in the next issue of this guide. The Jiekkevarri massif is best divided into 3 approaches (notes by G A Leaver):

The South-West Approach extends from Hundtind to the S ridge descending to Lyngsdal Skar. There are 5 ridges and 2 main glaciers, described from W to E:

Jiekkevarri from Hundtind — A ridge connects Hundtind with Vestre Jiekke-varri and the ice-cap, bending in an easterly direction. Hundtind is the highest point of a ridge running parallel with Sør fjord from the base of the moraine of Holmbukt glacier to Fugledal (Fauldalen on new map?) It lies W of Skarvknausen and is separated from it by a corrie glacier. Hundtind was climbed by its SW face in 1953 by B Blake, R Scott and J D J Wildridge.

Hundtind by SW Face — Ascend towards the large sheet of slabs from N bank of Andersdal river until a scree gully, bounded on its R by red slabs, is reached. The slabs are climbed easily to the ridge on generally sound rock to the ridge, which is followed to top. The ridge is shattered in parts and the two trolls on the ridge are hard, if climbed direct. Descend by a scree gully towards the fjord. Time from Holmbukt and back, 12 hrs. (J D J Wildridge).

Jiekkevarri from Skarvknausen — When seen from Holmbukt, Skarvknausen appears as a triangular black wall of buttresses, ribs and snowy gullies, culminating at the apex in a finely jagged top, but in reality it is a vast projecting spur from Vestre Jekkevarre, mistakenly called Holmbukttind by Mrs Main. It is unlikely that Caspari (see old guide) climbed the W face in 1896, as it presents considerable difficulties; the gullies are liable to falls of snow. Also, the W face does not connect with Fauldalen. In 1898, Hasting's party climbed it from the SW from Holmbukt glacier. The route lies up the gullies rising from the base of Holmbukt glacier. Mrs Main's variation went up to the R of Hasting's route. A glacier which once descended the N face towards Fugledal glacier, has since retreated, and this route is now impracticable.

Jiekkevarri from Vestre Jiekkevarri — This is the highest westerly point. It can be reached from Hundtind by a ridge which connects with the ice-cap. From the snow dome of Skarvknausen, an easy route leads to Vestre Jiekke-varri. 1st asc unknown.

Jiekkevarri by Holmbukt Glacier — This glacier which lies between Skarv-knausen and Kristianstind, leads to the ice-cap and gives access to Vestre Jiekkevarri on the L and to Søre Jiekkevarri on the R. It is much crevassed, and there is danger of falling seracs. The 1st asc by this glacier was made in 1951 by S G Moore and G Sutton.

Jiekkevarri from Kristianstind — The latter is a fine ridge-like mountain on the R of Holmbukt glacier. Its summit is connected via Hansentind to Jiek-kevarri ice-cap by a ridge which is still unclimbed in its entirety. Kristians-tind's W ridge was climbed in 1899 by Mrs Elizabeth Main with J and E Imboden. Firm slabby rocks. Descent by the same route or by the N face to Andersdalen or by the E ridge and then by scree and rock to moraine of SW Jiekkevarri glacier.

Jiekkevarri from Hansentind — The ice-cap is reached by descending the short rock ridge from Hansentind. This is a sharply pointed peak, rising from the northward running ridge that connects Kristianstind with the western ice-cap. Hansentind's NW face was climbed in 1899 by C V and L C Rawlence and E L Strutt. Great retreat has now made the "very steep snow slope" dangerous. A new route by the Kristianstind ridge was made in 1953 by R Scott and J D J Wildridge. This traverse must be one of the finest routes in Lyngen. It is chiefly on sound rock and gives some sensational situations. It is to be highly recommended to an experienced party. There are one or two short hard sections.

Hansentind by Kristianstind ridge — Ascend Kristianstind by its W ridge, drop sharply on to the Hansentind ridge, which is followed in its entirety to the summit of Hansentind. From the summit, the ridge continues until it abutts the ice-cap. Descent is made by a return along the ridge, and then descend the S face of the ridge. Descent can be made to Holmbukt glacier or via the ice-cap and one of the easy ridges. Other places of descent can be found easily without a complete return along the ridge. Time from Holm-bukt and back, 17 hrs. (J D J Wildridge).

Jiekkevarri by the SW Jiekkevarri Glacier — This glacier leads down from the ice-cap in a SW direction between Hansentind and V-tind. The terminal moraine of this glacier overlooks Andersdalen. The glacier is menaced by a great hanging glacier and is not to be recommended. It is unclimbed.

Jiekkevarri from Førstetoppen — From the SW Jiekkevarri glacier, a boulder-strewn ridge bounds the moraine to the E, forming a rounded pear-shape on the skyline. This is Førstetoppen. Its N ridge was climbed in 1953 by R Scott and J D J Wildridge.

Førstetoppen by N Ridge — The sharply defined ridge which rises from the SW Jiekkevarri moraine, can be reached by going up the moraine or traversing the slabs to L edge. The route starts at the extreme L edge of face just before some steep slabby faces are reached. The first 40 ft involves some hard climbing, but afterwards the route leads straight up to the summit on good rock, and provides 1000 ft of good continuous rock climbing. Descent by the W ridge. Time from moraine to top, 5 hrs. (J D J Wildridge).

Jiekkevarri from V-tind. A short ridge leads easily from V-tind via V-troll to the ice-cap. Søre Jiekkevarri lies easterly. V-tind rises SW of Søre Jiekkevarri and SE of Hansentind. It is only a spur of Jiekkevarri and has 3 ridges: The S ridge which rises from the moraine of the almost extinct Balgesvarre glacier, and the W ridge which rises from the R side of the terminal moraine of the SW Jiekkevarri glacier. Both ridges are unclimbed. Finally, there is the NW ridge, which is a steep spur of fine rock which rises from the SW Jiekkevarri glacier to the mile beyond the terminal moraine. The NW ridge was climbed in 1953 by B Blake, G A Leaver and J D J Wildridge.

V-tind by NW ridge — The climb starts on the ridge on the R of SW Jiekkevarri glacier, on the L of which is the Hansentind ridge. From R of glacier, the ridge runs up in a series of slabs and walls. Traverse L from foot of buttress and ascend the slabs towards an almost vertical black wall. Traverse L to where the angle of this wall eases off and ascend a thin crack which is delicate and hard. Traverse L to ridge itself and ascend until stopped by a series of overhangs. Again traverse L across the slabs to a gully. This can be ascended direct and is strenuous. Move R across boulders and ascend to the wall, which is climbed with difficulty to the broken rocks above. Traverse these upwards to R until the edge is reached and further progress is blocked by an overhanging wall. Move round the corner on to the exposed W wall and continue upwards to the ridge. Move R again and on to the W wall and ascend a groove with difficulty. The ridge is followed until some slabs are reached. These are climbed keeping R, and prove delicate. The easy rocks ahead lead to the summit. A beautiful climb on good firm rock almost throughout. Sufficiently difficult to necessitate moving singly almost through its entire length. Time from glacier to top, 10 hrs. Descent by a scree gully from the ridge behind the troll towards the glacier. (G A Leaver and J D J Wildridge).

V-troll from V-tind. The summit of V-tind lies 120 m E of the V-troll, which can be seen from Andersdalen. It was climbed in 1953 by B Blake and J D J Wildridge by a short route of some difficulty and exposure. Descend a slab to the gap. Climb the short wall on its exposed L edge to a perched block. Ascend the facing wall on its R corner (very hard). It can be climbed much easier by combined tactics. Ascend the final short wall on its exposed L edge. About 90 ft of climbing is involved. (G A Leaver and J D J Wildridge).

Jiekkevarri from Søre Jiekkevarri (1656) — This peak rises on the ice-cap, SW of Store Jiekkevarri, SE of Vestre Jiekkevarri and E of V-tind. The S ridge of Søre Jiekkevarri was climbed in 1898 by G Hastings with E Hogrenning. On the W side of Søre Jiekkevarri there is a narrow snow gully, broken in 3 pitches, which gives a good line of descent on to the Balgesvarre glacier.

The North Approach extends from Hundtind to Jiekke-varrinebba. Most of this face falls steeply into Faul-dalen, but it relents towards the E end (Fugledal Skar). Various ascents have been made from this end, details of which are not known. Routes on the western end are menaced by the condition of the ice hanging above the face.

Jiekkevarri from Skarvknausen — The route lay up the glacier which once descended to Fugledal glacier, but it is now impractical.

Jiekkevarri from Fugledal Skar — The pass between Fugledal glacier and Fornes glacier is called Fugledal Skar, not to be confused with Fornes Skar, which lies E of both glaciers between Jiekkevarrinebba and Tigertind. The route lies up the glacier which comes down from the N face of Austre Jiekkevarri, climbed in 1899 by G Hastings and E Hogrenning. Probably a variation of this route was made in 1954 by G Dàbakk and K Kristensen, when they started from Leirvik and went up Fugledal glacier towards the gap E of Fornes Skar and up on to the ice-cap. Fornes glacier no longer has an icefall as in Hasting's day. Instead there is a rock-step of nearly 1000 ft in height, easily ascended on its L. The hollow on the SW side of the skar still exists and is nearer 150 ft high and immensely corniced.

Jiekkevarri from Austre Jiekkevarri — This peak lies on the NE fringe of the ice-cap and is reached in an hour from Store Jiekkevarri by walking over hard snow. Its N ridge was climbed in 1897 by G Hastings and H Wolley. Its E ridge was climbed in 1954 by D A Christoffel, M J Howells, R S Knight and A G Troughton.

Austre Jiekkevarri by N Ridge — From Kvalvikdalen, skirt N shores of iceberg lake and ascend over scree, aiming for a traverse which leads through a line of crags up on to the second glacier which comes down in fine seracs into the iceberg lake. Follow glacier to its head and then on to the col above, from which the N ridge of Jiekkevarri rises. Halfway up, the ridge becomes too steep and is turned by crossing from W to E face and then up to the snow dome, whence the Austre Jiekkevarri is reached after 15 minutes walking up hard snow. Time from Kvalvikdal to top, 6 hrs. (G A Leaver).

Austre Jiekkevarri by E Ridge — Up from N branch of Lyngsdal glacier. The ridge is best gained by climbing R-hand snow couloir. It is a pleasant climb up sound rock and affords an easy and quick means of descent from the Jiekkevarri plateau to Lyngsdal. If desired, the summit of Skartind can be reached in about 15 min from the gap in the ridge between it and Austre Jiekkevarri. (D A Christoffel).

Jiekkevarri from Fornes Skar — This route was climbed in 1924 by E Barlindhaug and J Quigstad. No report.

Jiekkevarri from Jiekkevarrinebba — A sharp arete leads from Jkkevarrinebba towards Austre Jekkevarre, where it widens into a broad and stony ridge. Jiekkevarrinebba is a sharply pointed peak, very like Crast' Aguzza, when seen from the plateau above the labyrinth. It was traversed from Austre Jiekkevarri (not Vestre) in 1899 by Mrs Main and the Imbodens. Its N ridge was climbed in 1954 by K Griffiths, R Wilkinson and R Wyss.

The South Approach — The bulk of this side is the S face proper. It presents great difficulties. Storeggen which affords a magnificent climb, leads up the main SE ridge of the highest point, dropping 4000 ft to Lyngsdalen. It was climbed in 1953 by H Barber, M Fraser and J Heap, and a fortnight later by R A Brown, P B Cook and P R Falkner. The eastern end of the S side (called E face) is more easy of access, climbed in 1951 by P R Falkner and P C Parks. The SE face was climbed in 1959 by H Brunton, J Clarkson, G Hendry and G Lee.

Jiekkevarri by Storeggen — Start at true base of ridge (2200 ft), gaining height rapidly. The ridge bends to L with a little snow col (2900 ft) below the impressive main step of its lower part. Up the steep rock ahead, slightly L for 200 ft, then straight up 100 ft and back R 150 ft to ridge crest. Diff and exposed pitch up to L, an overshot groove, pitons at top, then L to a little nook (60 ft), then 60 ft more on easier stuff up to L to biggish triangular nook. A prominent band of bright yellow rock is passed just below the big nook. Then up to L on pleasant slabs for 200 ft, rather exposed, to a black mossy corner, with overhangs above and to L. The route escapes these by 60 ft of steep chimney up to R, to reach crest of ridge. 200 ft of easy rocks and then up steep rocks to another step. Very steep, exposed and outward tilted holds, on fine rock. Directly up for 70 ft, then L across an easy slab and 150 ft up and L and then 60 ft up direct, very exposed traverse to L, a severe pitch to a big ledge. Then easily up to R to outer end of level centre part of ridge. Time from foot to top of ridge, 6 hrs. Traverse level part of ridge, across easy but pleasant gaps and towers, rising a bit at inner end. Here is a large step, very steep and forbidding, grey and black rock. Good stance at base of step. Up 30 ft on L by easy cleft. Then a 40 ft pitch up and bending R, ending in a very exposed stance. 35 ft straight up wall to another stance, with piton belay up on R. Across to peg and up steep corner with overhanging finish to ledge and belay below steep black corner. Follow ledge below corner to R and continue R for 50 ft, very exposed, to wet gully. Go up this and regain ridge in 150 ft. Then direct up on crest on easy rock on L of big snow patch, to 40 ft wall, up its L side, then scrambling along levelling-off ridge to cairn at top of ridge. There is a steep short snow slope to summit plateau. The summit lies about ½ hour away to NW. Time from base of ridge to summit cairn, 10 hrs excl halts. Descent via Søre Jiekkevarri and its S ridge via Lyngsdal Skar and Lyngsdal glacier to camp. Time, 7 hrs. Allow 24 hrs for the whole trip. (Richard A Brown).

Jiekkevarri by SE Face — The route starts almost directly below the summit of S peak of Jiekkevarri at point where a rib of easy rock and rubble descends furthest out into the glacier. Climb this rib for about 1500 ft until it merges with steep snowfield. Climb snowfield diagonally to L to reach a rib of clean rock on the same line and immediately L of snow gully. The vertical face of Store Jiekkevarri lies just across this gully. Rib gives pleasant climbing of mod diff standard. At its top, it merges into more steep covered shelves leading upwards, still to L. Shelves end above an impressive ravine. Turn upwards to R and reach summit by very diff pitch of steep rock. Time, 6 hrs. (J Clarkson).

Jiekkevarri by E Face — This route probably leads up by the glacier between Jiekkevarrinebba and Tobretind. From the top and up to Store Jiekkevarri, there is a descent and re-ascent of at least 1000 ft.

Jiekkevarri from Tobretind — The latter is a prominent outlier of SE corner of Jiekkevarri to which it is connected by a ridge. Only a short length of this ridge has been traversed, but it would probably make an interesting expedition. Tobretind's E ridge drops steeply to a deep V-shaped col which is called Tobre Skar. This pass gives fairly easy access direct from the N tributary glacier ice bowl of Lyngsdal glacier to the Lille Jiekkevarri glacier above the icefall. The SW face above Lyngsdal glacier snout was climbed in 1951 by K Clarke and G A Sutton, up ribs to the summit ridge. Fairly loose rocks, but no great difficulty. The SE face was climbed in 1951 by R A Brown and N Dobson, up ribs and gullies. Loose rocks. The N face was climbed in 1951 by P R Falkner and S G Moore, up a prominent buttress and ridge overlooking Lille Jiekkevarri glacier. The lower section is fairly difficult, but the upper part is an easy scramble.

Jiekkevarri from Skartind — The latter is a sharply pointed summit on the ridge between Jiekkevarri and Tobretind. Its E face was climbed in 1953 by T Panther and R G Pettigrew. A route from Tobre Skar was made in 1956 by R M Middleton, J G G Stephenson and R J Wathen.

Skartind from Tobre Skar — A large tower blocks the view of the ridge from Tobre Skar. The tower has a long crack in the centre. Traversing up and left from a gully on its R, the party attempted to ascend this crack. Faced with a very hard chimney above a slab and lower chimney, they had to abseil off. This might give enthusiasts a good VS climb. The "15 min" descent to skar W of Skartind is diff. Steep couloir leads fairly easily to Lille Jiekkevarri glacier, but the bergschrund can be formidable. (R J Wathen).

THE BREDALSFJELL RANGES (maps 1633/4 Storfjord & 1634/3 Lyngen) are situated between Jiekkevarri and Lyngen fjord, N of Lyngsdalen and S of Klavikdalen. *Bredalsfjell* (1538) or Ruksisvaggegaissa is a magnificent rock massif, whose ice-cap throws down an icefall on its E side. There are several snow and ice slopes on the N face, with moraines which tell the tale of recessive glaciation. Its E ridge was climbed in 1897 by G Hastings and H Woolley, descending by steep crags to Lille Jiekkevarri glacier. The NE ridge was climbed in 1951 by R A Brown and S G Moore, a fine ridge which has the length, the dramatic setting combined with exposure, and the necessity for technique that go to form the hall-mark for the classic mountain route.

Bredalsfjell (Ruksis) by NE Ridge — The climb commences directly up the broad buttress above the screes, maintaining a direction in line with the knife-edged middle and upper sections. The ridge has several very hard pitches which are turned on the slabby N face. The ridge requires continuous climbing, in all nearly 4000 ft of rock climbing, which maintains the tension of uncertainty to its last pitch, which leads airily direct on to the summit plateau. (Harry Pretty).

Pollfjell (1213) or Dalfjell on old map is a prominent peak N of Dalen. Its summit is an elongated platau, reached from Dalen by a steep scramble. Its NE ridge was climbed in 1951 by S G Moore and H Pretty, an unsound route which cannot be recommended. Descent by the snow-covered W face.

THE DURMÅLSFJELL GROUP (maps 1534/2 Ullsfjord & 1634/3 Lyngen) rises in the NW corner of S Lyngen, a long ridge which runs N-S from Jøvik on the Kjosen fjord to Jiekkevarri. Its northernmost point is *Storfjell* (Litle Durmålstind on new map?), traversed in 1951 by P Parks, R G Pettigrew and G A Sutton. The ridge is over a mile long. *Leirbukttind* (1430) is a sharply pointed peak S of Storfjell on the ridge which circles round Leirbukt glacier from a high flat-topped peak between it and Durmåls-tind. It should not be confused with a miniature aiguille on the same ridge but nearer to Sør fjord. The summit ridge is about 20 ft long and very narrow. Climbed in 1899 by Mrs Elizabeth Main with the Imbodens from Holm-bukt via Fugledal river.

Durmålstind (1444) rises on the ridge S of Leirbukttind. A surprise meeting occurred in 1899 when two British parties, unknown to each other, met on the very top. G Hastings and E Hogrenning climbed it by the SW ridge at the same time as Mrs Main with the Imbodens climbed it straight up from Leirbukt, believing they climbed Loddevarre. Durmålstind was climbed in 1951 by A N Bartholomew, K Clarke and G Sutton, from Fornesdal glacier to a gap on the N ridge. From the gap, a 1000 ft climb, increasing in steepness and difficulty, leads to the summit. Descent by the E ridge. Time from Fornesdal and back, 12 hrs.

Loddevarre (1620) is a snow plateau, connected to Dur-målstind by a fine rocky ridge. A traverse from Jøvik was made in 1956 by K Blackwood and A C White. Walk up slopes due S of Jøvik, past twin lakes. Climb up scree slopes, traversing southwards round bottom of pinnacled ridge into large corrie. The pinnacled ridge forms the N side of the corrie, its S side being the SW ridge of Lodde-varre. Follow up corrie and glacier. The jagged ridge forming the head of the corrie connects Durmålstind and Loddevarre. For Loddevarre, ascend snow couloir on the S side of the ridge, but for Durmålstind aim for the S side of the highest point on the ridge. Upon gaining the ridge, the summits will be obvious — follow snow to the highest points. Descend from Loddevarre by going down the SW ridge to a snow couloir, which provides an easy route down to the glacier in the corrie. Time for traverse from Jøvik and back, 15 hrs. (A C White).

Fugledalstind (1550) is an outlying spire SW of Durmåls-tind, above Fuglevatn, climbed in 1899 by Mrs Main and the Imbodens, by steep but easy rocks on the S face, descending by steep and stony gullies direct to lake Fuglevatn.

THE STORFJELL GROUP (map 1634/3 Lyngen) is a long ridge E of Fornes glacier and S of Fornesfjell. Its northernmost point is *Salryggtind*, which was cairned in 1951 by R G Pettigrew and G Sutton, ascending by the NW face from Fornesdalen in 10 hrs from Jøvik and back. This route is feasible only under favourable snow conditions. The central peak on the ridge is *Hidden Peak* (Stortind on new map?), cairned in 1953 by R A Brown, P B Cook and P R Falkner.

Hidden Peak by N Ridge — Up by E side of Fornes glacier, then up a 1000 ft snow couloir to lowest part of N ridge between Salryggtind and Hidden Peak. Follow N ridge to small twin-topped summit. Descent by same route. Time, 4½ hrs up, 4 down. (Richard A Brown).

Tigertind (1492) is the southernmost point on the ridge, separated from Jiekkevarri through Fornes Skar. Its S ridge was climbed in 1953 by R A Brown, P B Cook and P R Falkner. The name is derived from the extremely strong stripping in the banded gneiss of which it is formed.

Tigertind by S Ridge — Up Fornes glacier and southwards nearly to top. Up prominent 1200 ft snow couloir at end of S ridge, then follow S ridge to top. Big but easy gap before summit. Some smaller gaps before top. Descent by same route. Time from glacier snout to top, 4½ hrs. (Richard A Brown).

THE RØDBERGDAL GLACIER RANGES (map 1634/3 Lyngen) are situated S of Kjosen fjord and E of Fornes-dalen, which twists itself into a hanging valley named "Hidden Valley", which joins Rypedalen to the S. It is bounded to the E by Rødberg Skar, which drops steeply northwards into Rødbergdalen, but falls gently southwards into Goalsedalen (N-S), which joins the broad Kvalvikdal (W-E) at the S slope of the main ridge. *Fornestind* (1478) is an impressive mountain on the main ridge. Its N ridge was climbed in 1898 by W P Haskett-Smith, G Hastings and Wm C Slingsby, reclimbed in 1956 by K Blackwood and A C White. Excellent rock scrambling for 3000 ft on very good rock.

Fornestind by N Ridge — From Kjosen fjord, follow N ridge to smaller summit, separated from main top by 200 ft gap, which is traversed easily. Follow ridge to main summit, except about halfway, where a 100 ft gap is turned by traversing ledges on E side of ridge to bottom of gap. A snow gully on NE side provides quick and easy descent towards Kjosen fjord. Alternative descent by snow gully on S face. Time from Jøvik and back. 12 hrs. (A C White).

156

The main ridge between Fornestind and Rødbergtind is broken by a central peak, *Sentraltoppen* (1467), which probably was climbed in 1946 by G Billing and O Bjørn, when traversing from Rødbergtind. Its S ridge was climbed in 1953 by R A Brown, P B Cook and P R Falkner.

Sentraltoppen by S Ridge — From camp in upper Fornesdal, up past boulders at mouth of Hidden Valley to foot of W wall of S ridge. Up this by slabs and gullies, loose rock, to a gap in S ridge with a grey troll in it. Difficult pitch out of the gap, then straightforward stuff on ridge, steepening towards the end, to top. Good rock on ridge. Descent by gully on W wall, some abseiling. Time, 7½ hrs up, 5½ down. (Richard A Brown).

Rødbergtind rises E of Sentraltoppen. Its N face which overlooks Kjosen fjord, is an enormous expanse of slabs, ribs and great buttressed ridges. The scope on this face alone is almost limitless. Rødbergtind's E ridge was climbed in 1946 by G Billing and O Bjørn by a severe route, but an easier variation was made a month later by S Synnergren and a Norwegian. The N face was climbed in 1953 by A R Brown, P B Cook and P R Falkner, a very long climb, though not difficult.

Rødbergtind by N Face — Start up nearly anywhere on the face. The trend is away to L, where the ribs fuse into the main ridge, eventually coming out on top of NE foretop. Then follow main ridge to top. Descent by S face to Rødberg glacier. Time from fjord to top, 11 hrs. (Richard A Brown).

Southwards from Sentraltoppen, there is a long ridge which comprises the *Kvalvikfjell* (Goalsevaggegaissa on old map). This ridge was traversed in 1951 by A N Bartholomew, R A Brown, S G Moore, R G Pettigrew and H Pretty. The first peak was cairned, but all other summits were found uncairned.

Traverse of Kvalvikfjell — Up by NE ridge to the easternmost summit, a first-rate climb of some 3000 ft of alpine character. From the first summit, abseil down a vertical 80 ft smooth-walled gash and follow ridge westwards across minor and major peaks. (Richard A Brown).

THE RØRNESFJELL RANGE (map 1634/3 Lyngen)
overlooks Lyngseid and Kjosen fjord. The horse-shoe ridge which rises behind Lyngseid is made up of Rørnesfjell and Kvalvikfjell (Goalsevarre on old map). *Gjertind* overlooks the head of Kjosen fjord, and a connecting saddle leads SW to *Rørnestind* (1247) and *Mellemfjell* (1304), which again connect with *Kvalvikfjell* (1278). A complete N-S traverse was made in 1888 by O Vorwerg, and in the reverse direction in 1954 by J Allen, T Panther and R G Pettigrew. The SE ridge of Kvalvikfjell is an unattractive assortment of ill-balanced boulders. The slabby W face of Rørnestind was climbed in 1951 by R G Pettigrew and G A Sutton, starting from Rørnes Skar — the pass which separates Rødbergtind from Rørnestind.

The uppermost 500 ft are quite interesting. A fine but short pinnacled ridge which runs NW from Rørnestind to Rørnes Skar, was climbed in 1951 by the same party.

THE KJOSTIND GROUP (map 1634/3 Lyngen) is the southernmost range in North Lyngen, situated NW of Lyngseid and immediately N of Kjosen fjord. The road between Tromsø and Lyngseid runs below the main ridge, which is bounded to the N by Tyttebærdalen and Fastdalen. There are 3 great glaciers — Kjos (same as Blåisen?), Giæver and Råttenvik. Urkjerringa Skar which lies below the SW face of Urkjerringa, facilitates the crossing from Tyttebærdalen on to Kjos glacier, and Kjosen Skar between Store Kjostind and Giævertind affords a passage from Kjos glacier to Råttenvik glacier.

Tyttebærtind (1150) is the westernmost point on the ridge. Its S face is nightmarish, with shattered and rotten ribs, broken off in overhangs and a myriad of stone-swept gullies. It was climbed by its E ridge from Urtind in 1899 by Mrs Elizabeth Main with J and E Imboden. The ridge is steep and narrow at first, crested with many peaks of loose rock. Descent by the W ridge into Tyttebærdalen. Its W ridge was climbed in 1951 by R A Brown and H Pretty. One or two interesting little walls and notches.

Urtind (1225) rises on the W fringe of Blåisen (Blue Ice) glacier, a prominent peak when seen from Lyngseid. Mrs Main and party climbed it in 1898 by the rock ridge which lies S of the snow couloir descending from its E face. It was climbed from Tyttebærtind in 1951 by A R Brown and H Pretty, descending by the S face, which is marked by a deep snow gully which descends from the ridge just N of Urtind, right down to Blåisen glacier bowl. They kicked 2250 steps in bad weather and rotten snow conditions. *Festningen* lies NE of Urtind on the ridge which forms a crescent above Blåisen glacier. It is a fine square-topped peak, climbed in 1898 by Mrs Main and the Imbodens, across the glacier and up by the SE face and E ridge in 5 hrs from Lyngseid. Its SW arete was climbed in 1953 by R A Brown, P K Cook and P R Falkner.

Festningen by SW Arete — From Lyngseid and up Blåisen glacier, then up the curving couloir of Urtind. Along the rising SW ridge until very steep wall, dropping from top of Festningen, blocks all progress. Descend 150 ft on W side, then up steep and loose rock wall; care required for 250 ft; one awkward bit near top. Then L about 30 ft and straight up easy rock, over sound pleasantly stepped ridge to 1st summit. Quite sharp pronounced verticality on Kjos side. Summit is chain of 3 tops, 1st and 3rd of equal height. One hour along the ridge in a NE direction leads to a very deep gap in front of Urkjerringa. The party did not find a route here, though with more snow it should be quite reasonable to go down on W side. They descended a snow couloir on SE face of ridge to upper Kjos basin and thence to the road. (Richard A Brown).

Urkjerringa (1399) is a magnificent peak, called the "Aiguille Dru of the North" by Slingsby, situated between Festningen and Store Kjostind (Istind on new map?) It was climbed in 1911 by K Endell and W Martin, and a winter asc was made in 4/1939 by G Billing and G Santesson, both ascents probably by the NE ridge from the col E of Urkjerringa. Its E face was climbed in 1954 by J Allen, B Nearn, R G Pettigrew and W Ruthven. There is no sign of the SE and SW sides ever having been attempted.

Store Kjostind (Istind 1550 on new map?) is a beautiful snow dome, climbed in 1898 by G Hastings and Wm C Slingsby, first by the N face and then by the N ridge, a pleasant route. A traverse from Giævertind was made in 1898 by Mrs Main and the Imbodens. Its S face was climbed in 1956 by P R Falkner, W J Cartwright and L Pratt, from Kjosen fjord and straight up long scree slopes to Kjosen glacier, then long snow slopes and finally a short rock scramble, a simple and direct route, made in 4 hrs.

Giævertind projects with very steep walls from Store Kjostind's SE ridge, between Kjos glacier and Råttenvik glacier. Its main ridge is so narrow that one can almost straddle it. The E ridge was climbed in 1888 by O Vorwerg with a porter; time from Lyngseid, 6 hrs up, 5 down. The N face was climbed by Mrs Main and party in 1898 via Råttenvik glacier and the saddle between Store Kjostind and Giævertind. She believed a route could be made by the W ridge from Kjos glacier.

Austre Kjostind (Store Kjostind 1489 on new map?) is situated SE of Giævertind and forms the central point of a horse-shoe ridge which embraces the Giæver glacier. It is cut off from Giævertind by a gap and a precipitous wall beyond, although Austre Kjostind rises merely 50 ft above the floor of the gap. Vorwerg must have passed over it when he climbed Giævertind in 1888. From Store Kjostind (Istind on new map?), another ridge runs northwards to *Nordre Kjostind*, climbed in 1951 by R A Brown and P R Falkner, when they made a traverse of Austre Kjostind — Giævertind — Store and Nordre Kjostind. The hardest section was the crossing of the gap between Austre and Giævertind. Encircling Råttenvik glacier, the ridge from Nordre Kjostind continues to *Fastdalstind* (1275). The ascent is merely a scramble.

The Isskartinder seen from the pass near Fastdalstind (Photo: Bolinder)

THE ISSKARTIND GROUP (map 1634/3 Lyngen) is situated above the promontory between Ulls fjord and Kjosen fjord, W of Tyttebærdalen and S of the Jegervasstinder. It is a fine group which affords good ridge climbs. Isskar glacier is contained within the network of ridges, and Is Skar between Sofietind and Austre Isskartind affords a passage from Tyttebærdalen on to Isskar glacier.

Sultind (1091) is the southernmost point, overlooking Kjosen fjord and Tyttebærdalen. It was climbed by the N face from the snow basin in 1898 by Mrs Elizabeth Main with J and E Imboden. *Sofiatind* (1222) lies N of Sultind, overlooking Isskar glacier. Its NE arete which rises from the glacier, was climbed in 1898 by Mrs Main and party. This arete is followed until steep cliffs necessitate a traverse to the E face, which is climbed until the arete is regained below the summit. Some pleasant climbing in chimneys is met with on the E face. The W ridge was climbed in 1951 by A N Bartholomew and P Parks. Very loose rock and an uninteresting route. The ridge between Sultind and Sofiatind has never been climbed.

Austre Isskartind (1272) forms the central and northernmost point on the ridge which envelopes Isskar glacier. Climbed in 1898 by W P Haskett-Smith and Wm C Slingsby with E Hogrenning, up by a gully to a place with a split block in the corner of a vertical face about 20 ft high — very similar to the E Pisgah climb on the Pillar Rock. Above this place, a series of gently inclined

slabs lead to the top. Descent by the W ridge into Slingsby Skar, which lies between Store and Austre Isskartind.
Store Isskartind (1441) (Trollvasstind on new map?) is the
highest peak, climbed in 1898 by W P Haskett-Smith and
Wm C Slingsby with E Hogrenning, probably by the E
ridge from Austre Isskartind. Mrs Main and the Imbodens
climbed it 4 days later, by the E ridge via Slingsby Skar
from Isskar glacier. Surveyor K S Klingenberg and M
Folsvik made 3 routes in 1904 — Store from Lille Isskartind, Store by N face and Store by W wall. *Lille
Isskartind* (1338) rises W of Store Isskartind, climbed in
1899 by G Hastings and E Hogrenning by the N ridge
and a long gully. Descent by the E ridge to the col
between Store and Lille Isskartind. A complete traverse
of the Isskartinder (also the 1st winter asc) was made in
3/1940 by G Billing and H Hammarsten.

THE JEGERVASS RANGES (map 1634/3 Lyngen):
The mountain ranges between Jegervatn in Ulls fjord
and Kopang in Lyngen fjord are bounded by Stortinddalen to the S and Strupendalen to the N. There are 3
distinct groups, connected with glaciers and a fine network of ridges. Jegervatn and Kopang hamlets can be
reached by road from Lyngseid. There is a small shop at
Jegervatn, but it does not sell bread. No accommodation.
Stortinddalen which runs easterwards from Jegervatn
(Hunter's Lake), provides a splendid passage right across
the peninsula. Magnificent scenery and easy going.
Strupendalen also provides a passage between both fjords
by way of *Strupen Skar*, but it is one of the stoniest passes
in Norway, and its approach involves laborious traversing
of blocks and boulders of all sizes. A passage from Stortinddalen to Strupendalen can be made by ascending
Stortinddal glacier — one of the most delightful icefields in Norway — and descending Lenangen glacier.
From the top of Stortinddal-Lenangen glaciers, the
Lenangen Skar leads on to the crest of Kopang-Strupen
glaciers. The Jegervasstinder lie E of Jegervatn and W of
Stortinddal—Lenangen glaciers. Dropping westwards,
there are 2 major glaciers — Forholt glacier W of Forholttind and Troll glacier W of Store Jegervasstind.
Forholt Skar lies between Stortind and Forholttind,
reached by a quick walk from Jegervatn up Forholt
glacier.

Stortind (1512) or Garjelgaissa rises E of Jegervatn, with
grand precipices from a ridge which runs W-E above
Stortinddalen. On its E side lies a round tarn of turquoise
blue, singularly like the Lac Bleu at Arolla. Stortind's

NW ridge was climbed in 1898 by C Caspari, W P Haskett-Smith, G Hastings and Wm C Slingsby with E Hogrenning, a first-rate climb, repeated in 1956 by R J Donovan and H B Francis. This ridge is a knife-edge in places and much pinnacled. The SW face was climbed from Jegervatn in 1898 by Mrs Elizabeth Main with J and E Imboden, up steep but easy rock. A descent by the W side was made in 1933 by A Næss and P W Zapffe. The 1st winter asc was made in 1940 by G Billing and H Hammarsten. The true NE ridge was climbed in 1956 by P R Falkner, W J Cartwright and L Pratt.

Stortind by NW Ridge — Through birch forest from Jegervatn and up by NW ridge until a gap has to be turned by a long descent on W face of ridge. Traverse over steep slabs, back to ridge, which follow to subsidiary summit, separated from Stortind by deep gap. A steep and jagged ridge leads down to snow col. Then follows an ascent of 500 ft up steep snow and finally 150 ft more over rocks to top. Return by same route. Good and fine rocks, very much like the huge slabs on N face of Scafell. (R J Donovan).

Stortind by NE Ridge — From Forholt glacier, ascend steep snow slopes to col between Stortind and Forholttind. Follow the NE ridge to top. The ridge rises fairly steeply and is partly snow and partly rock. There are a few steep and difficult sections in the direct line, but these can be avoided to the R. Time from Jegervatn, 6 hrs. (P R Falkner).

Forholttind is situated E of Stortind at the head of Forholt glacier. Its W ridge was climbed in 1898 by Mrs Main and party via Forholt glacier and Forholt Skar. *Tvillingtind* (1437) is a twin-topped peak on an outlier which stretches SE from Forholttind. It was climbed from Stortinddal glacier in 1899 by G Hastings with E Hogrenning. *Trolltind* (1425) is another double-pointed peak, situated N of Forholttind and W of Stortinddal glacier. Its W ridge separates Forholt glacier from Troll glacier. A spur on the S ridge, resembling the Dent du Giant, was climbed 1898 by Mrs Main and the Imbodens. The 1st asc of Trolltind was made in 1899 by G Hastings and E Hogrenning, up by the W ridge, a good climb. A new route by the W face was made in 1933 by A Næss and P W Zapffe.

Trolltind by W Ridge — The ridge begins as an abrupt cliff, which is turned by a snow gully. The crest above the cliff is easy for some distance, until a red triangular slab is reached. This requires care. A few hundred feet below the summit, the ridge becomes narrow and broken. The final tower appears unclimbable, but it has excellent holds. Diff. The tower is the main top, and the other top can be reached by easy circuitous routes, or — with considerable difficulty — straight along ridge. (P R Falkner).

Store Jegervasstind (1668) rises NE of Trolltind. It was climbed in 1898 by P W Haskett-Smith, G Hastings and Wm C Slingsby by a gully on the SW face, returning by the same route. *Lille Jegervasstind* rises on the ridge between Troll and Lenangen glaciers, NW of Store Jegervasstind. Probably fisrt climbed by Mrs Main and party in 1898. Its W ridge was climbed in 1951 by S G Moore and R G Pettigrew. This ridge is partly narrow and is

The Jegervasstind ranges consist of 3 distinct groups, connected with glaciers and ridges (Photo: Harstad)

broken into numerous pinnacles. The traverse of some of them is tricky and the rock is not good. The final peak rises steeply beyond the pinnacles, but the rock here is much better. A simpler way up is to ascend to the col between Lille and Nordre Jegervasstind, descend a short distance to the snow field on the Lenangen glacier, across snow to a little snow gully, which runs up into the final tower of Lille Jegervasstind, close to the final section of the W ridge route, which is then followed to the top. *Nordre Jegervasstind* (1044) joins the pinnacled W ridge of Lille Jegervasstind. It is a twin-topped peak, which may have been climbed by Mrs Main and party in 1898. Both points were climbed in 1934, Nordtoppen by E Thyholdt and P W Zapffe, Sydtoppen by K Antonsen and P W Zapffe.

A traverse (N-S) of the Jegervasstinder was made in 1951 by D Scott, A Watson and Tom Weir. Another traverse in the reverse direction was made in 1951 by P R Falkner, S G Moore, P Parks and R G Pettigrew. Starting from the S, this climb leads up from Forholt glacier by a steep snow gully and a forbidding tower (summit of Trolltind), which appears unclimbable until the last moment. The greatest difficulty on the ridge itself is a cleft about 100 ft deep. Abseil down the wall and regain the ridge after a severe move over an overhang. Across Store Jegervasstind, then descend by the N arete for about 1000 ft, whence a short-cut is taken down snow slopes to the glacier. There are 2 bergschrunds, and the second requires a powerful leap — 15 ft down and 6 across, with an ice chasm below. In 1953, the ridge from Nordre to Lille Jegervasstind was traversed by R A Brown, P B Cook and P R Falkner, a fine trip of 14 hrs. They believe it would be possible to traverse all peaks in one go from Nordre to Trolltind, a fine feat which would probably make an expedition of more than 24 hrs.

Bristling with petrified trolls on its 3 ridges, the *Lenangentind* (1596) (called Storbotntind by Slingsby) rises opposite Nordre Jegervasstind, the Lenangen glacier intervening. It was climbed in 1898 by P W Haskett-Smith, G Hastings and Wm C Slingsby with E Hogrenning by Hasting's Couloir — a wide and steepish gully on the SW side of the main S ridge. They descended by the SE face, contouring round the S ridge to Lenangen Skar. In 1934, three Germans (Bøhmer, Krueke and Schott) ascended by the route Hastings descended. Its NW ridge was climbed in 1953 by R A Brown, P B Cook and P R Falkner, incl the 1st asc of *Vestre Lenangentind*, which is the summit of the NW ridge. Miss Elizabeth Stark and party attempted the traverse from Strupentind in 1954. It looks like a feasible route, but the rock is rotten. A traverse from Lenangentind to Sturpentind was made in 4 hrs in 1956 by N Aitkenhead, D Langley and L Sharratt. They also climbed the Lenangentind by the SE ridge, the short and steep ridge from Strupen glacier to a subsidiary peak on the main E ridge.

Lenangentind by NW Ridge — From Lenangen valley, up screes and then up steep snow in gully between small outlier and main peak, hitting NW ridge at its lowest point. Direct up exposed ridge, a stiff bit at about 4000 ft, then up on crest which eventually eases, giving a shoulder with 4 sharp pinnacles. Cross these, second has tricky descent, then on and up steep final spire to Vescre Lenangentind. From this point (4½ hrs from bergschrund below gully), the main peak to the E looks very impressive and stiff. Descend along arete to E, very narrow but good rock, to a gap, then 2 pinnacles and a descent to ice couloir, across this and up steep exposed slabs to top (1½ hrs from Vestre). Descent by SE face, quite easy except for big icefall, where route hard to find. Then round to Lenangen Skar. (Richard A Brown).

Lenangentind's S ridge terminates in *Søre Lenangentind* which overlooks Lenangen Skar, the pass between Stortinddal glacier and Strupen glacier. It was climbed from Strupen glacier in 1956 by N Aitkenhead and L Sharatt, up by the longest and most obvious buttress just S of the summit on the E face. The traverse from Søre Lenangentind to the main peak presents no difficulty. *Strupentind* rises E of Lenangentind, between Strupen glacier and Strupen Skar. It was climbed in 1901 by Hastings and Hogrenning and in 1927 by Guy Barlow (alone, in 9 hrs from Kopang), both routes unknown. K Clarke and H Pretty climbed its S ridge in 1951, descending by the W ridge. Miss Elizabeth Stark and party climbed the E ridge in 1954, but tried in vain to traverse to Lenangentind. This traverse was made in the opposite direction in 1934 by 3 Germans and in 1956 by N Aitkenhead, D Langley and L Sharratt. This ridge is interestingly airy in places. Peak 1152 which lies on the ridge E from Strupentind, was climbed in 1956 by L Sharratt. The long ridge which rises S of Lenangen Skar and E of Stortinddal glacier, forms a truncated peak called *Taffeltind* (1395), which has a flat glacier on its top. It was climbed up easy snow slopes from Kopang glacier in 1898 by Mrs Main and her guides. A new route was made in 1924 by E Barlindhaug and P W Zapffe. The N ridge was climbed in 1956 by W A Elders and D W Langley.

Taffeltind by N ridge — From Strupen glacier, Taffeltind appears as 2 steep ridges separated by a snow slope. The northern ridge, lying due W of confluence of Strupen and Kopang glaciers, should be climbed from glacier level, on sound and fairly steep rock for several rope lengths, until N summit is reached. Traverse along shattered ridge to main summit. Magnificent views. It is possible to glissade almost from summit cairn to glacier, down the NW side. Taffeltind is easily climbed from W and NW. (Les Sharratt).

A long ridge connects Taffeltind with *Goalbårri*, a disintegrating mountain behind Kopang, overlooking Lyngen fjord. Its E ridge which is fairly steep at top, was climbed in 1927 by G Barlow and party. Its SW face was climbed in 1951 by K Clarke and H Pretty, starting from Kopang river. *Kopangstind* (1224) rises on a long ridge which wedges into Kopang and Strupen glaciers. Its sides are crammed with boulders, but where the rock is steep, it is reasonably firm. Climbed in 1914 by O D Tauern and H von Tappeiner. Its N face was climbed in 1957 by N Aitkenhead and J Cheesmond.

Kopangstind by N Face — From Strupen glacier, the climb starts on the lowest rocks of prominent buttress below summit. The rocks are steep at first with 2 V Diff pitches. Loose rock in places. About 2/3 of the way up, the buttress gives way to a short but spectacular knife-edged ridge which leads via an upper buttress to summit. (Neil Aitkenhead).

THE REINDALSTINDER (maps 1634/3 Lyngen & 1634/4 Lyngstuva) lie E of Sørlenangen fjord, between Strupendal and Reindal valleys. There are several glaciers, the largest being Reindalsblåisen (Reindal Blue Ice). There are 2 ranges — the Reindalstinder to the E and the Veidalstinder towards Sørlenangen fjord. Neil Aitkenhead of Durham University reported in 1958 that there are still some new minor peaks and new faces and ridges to be climbed in this wonderful district.

Reindalstind (1334) is a fine peak N of Støvel glacier, above an ice-dammed lake. It was climbed in 1899 by G Hastings and E Hogrenning, up from Strupen fjord via the SE gully. It was climbed from Strupen in 1956 by R J Donovan and H B Francis. Its S face was climbed in 1956 by N Aitkenhead and L Sharratt, a fine cliff with great possibilities. This is a direct route from the corrie N of the ice-dammed lake, affording 3000 ft of pleasant rock climbing. Another route by the S face was made in 1957 by N Aitkenhead and B Burrough. The 1956 route followed a ridge E of the great amphitheatre on the S face, whereas the 1957 route was by the prominent ridge flanking the W side of the amphitheatre. The upper part of the N face is vertical and looks as if it would provide a really high standard climb on good rock.

Reindalstind from Strupen Skar — The route leads N from the skar to the highest point in the ridge, which is continuous with the true W ridge of Reindalstind. Then E along ridge, descending to its lowest point, then climbing Reindalstind itself. Good rock and narrow ridge with impressive drops on each side. Two steep steps are easily detoured to R. The gendarme in gap is easily turned on L. There is a short diff pitch about 100 ft above this, otherwise the route is easy. Time from skar to top, 5½ hrs, down 4½ hrs. (H B Francis).

Reindalstind by S Face (E Sector) — Start from highest point of small corrie glacier where main water course from large amphitheatre E of summit enters bergschrund. 2 pitches on R of stream, then continue L till rocks become much steeper, just below obvious terrace rising across face from W to E. Then 2 pitches on R up to terrace. Cairn. Awkward traverse L to recess. Climb small grey tower on L. Several pitches on slabs upwards and over to L to ridge which leads straight to top. Descent via E ridge with some recourse to snowfield on N side. Some unpleasant loose gullies on E end of S face. Time, 3 hrs up, 2½ hrs down. (Les Sharratt).

Reindalstind by S Face (W Sector) — This route starts on the lowest rocks to L of amphitheatre. Cairn. 100 m of scrambling leads to severe pitch on steep rock below very broad ledge which runs diagonally right across S face. From ledge, diff climbing across gully at a point where the ridge proper commences. The ridge is then climbed, keeping as much as possible to the natural route. Rough but sound rock. 3 severe pitches. It is a really splendid route and must rank as one of the best rock routes in Lyngen. (Neil Aitkenhead.)

Reindalstind's E ridge has many gendarmes, but these can be avoided by a short descent onto a corrie glacier on the NE side. *Austre Reindalstind* (930?) lies at the end of this ridge. It was climbed in 1957 by N Aitkenhead, B Burrough and J Tarney. The same party also climbed *Sybilstind* and *Nordre Sybilstind*, which lie on the ridge running NNE from near the main summit of Reindalstind. They are minor summits. *Støveltind* (1306) or Oxaltind is the 2nd highest peak on the ridge flanking the N side of Strupen Skar, opposite Lenangentind. Climbed by the Oread party in 1953. Its N face was climbed in 1957 by N Aitkenhead, J Cheesmond and J Tarney. From Støveltind they traversed the narrow and spectacular ridge to the W and returned to Sørlenangen.

Støveltind by N Face — From Sørlenangen by way of Støveldalen and a small glacier below N face. After scrambling up the lowest rocks, a traverse is made along ledge to R for about 130 m on to N face proper. The route then leads directly up the face on diff rock with one V Diff pitch. Time, 4½ hrs. (Neil Aitkenhead).

From about the middle of the long Veidalstind—Reindalstind ridge, another ridge, broken by a fine pass, leads northwards and on to *Bryllupstind* (1327), which rises in the range which forms the S boundary of the Reindal. It was cairned in 1914 by Oda and O D Tauern (during their honeymoon, hence the name). In 1951 it

View from Spisshorn. On the skyline (left to right): Kopangstind (far distance), Bryllupstind, Strupentind, Lenangentind, Store Jegervasstind, Trolltind (only just visible), Stortind and Veidalstind. In the foreground Isvasstind (Photo: T J C Christie)

was climbed by P R Falkner and S G Moore, ascending its W ridge, descending by the glacier on the N face. Mod diff. A new route from Isvasstind was made in 1957 by T J C Christie and P M Gerrard. The main difficulty was the steep W face, which was covered in snow. Traverse the face until the SW ridge is gained. It gives an interesting but not very diff climb to the top. Descent by the NW ridge to Veidalsfjell.

Isvasstind (1134) rises NNE of Bryllupstind, overlooking Reindal Skar. It was climbed by the N ridge in 1957 by T J C Christie and P M Gerrard, an interesting climb, difficult in places due to new snow. From the summit, descend SW, and a sporting ridge ("The Corridor") leads to a less distinct second summit (1114), then on to Bryllupstind. Between Bryllupstind and Isvasstind, a ridge sets off in a NW direction, terminating in *Veidalsfjell*. This ridge whose highest point lies SE of pt 835, was climbed in 1957 by T J C Christie and P M Gerrard.

SØRLENANGEN AND THE GREAT WALL (map 1634/4 Lyngstuva): The "Great Wall" is an extensive face of broken rock forming the N side of Reindalen, which stretches from Reindal on the Sørlenangen fjord to Reindal on the Lyngen fjord. This valley provides an easy and delightful passage right across the peninsula. It leads through *Reindal Skar*, which lies between Isvasstind and Spisshorn. Five outliers with many peaks and glaciers shoot off northwards from the Great Wall. Each outlier forms a distinct group of peaks — Vaggastind group, Kløfttind ridge, Kvasstinder, Bjørndalstinder and Rundfjell. The Great Wall can be crossed either at its lowest point SE of Stetind (Stetind Skar) into Raud-tinddalen, or by the high pass between Ilfrastind and Spisshorn (Spisshorn Skar, 1100). The latter provides a pleasant route from Vaggasvatn to Reindal and Sør-lenangen by way of the Spisshorn glacier (Vestre Vaggas-blåisen), but would be an arduous crossing in the S-N direction. The pass E of Spisshorn might be better. Another pass, *Vassdal Skar*, opens access from Reindal in Sørlenangen via Bjørndalen between Rundfjell and Bjørn-dalstinder, across Vassdal Skar and down the Vassdal to Nordlenangen fjord. From Nordlenangen fjord, the magnificent Vaggasdal runs SE to the Troll Valley with snowy mountains all round.

Vaggastind (1398) is a fine snow peak which dominates the Troll Valley. Three glaciers emerge from magnificent cirques to the S of this valley. The 1st recorded asc was made in 1951 by the Oread party — P R Falkner, S G Moore, P Parks and R G Pettigrew, ascending from Reindal Skar, up scree and broken rocks to the W ridge which is 2 miles long and gives pleasant and exposed but not seriously difficult climbing. Its NE ridge was climbed in 1955 by G B Phillips and G M Treacher, a mod diff ascent full of character and highly recommended. The N face was climbed from Blåvasshorn col (MR 714417) in 1956 by R V Adamson, T J C Christie, A P D Ouvry and G H M Wilcox, ascending directly over firm rock at a fairly gentle angle to a long and steep but easy snow slope leading to the top. The same face was climbed again 2 months later by P R Falkner, W J Cartwright and L Pratt, by a route further W (see below).

Vaggastind by NE Ridge — From Vaggasdalen the peak resembles a triangle, the R side of which divides into two, with a high level ridge running west-wards (ascended by the Oread group), and the L side curving towards E cove and partly hidden by the mass of Blåvasshorn. This is the NE ridge. Ascend scree and loose rock on lower half of ridge, leading to terrace (cairn) with magnificent views. Ascend over good rock up ridge to high level terrace, terminating in vertical rock face plunging into Vaggasdal. The rocks above are generally snowed up, leading to snow cwm below summit. Continue up snow arete to summit rocks. Mod diff. The descent by the Great Gully is diff but of considerable charm. Traverse down snow towards Blåvasshorn gap. Move W and down awkward rocks to upper branch of Great Gully, leading down to Vaggastind glacier. Descend through seracs to small rock island in middle of main gully. Continue to glacier. (G M Treacher).

Vaggastind by N Face — This face is divided by 2 great snow couloirs, run-ning up the whole height of the face. The route starts up L couloir and at about $^1/_3$ of the height breaks out L into broader shallower couloir which is followed to top. Straightforward climbing on steep snow slopes all the way. (P R Falkner).

Blåvasshorn (1196) rises S of Vaggasvatn in the upper Troll Valley. It was "discovered" by Showell Styles in

1953 and climbed in 1954 by Rosemary Baker, J C H Davis, P M Hewlett and Gillian E Northfield, climbing the S ridge, which leads from the col between Blåvasshorn and Vaggastind. The same party also climbed the NW ridge. It is a good, interesting and direct route to the top from Vaggasvatn. This route was repeated 1 hour afterwards by J Allen and R G Pettigrew. One hour in a hundred years of mountaineering counts as a dead heat, so it merits mention! The N face gully was climbed in 1955 by G B Phillips and G M Treacher. This gully resembles its Clachaig counterpart in Glencoe, and the character of the climbing is similar.

Blåvasshorn by S Ridge — There is a gully leading direct to the col between Blåvasshorn and Vaggastind, but the route leads up by another gully to its L, from Vaggastind glacier to the col. This gully is loose, but often provides alternative routes of moderate standard on firm rock. The ridge is easy. (J C H Davis).

Blåvasshorn by NW Ridge — From Vaggasvatn, easy climbing leads to a 120 ft wall halfway up ridge. This is the main difficulty, the easiest line being a diagonal crack to R (standard diff). The ridge ends on good rock over a series of pinnacles which are interesting and very exposed on one side. (J C H Davis).

Blåvasshorn by N Face Gully — From Vaggasvatn there are 3 conspicuous details: The 2 steep ridges on L and R skylines, and a dark cleft formed by a twist in the summit mass, with a rake beneath it, running down towards L bottom. From the rake, rock leads down to the upper scree slope, and a band of red rocks cuts across to the middle of the peak from lower L edge to detached slab of red rock in centre of peak on scree. The route starts by this slab. Up lower rocks into upper section of rake. A variety of routes is possible. Up gully until it narrows into a crack with large overhang above. Crack is awkward, as a traverse has to be made onto black slab on L at one point. This is severe when wet. Ascend first snow patch and step from lip of bergschrund up steep rocks. This leads to 2nd snow section and out onto E ridge beneath 2 conspicuous rock pillars resembling Svolværgeita. Up ridge to top. Between twin summits an easy scree slope gives access to Vaggastind glacier. Under good conditions it should be possible to continue above upper snow section over steep rocks to summit, thus adding direct finish. The 1st section is mod diff; end section is very diff to severe. (G M Treacher).

The second outlier from the Great Wall runs between Spisshorn and Vaggas glaciers, and terminates in a peak called *Kløfttind* (MR 698423). It was climbed in 1953 by Showell Styles, D H Jones and J H Welbourn. The E upper branch of Spisshorn glacier was followed right to the snow col between the glaciers, from which the S ridge was climbed up easy rocks in less than 1 hour. The peak has 2 summits, and the lower or N summit was also reached. Its SE ridge was climbed in 1954 by R Baker, J C H Davis, P M Hewlett and G E Northfield. This ridge rises in a series of steep steps, whose faces show few lines of weakness.

Kløfttind by SE Ridge — Follow N side of ridge where angle is continuously steep, but where there are many possible lines. Rock is rough and mainly firm, but there is loose debris on ledges. The difficulty is mainly in route finding. Passages of diff standard. The buttress levels finally into an interesting and airy ridge. Descent by N ridge. The lower part of this ridge is an uninteresting boulder slope facing NE on to Vaggasvatn. Higher up, a col is reached, from which the ridge appears to be composed of unclimbable slabs, but they provide excellent climbing on only diff standard. Surprisingly, they appear much easier when descending. (J C H Davis).

Following the Great Wall westwards, *Spisshorn* (1233) rises splendidly from the wedge between the two limbs of the giant Spisshorn glacier, overlooking Reindal Skar. It resembles the Matterhorn and offers grand climbing. It was climbed in 1952 by Showell Styles and J H Welbourn, ascending the snow and ice slopes beneath its N face to gain its W ridge, which was then followed to the spire-like summit. Difficult climbing is encountered at two places, but for the most part the ridge is not hard, but always interesting. Its E ridge was climbed in 1954 by R Baker, J C H Davis, P M Hewlett and G E Northfield. This is a straightforward ridge, reached from Spisshorn glacier. The N ridge was climbed in 1955 by G B Phillips and G M Treacher, a very attractive route direct from the glacier. Another route by the NE rake was made in 1956 by R V Adamson, T J C Christie, A P D Ouvry and G H M Wilcox.

Spisshorn by N Ridge — The route follows the ridge to R of gully splitting N face. Ascend glacier to a point opposite an island of rock at foot of upper snowfield leading to W ridge. Across bergschrund and up excellent rock to loose scree. Scrambling for some distance until ridge narrows and climbing becomes very pleasing. At least 2 VD pitches. (1) Traverse R over smooth slabs into crack and ascend it until it becomes vertical. Move out L and ascend to perched spike of rock. Balance awkward. (2) Near top a move is made out onto exposed face sweeping down to gully. Ascend directly above on good but doubtful holds. Towards summit, the angle eases off, but is always interesting. (G M Treacher).

Spisshorn by NE Rake — The route leaves Spisshorn glacier at foot of N ridge and curves upwards to L of main NE gully, following rake to top of gully. Traverse R and then 2 harder pitches lead onto fine NE shoulder, pleasantly exposed. A narrow ridge leads to gap in main N ridge, which is followed to top. An enjoyable climb. (T J C Christie).

Ilfrastind (1154) is a minor rock peak on the Great Wall, just W of Spisshorn, climbed in 1955 by D H Jones, Showell Styles and J H Welbourn, by upper western snow slope of Spisshorn glacier and W ridge of Ilfrastind. Half an hour's interesting rock work from the col, and a very fine view.

The third outlier from the Great Wall starts W of Ilfrastind and runs northwards between Rautinddalen and Vaggasdalen, terminating in the Kvasstinder. *Bretind* (1184) is the highest point. Its E ridge which rises from Spisshorn glacier, was climbed in 1954 by R Baker, J C H Davis and P M Hewlett.

Bretind by E ridge — Up by the loose but mainly easy E ridge leading from Spisshorn glacier. It steepens near top. Here, a traverse is made round a tottering pinnacle, up to large sloping platform. Standard diff. The steep wall ahead can be avoided easily to R and behind. The route ends with a series of pinnacles, which look much nastier than they are. Descent by N ridge which leads from col between Bretind and Ruthtind. The rock is good and of brightly varied colours. The col may be reached easily either up a snow gully from Spisshorn glacier or by a gentle boulder slope from Rautinddalen. (J C H Davis).

Ruthtind rises N of Bretind. It was climbed in 1953 by Showell Styles, J H Welbourn and D H Jones by the N face (snow gully beside hanging glacier) and the NW ridge, a very fine climb. Rock climbing of diff standard leads to the first of 3 summits, of which the third is the highest. The peak was traversed, with descent into Rautinddalen. Its S ridge from the E summit was climbed in 1954 by R Baker, J C H Davis and P M Hewlett, an easy and quick climb from the col which separates it from Bretind. Descent by the E ridge from the E summit. The E ridge proper can be gained up an uninteresting boulder slope from the snout of Spisshorn glacier. Later it becomes narrower and more interesting but always easy. *Kvasstind* (1015) (Rødtind in guide, Middagstind in addendum) is a distinctive conical peak of red-brown rock at the junction of Rautinddalen and Vaggasdalen. Climbed in 1953 by D H Jones, Showell Styles and J H Welbourn by way of a 2000 ft snow gully on the N face. From the col above, the S ridge gives very interesting climbing for about half a mile, until a traverse on the L allows the peak's W ridge to be gained a few hundred feet below the summit. A winter asc by the N face was made in 1/1955 by D Aldridge and N C Negri.

The fourth outlier from the Great Wall runs between Vassdalen and Rautinddalen, starting from *Stetind* (921), and then northwards to *Bjørndalstind* (915), called Storrødtind in addendum. The latter was climbed in 1957 by T J C Christie, P M Gerrard and M C Prestige, an easy climb up the N ridge to the corniced summit. The ridge continues to *Rautind* (Rødtind in addendum), which is a small conical peak NE of Rautinddal glacier cirque. Its E ridge was climbed in 1/1955 (also 1st winter asc) by D Aldridge and D Barnes. Mod diff. Danger from windslab during winter.

Finally, the fifth and westernmost outlier is formed by *Rundfjell*, the whale-backed mountain which runs parallel with Sørlenangen fjord and dominates the W coast of Nordlenangen fjord. 1st winter asc by the E face in 12/1954 by D Barnes and N C Negri, up by a snow gully rising from the main corrie to an elevation of 1900 ft, then up indefinite buttress of loose rock to approx 2200 ft. Last 70 ft unclimbed. There are 3 minor peaks, perhaps more accurately described as nunataks, which form the highest part of the ridge connecting Rundfjell with Rautinddalen. 1st winter asc of Nos 1 & 2 in 12/1954 by D Aldridge and No 3 in 2/1955 by D Aldridge and N C Negri.

THE TROMMA RANGES (map 1634/4 Lyngstuva) are the northernmost peaks in Lyngen, E of Nordlenangen fjord and Vaggasdalen. Nordlenangen village is reached by steamer from Tromsø or Lyngseid. There is a walk of about 6—8 hrs from Nordlenangen up Vaggasdalen to the Troll Valley between the Kvasstind—Vaggastind chain and Nordausttind. *Nordausttind* (1132) or Lilleskå is the first peak N of Blåvasshorn. It was climbed from Vaggasvatn in 1952 by M J Barber and J N Hutchinson. Showell Styles and J H Welbourn climbed it in 1952 by a snow gully on the NW side and finally by the W ridge. A new route by the Central Rib was made in 1955 by G B Phillips, W Ritson and G M Treacher.

Nordausttind from Vaggasvatn — From E end of lake, a steep but easy ridge leads to short 3-pitched arete, where rope is necessary. Descent by 1800 ft snow gully on W face. This route of descent is subject to falling rocks and there are 2 rock steps in gully which are insecure. (M J Barber).

Nordausttind by central rib — From Vaggasvatn, the Nordausttind is divided into a series of impressive ribs and buttresses. The central rib is the most impressive of all, and appears vertical from the scree to a pinnacle beneath summit ridge. This is not so, the climbing being at a very comfortable angle throughout. The route offers the most direct ascent to the summit. Mod diff. (G M Treacher).

Stortind (1235) or Storskå rises NE of Lilleskå. Its NW ridge which connects with S Tromma, is cut by a deep cleft called V Col. It was climbed in 1952 by J N Hutchinson, Showell Styles and J H Welbourn by a side glen (V-Cwm) and snow gully from upper Vaggasdalen. Climbed in 1953 by D H Jones, Showell Styles and J H Welbourn by a longer route up the SE ridge of Nordausttind and easy snow and boulder slopes to the final spectacular SW ridge of Stortind. Moderate climb of great scenic interest. A new route by the NW ridge from the V Col was made in 1956 by R V Adamson, T J C Christie and G H M Wilcox. The S face was climbed from Lyngen fjord in 1957 by T J C Christie, P M Gerrard, M C Prestige and D Rhodes, a really splendid climb of over 4000 ft. Due to freak snow conditions, they found the easy SW ridge blocked by a barricade of 30 ft cornices, but they found a gully leading into V cwm from near the summit. There are two fine cwms SE and E of Stortind, which may afford magnificent climbs. The E cwm (Goddeskora) has never been entered.

Stortind by NW Ridge from V Col — The climbing begins a few hundred ft above V Col. Rock very loose and often mossy. Awkward but not V Diff. Traverse L for several pitches to slightly firmer rock E of crest. Diff. Ascend directly on W of couloir, prone to falling rock, to shelf at foot of smooth vertical wall. This is turned by moving to W side of crest. Here the angle decreases, and a large number of delightful pitches on firm gabbro lead up the crest to summit. Descent by SW arete and a long snow gully leading down opposite gap between guardian bluffs. (T J C Christie).

Stortind by S Face — Start at the cove marked Mittalegga between Nordausttind's E ridge and Stortind's SE ridge. Climb snow gully that calves into sea for some 1000 ft, taking R fork. At narrowest part, traverse R onto main southern buttress and climb directly upwards. Follow crest, and after a couple of hundred feet the climbing gets harder. Diff rock steps alternate with exposed knife-edge snow aretes. The climbing is delightful and there are sensational situations throughout. Just before top, one suddenly looks down through 4000 ft of uninterrupted space to eastern cwm between Stortind's SE & NE ridges. (T J C Christie).

Goddeskortind or Lilletårnet is no more than a knoll at the end of a fine ridge which joins Stortind's NW ridge just S of the V Col. It forms the S wall of the Storskål valley. Goddeskortind is unclimbed, but an ascent looks well worth doing.

The *Pinnacle ridge* is a fine ridge which runs NE to Lyngen fjord from the main Tromma ridge between the V Col and Søre Tromma. From the V Col, an easy snow gully gives access to the Storskål valley and thus to the more easterly pinnacles. The Pinnacle Ridge was explored in 1955 by G B Phillips and G M Treacher.

Pinnacle ridge from Tromma ridge: Broken scree and loose rocks lead from Tromma ridge down to Pinnacle Col at foot of 1st pinnacle. The col also provides an easy route into Glacier Cwm, which lies N of Pinnacle Ridge. The 3 pinnacles of *Alpha, Beta and Gamma* afford straightforward climbing with gabbro pitches. Mod. diff. The *Red Slab Pinnacle* is highest point on ridge. Diff. Its final tower is v diff. From Gamma pinnacle, down into gap and up red slab on good holds. From a distance the slab looks impossible but is very pleasant. Traverse carefully over loose boulders to ridge. Final tower: Ascend edge on good holds to terrace. Traverse across face and round into vertical crack, and so to top. *Grandstand* provides a straightforward ascent from needle gap. It leads on to remaining pinnacles and offers superb grandstand views on *Nantlle Needle*, a magnificent pinnacle overhanging Storskål valley. It resembles the Campaniles in the Dolomites. On its N side are 2 vertical faults leading to boulder-strewn terrace, by anvil-shaped minor pinnacle. Climb R crack to terrace and move R to foot of Flake Crack. The first 12 ft or so are overhanging, and steep climbing leads to Flake. Ascend behind Flake and step across onto N wall. This is vertical, and route inclines towards R edge. The rock in most places is most treacherous, and on the 1st asc the use of a loose foothold was found essential without a traverse away from edge. The situation throughout is superb. The Flake Crack and the N wall are very severe (300 ft). From the summit, two 60 ft abseils down W face lead to Pinnacle Gap. From Grandstand, continue over ridge to *Glyntind*, a curious collection of perched pinnacles. Traverse L by good flake and up wall. Ridge terminates with 4 pinnacles, the *Four Apostles* (John, Luke, Matthew and Mark), the first and last from Glyntind being pointed, and the middle two having flat summits and smooth sides. The climbing on John and Luke is straightforward and moderate. Matthew and Mark are unclimbed and would be best approached from Apostles' Col at the extreme end of the ridge between Rappgamtind and the end pinnacle. From Luke, the climbing would be severe. (G M Treacher).

Rappgamtind or Stortårnet rises at the end of the Pinnacle Ridge among some of the wildest and most spectacular sceneries in Lyngen. Its SW face was climbed in 1957 by T J C Christie and P M Gerrard.

Rappgamtind by SW Face — From V Col, descend to just below Nantlle Needle, where a gully leads NW for 1000 ft to Apostles Col under Rappgamtind. Its SW face ("The Cathedral") looks fearsome, but is much easier than it appears. From col, traverse R and climb face just S of main tower feature. Diff. Loose rock to begin with, but it improves. One comes on to summit ridge almost unexpectedly and is deprived of final hard climb which hitherto appears unavoidable. Summit ridge is followed easily to top. (T J C Christie).

Hattetind or Søre Tromma rises between the V Col and Midtre Tromma. It was climbed in 1955 by G B Phillips and G M Treacher, when they made a N-S traverse of the Tromma ridge. From the snow cap, the rocks overhanging Glacier Cwm and Storskål Valley were followed to the V Col. The S face from the V Col was climbed in 1956 by R V Adamson and T J C Christie.

The N face of Hattetind (Photo: T J C Christie)

Hattetind by S Face — From V Col, traverse diagonally L until rock slabs are met. Large number of interesting pitches of diff and v diff standard up these rocks, which are clean and firm. A traverse is made just below first shoulder onto main S face, where easy climbing leads to snow-cap and summit. Magnificent views in all directions, incl Jiekkevarri ice-cap. (T J C Christie).

Tverrbakktind (1390) or Midtre Tromma is the highest point on the ridge. It was climbed in 1954 by J Allen, K Griffiths, J Hutchinson and R G Pettigrew by the S ridge from a col which was reached from Vaggasdalen. Descent by the same route. In 1955 the N ridge from Terminal Col was climbed by G M Treacher. Attempts have also been made on the NW ridge, but this is only feasible under favourable snow conditions.

Between Tverrbakktind and *Storurdtind* (1219) or Nordre Tromma, the ridge leads around Terminal Cwm (Bruelvdalen), which provides a passage between Nordlenangen and the cwms of E Tromma, as well as the Peppartind region. Storurdtind was climbed in 1954 by J Allen and R G Pettigrew from NW Tromma. The very jagged ridge running eastward from the summit, was traversed by G M Treacher in 1955, and the E peak of the same ridge was reached from Terminal Col by T J C Christie and P M Gerrard in 1957.

Stor-Galten (1224) or Stortind is the most northerly major peak of the Tromma range. A complete N-S traverse from Stor-Galten to V Col was made in 1955 by G M Treacher, a very fine expedition of 9 hrs, with superb views in all directions. G B Phillips left Treacher at the first col to traverse S through all the cwms E of the Tromma ridge.

Peppartind (1253) rises E of the Tromma ridge but is connected to it by a ridge which joins the main network between Terminal Col and Storurdtind. Climbed in 1899 by G Hastings and E Hogrenning, by the SW ridge from Peppartind glacier, an interesting climb on firm rock, with a magnificent precipice on the L. The NE ridge which is a grand arete of steep rock, was climbed in 1953 by D H Jones, Showell Styles and J H Welbourn. Starting from the E side of the Peppartind glacier snout, the ridge was gained and followed without great difficulty to the big cleft between it and the final wall, where a slight descent of the snow gully on the W enabled a lodgement on the wall to be effected. Loose troughs and exposed traverses led to the crest about 100 ft S of the summit. (Showell Styles).

THE SKJERVØY REGION

This region covers the islands and outer mainland N of Lyngen, best approached by coastal express steamer from Bergen to the fishing village of Skjervøy, a journey of 4 nights. Local fjord steamers will take you to any fishing village in the area, or you may hire small fishing boats to take you to any out-of-the-way island. Camping is a necessity almost anywhere. Starting from the Arctic Highway, these is a bus service to Hamneid (18 km) and boat service to Skjervøy (1 hr).

ARNØY ISLAND (maps 1635/3 Karlsøy & 1635/2 Arnøy) lies just N of Lyngen, reached by boat in an hour from Skjervøy or in 3 hrs from Nordlenangen in Lyngen. The island contains a number of fine mountains rising to 4000 ft, but it has only been visited by few climbing parties, two in 1957 — the Cambridge expedition in July and the Young Unitarians expedition in August. The following notes are based on reports from the two leaders — T J C Christie of Cambridge and K C Treacher of the Young Unitarians. The best places to land are Årviks and, Unitarians. The best places to land are Årviksand, Akkarvik and Arnøyhavn, which have regular boat connections with Skjervøy, as well as shops, also telephone and post offices.

The Arnøy NE Group (map 1635/2 Arnøy) is bounded by the coast and the valleys of Tjyvdalen and Nord-Rekvikdalen. *Tjyvtind* (693) is the jagged ridge forming the N wall of Tjyvdalen. 1st asc 7/1957 by T J C Christie and P M Gerrard, traversing SE-NW. Loose rock. *Arnøy-høgda* (1168) rises N of Isbakkdalen. Its heavily corniced

SE ridge was climbed from the Langtind Col in 7/1957 by T J C Christie, P M Gerrard and D Rhodes. Both the NW ridge and the N ridge from Tarenesfjell should make excellent climbs. The W face of the NW ridge was climbed in 8/1957 by E H Hutton, L Noble and R Thompson. The buttress to the immediate L of the central gully provides a climb of 1400 ft with many fine pitches on excellent coarse rock. Very diff, but very severe on crux. The *Delta Needle* (200 ft) is a slender and dramatic looking obelisk at the end of the SE ridge, the biggest of 6 pinnacles. The SE ridge was traversed to the gap leading to the Needle on 8/1957 by P Adams, R Bambridge and R Mason. They reported that a possible route might go up the SE side of the Needle, or it can be gained from the slopes beneath it, leading from Lauksletta on the E. The unclimbed *Rødhetta* stands NE of Arnøyhøgda, with a very spectacular E face. Its N ridge appears to offer the only feasible route, but it might perhaps also be tried from Arnøyhøgda's N ridge. It would still provide a hard climb. *Brattfjell* (1053) or Slettfjell, is a large broad-backed peak N of Rødhetta, climbed in 1937 by Norwegians. Its S ridge was climbed in 7/1957 by T J C Christie and M C Prestige, descending by the narrow E ridge to *Flutind* (833). Descent into the W corrie. *Svarttind* (933) or Onsdagstind is a peak on the continuation of the NW ridge of Arnøyhøgda. 1st asc 7/1957 by T J Christie, M C Prestige and D Rhodes, up by the S ridge, down by the N ridge. Its W side was climbed in 8/1957 by B Bambridge, A Rogers and K Treacher. There is still room for good routes on sound rock.

Arnøyhøgda by W Face Route — The W face of the NW ridge is divided by wide gully with broad and formidable cliff on R and a ridge on L, the lower end of which is broad and spatulate, coming lower down the scree than another rib of rock. The buttress to immediate L of central gully provides the climb. Keep to R edge. The crux occurs in the first third of the climb and is exposed: The leader cannot be adequately protected. When 1400 ft is done, 300 ft of ridge leads to top, a deep gap being turned on L. The ridge would be serious under heavy snow. (K C Treacher).

The Arnøy SE Group (map 1635/2 Arnøy): *Singeltind* (741) or Grunnfjordtind rises on the SE extremity of the island. Its easy N ridge was climbed in 7/1957 by T J C Christie. *Skartind* (768) is situated NW of Singeltind. 1st asc 8/1957 by R Bambridge, R Mason, A Rogers and N Williamson. *Tågtind* (867) is a conspicuous peak E of Grunnfjorddalen, climbed from the N in 1957 by T J C Christie and M C Prestige. *Lyngnestind* (878) is a ridge with 6 peaks E of Lang fjord. It was traversed N-S in 7/1957 by T J C Christie. *Fosstind* (880) is a beautiful peak E of Lang fjord. 1st asc 7/1957 by T J C Christie and P M Gerrard by the N ridge from Foss col, nearly 800 ft

Midnight Sun scene in Kongsfjord, West Spitsbergen (Photo: Bolinder)

SVALBARD (SPITSBERGEN)

Svalbard — or Spitsbergen — is a large group of Arctic islands, covering an area of 61.300 sq km, situated only 600 miles below the North Pole. It was discovered by Norwegian fishermen in 1194 and rediscovered by Sir Hugh Willoughby in 1533 and by Willem Barents in 1596. The Russians claim it was discovered by Alexei Khimkow in 1743. By the Paris Treaty of 1920, Norway was given the sovereignty over Svalbard, and the entire group is now Norwegian territory.

West Spitsbergen is the largest island, 40.000 sq km, and the only island where people live all the year round. Longyearbyen in the Ice fjord has 1000 inhabitants, and Ny-Ålesund in King's Bay has 70. The Norwegian governor resides in Longyearbyen, which also has a permanent radio station. There are three Russian mining settlements in the Ice fjord. The North-East Land (Nordaustlandet) of 17.000 sq km is entirely uninhabited.

Svalbard is visited by several cruise vessels during the Midnight Sun season, but the usual route is either by air from Oslo or Bergen to Tromsø, or by coastal express steamer from Bergen to Tromsø in 4 nights. From Oslo by train to Fauske and express bus to Tromsø in 3 nights. The Troms S/S Co of Tromsø operates a series of sailings each summer by the ms "Lyngen" between Tromsø and Svalbard, calling at Longyearbyen and Ny-Ålesund, a journey of 3 nights each way. The coal freighters which sail between Norway and Svalbard do n o t accept passengers.

There are no formalities or restrictions when travelling on a round trip to Svalbard, and no permit is required for shore excursions, but as there is no hotel accommodation on the islands, visitors cannot stay ashore without a permit. This can be obtained in advance from the coal mining company — Store Norske Spitsbergen Kulkompani A/S, Tordenskjoldsgate 6, Oslo. Visitors wishing to take their own guns and ammunition to Svalbard, must first obtain a permit from Den Sivile Våpenkontroll, Akersgaten 44, Oslo. Provisions and bread can be bought from the mining company's shops at Longyearbyen and Ny-Ålesund.

The climate is surprisingly mild in summer, influenced by the Gulf Stream and the Midnight Sun. The sun never dips below the horizon from April 21 to August 24. The clear air and brilliant sunshine against a background of white snow, black peaks and blue fjords provide an unforgettable experience, and there is no equivalent in lower latitudes. The opportunity for taking spectacular movies and snapshots is unlimited.

The Svalbard fauna comprises polar bears, blue fox, white fox and reindeer. Experiments have been made to introduce musk ox into the Advent Valley, and they seem to thrive. There are about 30 different bird species including ptarmigan. In the sea there are whales, seals and walrus. The flora comprises about 130 species of plants. There are no trees, only two bush species. The richest vegetation is found below the bird sanctuaries. From a scenic point of view, Svalbard provides a grand mixture of fjords, mountains and glaciers. Over half of it is covered by eternal snow and ice, many glaciers stretching right down to the sea. As a result of the milder temperatures during recent years, Svalbard is undergoing rapid changes. Several glaciers have retreated enormously, for instance the Horn glacier has retracted about 3 miles since 1936. Before the war, ice blocked the Svalbard approaches until about August, but now the shipping lanes are open in May.

There are several virgin peaks which have never been climbed. The highest peaks are *Newtontoppen* of 5630 ft and *Hornsundtind* of 4700 ft. The snow line lies at about 950 ft. In summer, the western valleys are easily accessible, and the rivers afford good fishing — with fine catches of "Spitsbergen salmon".

Svalbard has been an important stepping stone for historical polar expeditions — with famous explorers such as S A Andree, Roald Amundsen, Lincoln Ellsworth, Admiral Richard E Byrd, General Umberto Nobile, Sir George Wilkins and Carl Ben Eielson. There has also been a number of scientific expeditions, most of them combined with rock climbing and glacier exploration.

Professor B M Keilhau was the leader of the first Norwegian expedition in 1827. Several Swedish and German expeditions visited Svalbard between 1850 and 1880. V H Gatty and A Nathorst made ascents in the Ice fjord area in 1895. The Hornsundtinder were explored in 1896 by E J Garwood and T Battye. Lord Conway explored the Nordenskiøld glacier in 1897. The Prince of Monaco and A H Isachsen surveyed Cross Bay and Liliehøk glacier in 1907. J M Wordie and party visited Bille fjord in 1919 and 1920. The universities of Oxford and Cambridge have sent a great number of expeditions to Svalbard since 1921. Other countries incl USA have also sent parties to Svalbard since the war.

18 survey maps are planned to cover the Svalbard islands, but only 7 are available as yet, covering the SW sector from South Cape to Ice fjord. No maps exist of the territory N of latitude 79, nor of the Barents island, Edge island, Kong Karls Land and Kvitøya. Available maps can be bought from the Norwegian National Tourist Office, 20 Pall Mall, London SW 1.

Miscellaneous

LODGES, HOSTELS & HOTELS

THE ROGALAND — SETESDAL
HIGHLANDS

	Beds	Rooms	Altitude Ft.	M	Maps
Ådneram Lodge, Fidjeland	30x	5	1960	600	K 480
Årdal Pensjonat, Årdal (tel. Årdal 3a)	15	7	—	—	E 690
Bjåen Fjellstove, Byklehei (Bjåi 2)	20	10	2950	900	K 480
Bjørnevass Lodge, Oveinang, Bykle.........	14x	2	2400	740	»
Blåfjell hut, Jøsenfjord (no staff)	12x	3	3470	1060	»
Bleskestad hut, Roaldkvam (no meals)	10x	2	1960	600	»
Bossbu hut (unstaffed)	8x	2	3400	104	»
Bråtveit farm (meals only, no rooms)	—	—	325	100	»
Bratteland hut, Bykle (closed down)	—	—	1850	565	»
Breifonn — see hotel list and YHA list	—	—	1640	500	»
Brekke hut, Ålgård (Ålgård 6a) (no meals) ..	22x	4	800	250	D 260
Bykle — see hotel list and YHA list	—	—	2085	635	K 480
Fisketjønn hut, Ålgård (no staff)	36x	8	1960	600	D 260
Flateland hut, Oveinang, Bykle	14	7	1310	400	K 480
Førrevass — closed down, see Undeknut	—	—	3280	1000	K 480
Gaukhei hut, Granheim	28x	7	2725	840	»
Granheim Pensjonat, Granheim (Langeid 4) .	20	2	2750	840	»
Håhellern hut, Rysstad (no meals)	4	1	2860	875	»
Haugen farm, Øvre Sirdal	16x	3	1800	550	»
Haukeli seter, Haukeliseter (Haukeliseter 1) .	24	18	3220	986	»
Helle — see YHA list	—	—	2085	635	»
Hovden hut, Byklehei	90x	15	2400	740	D 260
Jørpeland Gjestgiveri, Jørpeland	16	10	—	—	»
Kvandal hut, Roaldkvam (no meals)	10x	2	2300	700	K 480
Kvilldal hut, Kvilldal (Kvilldal 6a)	12x	4	325	100	J 450
Kvina hut, Øvre Sirdal...................	18x	4	2290	700	K 480
Ljosland hut, Åseral	50x	10	1700	520	»
Lysebotn Lodge, Lysebotn	18x	8	50	15	E 447
Lysebu Lodge, Lysebotn	36x	6	2625	800	K 480
Mostøl hut, Bråtveit (no meals)	18x	3	1960	600	J 450
Nesflaten — see hotel list and YHA list	—	—	325	100	K 480
Nilsebu hut, Årdal.......................	36x	6	2300	700	E 447
Ørekvam hut, Jøsenfjord (no meals)	12x	2	1640	500	J 450
Øyulvsbu hut, Rysstad (no staff)	12x	2	2860	875	K 480
Prekestol Lodge, Jørpeland	70x	20	815	260	J 402
Roaldkvam farm (meals only, no rooms).....	—	—	325	100	K 480
Røldal — see hotel list and YHA list	—	—	1640	500	»
Rysstad: Helle youth hostel, Rysstad	25	5	985	300	»
Rysstad Pensjonat, Rysstad	14	7	985	300	»
Salmelid hut, Fjotland	12x	3	1640	500	»
Sand — see hotel list and YHA list	—	—	—	—	J 450
Sandeid — see YHA list	—	—	—	—	E 986
Sandsa Lodge, Jøsenfjord	40x	12	1960	600	J 450
Sandvatn hut, Roaldskvam (no meals)	8x	2	2950	900	»
Sinnes: Sirdølen youth hostel	27	4	1800	500	K 480
Stranddal Lodge, Kvilldal	28x	7	3100	950	J 450
Suldal: Hårenes Pensjonat, Suldal	13	8	325	100	»
Trodlatysdal hut, Årdal (no meals)	9	2	260	80	»
Ullatun hut, Ulladal (no staff)	16x	5	320	100	J 450
Undeknut hut, Førrevass (no staff)	12	2	3280	100	K 480
Valle: Vallarheim hut, Valle (Valle 8)	24	14	985	300	K 480
Viglesdal hut, Årdal (no meals)	12x	2	1300	400	E 447

(x) Owned by DNT or associated clubs.
(y) Privately owned, but DNT members are admitted at reduced rates.

FOLGEFONN GLACIER

Herand Gjestgiveri, Herand 20	11	—	—	E 275
Mauranger: Sundal Gjestgiveri, Mauranger ..18	10	—	—	»
Odda — see hotel list and YHA list ....—	—	—	—	»
Utne — see hotel list ....—	—	—	—	»

HARDANGER MOUNTAIN PLATEAU

Åan Lodge, Dagali near Geilo 14y	6	3150	960	J 400
Bjoreidal Lodge, Eidfjord Øvre 43	15	3740	1130	»
Breifonn — see hotel list and YHA list......—	—	1640	500	K 480
Brøstrud Pensjonat, Brøstrud—Uvdal 15	7	2625	800	J 400
Dagali Pensjonat, Dagali near Geilo 17	9	2820	860	»
Dyranut Fjellstove, Eidfjord Øvre 15	5	4060	1240	»
Dyranut hut, Eidfjord Øvre 50y	10	4060	1240	»
Eidfjord — see hotel list and YHA list .....—	—	—	—	»
Eidfjord Øvre: Eidfjord Gjestgiveri 20	10	100	30	J 400
Fagerheim Fjellstove, Krekja 60	30	3840	1170	»
Finse Lodge, Finse 100x	32	4010	1222	»
Fossli Hotel, Vøringfoss 100	62	2460	700	»
Geilo — see hotel list and YHA list ....—	—	2625	794	»
Hallingskeid Fjellstove, Hallingskeid 25y	15	3640	1110	E 345
Hallaskard Lodge, Eidfjord Øvre 20	8	3280	1000	J 400
Halne Fjellstove, Haugastøl 23	9	3740	1130	»
Haugastøl Kafe, Haugastøl 6	2	3240	982	»
Haukeli Seter, Haukeliseter 52	24	3220	986	»
Hedlo Lodge, Eidfjord Øvre 30y	11	3120	950	»
Hein seter, Uvdal 10y	4	3500	1070	»
Hellevassbu hut (no meals) 6	1	—	—	»
Hjølmo farm, Eidfjord Øvre 6	3	980	300	»
Instestøl hut, Vøringfoss 18x	3	2880	880	»
Kalhovd Lodge, Tinn 90x	10	3280	1100	»
Kinsarvik Pensjonat, Kinsarvik 19	13	—	—	»
Kongsbergseter YH, Tinn — see YHA list .. —	—	—	—	»
Krekja hut, Haugastøl 64x	12	3770	1150	»
Lågaros hut (unstaffed) 20x	7	4270	1300	»
Litlos Lodge, Espe 30x	8	3800	1250	»
Lofthus — see hotel list and YHA list ......—	—	—	—	»
Mårbu hut, Uvdal 50x	10	3770	1086	»
Maurset Hotel, Vøringfoss 50y	29	2570	800	»
Midtleger youth hostel, Midtleger 6	2	—	—	»
Mogen hut, Møsvatn 50x	7	3020	920	»
Møsvatn Lodge, Møsvatn 20	11	3020	920	E 725
Odda — see hotel list and YHA list ....—	—	—	—	J 400
Ørterstøl Lodge, Geilo 18	7	3675	1120	»
Rauhellern Lodge, Haugastøl 50x	15	4590	1400	»
Reinsnos seter, Skarde 4	2	2000	650	»
Rembesdal seter (unstaffed)................20x	4	3050	930	»
Rjukan — see hotel list and YHA list.......—	—	980	300	»
Sandhaug Lodge, Vøringfoss 60x	25	3800	1250	»
Seljestad — see hotel list ....—	—	1960	600	»
Skiftesjøen hut, Vøringfoss (closed down) ...—	—	3930	1200	»
Solheimstul seter, Uvdal 50	26	3280	1000	»
Stavali hut, Kinsarvik 28x	7	3500	1070	»
Tore hut (unstaffed) 12x	3	4420	1346	»
Tråastøl hut, Eidfjord Øvre................12	3	4060	1240	»
Tuva seter, Skurdal near Geilo 20	9	3930	1200	»
Ustaoset — see hotel list and YHA list......—	—	3250	1000	»
Uvdal: Dagsvind Pensjonat, Uvdal 15	6	1640	500	»
Valldal seter, Røldal 34x	8	2300	740	»
Vasstulan Fjellstove, Brøstrud 18	7	3600	1100	»
Vasstulan seter, Brøstrud..................50	20	3600	1100	»
Viveli farm, Eidfjord Øvre.................12y	5	2870	880	»
Vøringfoss — see hotel list................—	—	2460	700	»

MJØLFJELL RANGES

Flåm — see hotel list ....—	—	—	—	E 270
Gudvangen — see hotel list and YHA list ... —	—	—	—	»
Mjølfjell — see hotel list and YHA list .....—	—	2058	627	»
Oppheim: Stalheim Pension, Oppheim 20	10	980	300	E 994
Reimegrend youth hostel, Reimegrend (J430) 30	8	1525	465	E 270
Stalheim Hotel, Stalheim (J500)............162	99	1250	375	E 994
Ulvik — see hotel list ....—	—	—	—	E 935
Vatnahalsen — see hotel list and YHA list .. —	—	2670	811	E 994
Vinje Hotel, Voss (J500) 38	22	980	300	E 994
Voss — see hotel list and YHA list ....—	—	186	57	E 992

(x) Owned by DNT or associated clubs.
(y) Privately owned, but DNT members are admitted art educed rates.

FINSE—BYGDIN MOUNTAIN RANGES

	Beds	Rooms	Altitude Ft.	M	Maps
Aurland — see hotel list and YHA list	—	—	—	—	E 270
Bergsjø Hotel, Ål	70	44	3610	1100	E 385
Bjøberg Fjellstove, Hemsedal	27	16	3325	1013	E 210
Bjordalsbu (unstaffed)	22x	3	5100	1575	E 210
Breistøl Fjellstove, Hegg—Hemsedal	45	25	3350	1024	E 245
Finse Lodge, Finse	100x	32	4010	1222	E 345
Gamlestuen seter, Nystova	30	15	3280	1000	E 245
Geiterygg Lodge, Finse (J300)	45x	16	3940	1200	E 120
Gullhaug Pensjonat, Hovet (Hol 1004)	25	14	1900	600	E 330
Hallingskeid Fjellstove and YH	25	15	3640	1110	E 345
Hydal seter, Hemsedal	8y	3	3110	950	E 385
Iungsdal Lodge, Ål	35x	14	3670	1120	E 210
Kljåen seter, Hemsedal	4y	2	3230	1011	E 965
Øvstebø Fjellstove and YH, Aurland	40y	10	2625	800	E 120
Øvstebø hut and YH, Aurland	40y	15	2710	825	E 120
Raggsteindal Lodge, Hovet (Hol 1012a)	60y	31	3280	1000	E 210
Reine seter, Leveld—Ål (Leveld 12)	11y	3	3900	1188	E 385
Smådal seter, Grindaheim	4y	1	3610	1100	»
Steinbergdal hut, Aurland	17y	2	3640	1110	E 120
Steine Lodge, Aurland (Vassbygdi 6a)	21y	10	120	35	»
Storeskar Fjellstove, Hemsedal	16	10	2920	960	E 385
Vats Turistheim, Leveld (Leveld 5)	24	12	2460	750	»

JOTUNHEIMEN

	Beds	Rooms	Altitude Ft.	M	Maps
Bessheim Lodge, Bessheim (Vågå 3)	56	38	3160	963	E 775
Bøverkind seter, Bøverdal (Lom 41)	20	10	3440	1050	E 870
Bøvertun Lodge, Bøverdal (Lom 30)	50y	26	3180	950	»
Bygdin Hotel, Bygdin (Bygdin 3)	70y	50	3490	1065	E 810
Eidsbugaren Hotel, Eidsbugaren	65	40	3480	1062	E 305
Elveseter Hotel, Bøverdal (Bøverdal 39)	85	52	2290	700	E 550
Fanaråk hut, Turtagrø	16x	5	6790	2069	E 870
Fortun tourist station, Fortun (Fortun 12a)	23	12	2625	735	K 430
Gjendebu Lodge, Gjendebu (Lom 21a)	77x	24	3250	990	E 305
Gjendesheim Lodge, Gjendesheim	130x	30	3250	990	E 775
Glitterheim Lodge Glitterheim (Lom 35)	72x	23	4540	1384	E 305
Haug seter, Bygdin	50y	20	3000	925	E 775
Hind seter, Hindseter	43	30	3120	950	»
Høydal seter, Bøverdal	34y	18	3000	925	E 870
Jotunheimen Hotel, Bøverdal (Lom 45)	38	20	3120	950	»
Juvass Lodge, Bøverdal (Lom 15b)	70	33	6030	1840	E 550
Krossbu tourist station, Krossbu (Lom 10)	40	20	4975	1365	E 870
Leirvassbu Lodge, Bøverdal	100y	56	4600	1400	E 305
Memurubu Lodge, Memurubu	40y	12	3280	1000	E 305
Nørdstedal seter, Fortun	29x	10	3280	1002	E 870
Olavsbu hut, Eidsbugaren (unstaffed)	30x	7	4658	1450	E 305
Randsverk tourist station, Randsverk	28	14	2625	735	E 995
Røysheim tourist station, Bøverdal (Lom 31)	56	27	1680	510	E 550
Sikkilsdal seter, Vinstra	58	26	3339	1017	E 775
Skagastøl hut, Turtagrø (unstaffed)	6	1	6230	1900	E 870
Skogadalsbø Lodge, Skogadalsbøen	57x	16	2740	834	»
Sota seter, Nordberg	30y	13	2600	750	E 793
Spiterstul Lodge, Spiterstul (Lom 25b)	110	42	3610	1100	E 305
Torfinnsbu hut, Torfinnsbu	30y	15	3480	1062	»
Turtagrø Hotel, Turtagrø (Turtagrø 1)	80	44	2950	930	E 870
Tyin Hotel, Tyin (Tyin 9 or 10)	75	44	3550	1080	E 965
Tyinholmen Hotel, Tyin	60y	40	3550	1080	E 305
Tyinstøl Lodge, Tyin (Tyin 6)	25	10	3550	1080	E 245
Valdresflya YH, Bygdin — see YHA list	30	5	4250	1400	E 995
Vetti farm, Farnes	14y	7	1035	317	E 870

JOSTEDAL GLACIER

	Beds	Rooms	Altitude Ft.	M	Maps
Åmot farm, Jølster	6y	2	1310	400	K 430
Arentzbu hut, Jostedal	8x	2	3250	900	»
Bødal seter, Lodal (unstaffed)	12x	6	1700	580	»
Fåberg farm, Gjerde—Jostedal	6y	4	1120	344	»
Fjellsli seter, Skjolden	8y	3	2750	840	»
Fjerland — see hotel list	—	—	—	—	»
Flatbre hut, Fjerland (unstaffed)	5x	1	3280	1000	»
Fortun tourist station, Fortun (Fortun 12a)	23	12	2625	735	»

(x) Owned by DNT or associated clubs.
(y) Privately owned, but DNT members are admitted at reduced rates.

	Beds	Rooms	Altitude Ft.	M	Maps
Grotli Hotel (and YH), Grotli (Grotli 1) 75	40	2952	900	»	
Hjelle Hotel, Stryn (Hjelledal 5)............	30	20	100	30	»
Jostedal tourist station, Jostedal (Gjerde 2) .	30y	16	810	250	»
Loen — se hotel list......................	—	—	—	—	»
Lunde farm, Jølster	6y	2	750	230	»
Marifjøra: Tørvis Hotel, Marifjøra	51	32	—	—	»
Nørdstedal seter, Fortun (E810)	29x	10	3280	1002	»
Olden — see hotel list and YHA list	—	—	—	—	»
Pollfoss tourist station, Pollfoss (Lom 606a) .	35	27	2290	700	»
Skåla tower, Loen (stone hut, unstaffed).....	3	1	6360	1938	»
Skei Hotel (and YH), Jølster (Jølster 7)	32	24	657	200	»
Skjolden Hotel (and YH), Skjolden	32	20	—	—	»
Skridulaup hut, Skjåk (unstaffed)	4x	1	3050	930	»
Sota seter, Skjåk (E 793)	30y	13	2600	750	»
Sperle farm, Myklemyr—Jostedal	4	3	570	175	»
Stryn — see hotel list and YHA list	—	—	—	—	»
Styggevass hut, Jostedal (unstaffed)	14x	4	3800	1163	»
Sunndal seter, Stryn	9y	2	1500	550	»
Tunga seter, Veitastrond—Hafslo	8y	3	250	45	»
Turtagrø Hotel, Turtagrø (E870)	80	44	3250	900	»
Vetledal seter, Stryn (unstaffed)	4	1	1970	600	»
Videseter Hotel, Videseter (Skåra 3)	40	25	1970	600	»
Vigdalstøl (unstaffed)....................	6 x	2	2710	825	»

ÅLFOT GLACIER

	Beds	Rooms	Ft.	M	Maps
Hyen: Rønnekleiv Pensjonat, Hyen	14	8	—	—	B 29/30
Hyen: Straumes Pensjonat, Hyen	10	7	—	—	»
Svelgen: Sandnes Kafe, Svelgen	6	4	—	—	»

SUNNMØRE

	Beds	Rooms	Ft.	M	Maps
Ålesund — see hotel and YHA lists	—	—	—	—	B 27/28
Bjørke: Tyssheim Pension	10	5	—	—	C 28/29
Djupvass Hotel — see hotel list (Geiranger) .	—	—	3380	1030	K 430
Eidsdal, near Geiranger — see YHA list	—	—	—	—	»
Fokkhaugstova, Stordal	40x	11	1970	600	D 27/28
Friisbua, Nordberg (unstaffed)	4x	1	4266	1300	»
Geiranger — see hotel list	—	—	—	—	C 28/29
Hellesylt — see hotel and YHA lists	—	—	1—	—	»
Kaldhus seter, Tafjord	35y	11	970	600	D 27/28
Norangdal Tourist Station, Øye	24	10	980	300	C 28/29
Ørsta — see hotel and YHA lists	—	—	—	—	B 27/28
Øye — Union Hotel	90	60	—	—	C 28/29
Patchell hut, Øye (unstaffed)	2x	1	2625	800	»
Pyttbua, Stuguflåten	11x	4	3775	1150	D 27/28
Reindal seter, Tafjord.....................	34x	7	2400	700	»
Stordal: Vinje Gjestgiveri	15	7	—	—	C 26/27
Stranda — see hotel list	—	—	—	—	C 28/29
Straumgjerde: Bergheim Gjestgiveri	15	7	—	—	»
Sykkylven: Fjellseter hut	20	8	1475	450	»
Sykkylven Hotel, Sykkylven	19	10	—	—	»
Syvdsbotn: Almklovs Pension	24	12	—	—	B 27/28
Tafjord: Kvilhaug Gjesteheim	22	65	65	20	D 27/28
Torsbu (unstaffed)	10x	3	4260	1300	»
Trollstig Hotel, Åndalsnes	40	21	2790	850	»
Tunga seter, Stuguflåten - no accommodat. .	—	—	3215	980	»
Urke — see hotel list	—	—	—	—	C 28/29
Vakkerstøylen, Stuguflåten	20x	4	2855	870	D 27/28
Valldal — see hotel and YHA lists	—	—	—	—	»
Veltdal hut, Tafjord (unstaffed)	4	1	3935	1200	»
Volda — see hotel list....................	—	—	—	—	B 27/28
Ytterdal: Eides Pension, Eidsdal...........	10	6	—	—	D 27/28

ROMSDAL

	Beds	Rooms	Ft.	M	Maps
Åndalsnes — see hotel and YHA lists	—	—	—	—	G 220
Eidsvåg: Sverdrup Gjestgiveri, Eidsvåg	14	10	—	—	D 25/26
Eikesdal — see Finnset or Reitan	—	—	100	30	K 400
Finnset tourist station, Eikesdal............	22y	14	610	185	»
Hen Gjestgiveri, Hen	12	8	510	156	G 220
Hoemsbu, Eikesdal	36	11	100	30	K 400
Lesjaskog — see hotel and YHA lists	—	—	2050	625	»
Måsvassbu, Molde	28x	4	1790	545	G 220

(x) Owned by DNT or associated clubs.
(y) Privately owned, but DNT members are admitted at reduced rates.

	Beds	Rooms	Altitude Ft.	M	Maps
Molde — see hotel and YHA lists .... —	—	—	—	C 26/27
Nauste: Eira Pension, Nauste 8	6	—	—	D 25/26
Reitan Pension, Eikesdal 22	16	100	30	K 400
Stuguflåten Gjestgiveri, Stuguflåten 25	18	1740	530	»
Sunndalsøra — see hotel list .... —	—	—	—	»
Tredal — see hotel list (Sunndalsøra) .... —	—	—	—	»
Verma: Kylling Kvarter, Verma 12	8	895	273	D 27/28

NORDMØRE—TROLLHEIMEN

	Beds	Rooms	Altitude Ft.	M	Maps
Ålvundeid: Buvang Pension 10	6	65	20	E 2/526
Fale Gård, Fale 25	17	330	100	E 27/28
Gjevilvass Lodge, Oppdal 52y	—	2390	728	D 380
Gjøra Farm, Gjøra 9	7	655	200	D 380
Grindal hut, Berkåk .... —	—	—	—	D 520
Innerdal Lodge, Ålvundeid 28	13	1310	400	E 25/26
Jøldal Lodge, Grindal 43y	—	2470	754	D 520
Kårvatn Lodge, Todal 28	14	685	208	E 27/28
Kåsa hut, Lønset (unstaffed) 16y	2	2035	620	»
Kristiansund — see hotel and YHA lists .... —	—	—	—	D 25/26
Lønset: Elvelund Gjestgiveri 12	6	1705	520	D 380
Oppdal — see hotel and YHA lists .... —	—	1790	545	D 380
Rauberg hut, Sunndalsøra 8x	—	3610	1100	
Renndøl seter, Ålvundeid 20	8	1310	400	E 27/28
Storli hut, Lønset 12y	—	2130	650	D 380
Sunndalsøra — see hotel list .... —	—	—	—	E 25/26
Todal Lodge, Todalen 35x	12	165	50	E 27/28
Trollheim Lodge, Rindal 50y	—	1740	531	D 520
Vassli farm, Lønset 20	10	2050	625	
Vognill: Stensheim Pension, Vognill 25	11	2200	670	D 380

DOVRE MOUNTAIN PLATEAU

	Beds	Rooms	Altitude Ft.	M	Maps
Åmotsdal hut, Drivstua 30x	2	4300	1310	D 145
Alfheim Lodge, Gjøra 18x	10	2590	790	D 380
Aursjø hut, Lesjaverk 18x	2	2820	860	K 400
Dindal hut, Lønset 16y	2	2790	850	D 380
Drivstuen Fjellstue, Drivstua 15	8	2265	690	»
Gautsbu seter, Lesja 6y	3	2800	850	K 400
Gruvedal hut, Gjøra (Gjøra 18a) 15x	2	2860	875	D 145
Hjerkinn Fjellstove, Hjerkinn 75	45	3150	960	»
Hjerkinnhus Lodge, Hjerkinn 30	15	3480	1060	»
Jenstad farm, Gjøra 7	5	1570	480	D 380
Kongsvoll — see hotel and YHA lists ...... —	—	2950	900	D 145
Lesja Gjestgiveri, Lesja (Lesja 519a) 16	10	2075	634	K 400
Lesjaverk farm, Lesjaverk (Lesjaverk 1216a)	26	15	2065	630	»
Loennechen hut, Gjøra (unstaffed) 2x	1	4100	1250	D 380
Reinheim hut, (unstaffed) 26x	6	5500	1675	D 145
Skamsdal hut, Lesja (Lesja 525a) (J470) 9x	2	3160	950	»
Vålåsjø: Dovregubbens Hall, Vålåsjø 22	9	3160	950	»
Vangshaugen Lodge, Gjøra (Gjøra 14f) 24x	9	2570	785	D 380

RONDANE MOUNTAIN RANGES

	Beds	Rooms	Altitude Ft.	M	Maps
Bjørnhollia Lodge, Atnedal Nordre 50x	15	2970	907	J 440
Breisjø seter, Atnedal Nordre 14	7	3120	925	»
Dørål seter, Brennhaug (Dombås 414) 16	8	3280	1000	»
Eldå seter, Hundorp 15	7	2460	750	E 735
Flat seter, Alvdal (Alvdal 1027) 10y	4	3240	994	J 440
Follansvangen seter, Alvdal 11	6	2900	830	»
Grimsdal Lodge, (Dovre 252) 34x	10	3260	995	»
Høvringen Fjellstue, Sel 65	35	3282	1000	»
Høvringen: Laurgård seter, Sel 60	33	3282	1000	»
Kvislå seter, Alvdal (Alvdal 1064) 17y	7	3500	1100	D 485
Mysu seter, Otta (Otta 108b) 15	8	2950	900	E 765
Nesset farm, Sollia (Atnebru 14a) 20	13	2360	720	J 440
Peer Gynt hut (or Uløy hut), Høvringen 6	2	3609	1100	»
Rondablik Hotel, Kvam (Kvam 457)........ 75	45	3051	930	E 735
Rondvassbu Lodge, Otta 38x	6	3840	1170	J 440
Stadsbu farm, Atnedal 20	8	2400	800	»
Veslesøln seter .... —	—	3246	989	D 485

(x) Owned by DNT or associated clubs.
(y) Privately owned, but DNT members are admitted at reduced rates.

	Beds	Rooms	Ft.	M	Maps

ØSTERDAL — FEMUND

	Beds	Rooms	Ft.	M	Maps
Elgå Gjestgiveri, Elgå	14	7	2300	700	D 365
Femund Gjestgiveri, Femundsenden	24	15	2175	663	D 490
Galten farm, Engerdal	—	—	2109	643	»
Misterdal seter, Øvre Rendal	8y	2	2307	703	D 590
Svukuriset Lodge, Elgå	33x	6	2667	813	D 365
Vesterheim farm, Engerdal	10	2	2300	700	D 490

RØROS — SYLENE

	Beds	Rooms	Ft.	M	Maps
Ålen youth hostel, Ålen	10	4	1566	477	D 235
Haltdalen: Morkenes Kafe, Haltdalen	3	2	984	300	»
Kjøli hut, Reitan—Ålen	12x	4	3492	1065	D 480
Nedal hut, Tydal	34x	5	2298	700	»
Nordpå hut, Aunegrenda—Haltdalen	36x	10	1803	550	D 235
Røros — see hotel and YHA lists	—	—	2060	628	D 415
Storerikvoll hut, Tydal	32x	6	2493	761	D 175
Stormoen hut, Flora	30x	4	1911	583	D 435
Stugudal Lodge, Tydal	24	10	2034	620	D 480
Vektarstua tourist station, Tydal	100	33	1968	600	»

OKSTINDAN — RØSSVATN

	Beds	Rooms	Ft.	M	Maps
Bleikvassli — see Stekvasselv	—	—	820	250	J 420
Kjensvass Lodge, Leirskardal	20	4	1705	520	»
Korgen Gjestgiveri, Korgen	—	—	100	30	»
Mosjøen — see hotel & YHA lists	—	—	—	—	E 595
Røssvassbukt — no accommodation	—	—	1230	375	J 420
Stekvasselv Lodge, Bleikvassli	30	8	1230	375	»

MO I RANA — SVARTISEN

	Beds	Rooms	Ft.	M	Maps
Blakkådal Lodge, Røvassdal	20	4	985	300	E 215
Glomfjord: Kleivstua Gjestgiveri	22	16	260	80	E 590
Grønli caves — no accommodation	—	—	820	250	E 215
Mo i Rana — see hotel & YHA lists	—	—	—	—	E 700
Ørnes: Skogstua Gjestgiveri	14	8	80	25	E 590
Plurdal Caves — no accommodation	—	—	1610	490	E 940
Svartisdal Lodge, Røvassdal	10	3	330	100	E 215

KAUTOKEINO — KARASJOK

Please note that every «fjellstue» is also a youth hostel.

	Beds	Rooms	Ft.	M	Maps
Aiddejavre Fjellstue, Kautokeino	4	—	1233	376	E 525
Alta — see hotel list and YHA list	—	—	—	—	E 105
Bassevuovde Fjellstue, Karasjok	4	—	625	190	E 410
Biggeluobbal Fjellstue, Alta	8	—	1236	377	E 585
Gargia Fjellstue, Alta	8	—	243	74	E 105
Jergul Fjellstue, Karasjok	2	1	1950	230	E 440
Jotkajavre Fjellstue, Alta	4	—	1340	400	E 105
Karasjok — see hotel and YHA lists	—	—	440	130	E 450
Kautokeino — see hotel and YHA lists	—	—	1040	320	E 460
Lakselv — see hotel and YHA lists	—	—	—	—	E 825
Lappoluobbal Fjellstue, Alta	6	—	1100	335	E 520
Levajok Fjellstue, Karasjok	4	—	330	100	E 710
Mollisjok Fjellstue, Karasjok	4	—	1250	382	E 440
Nattvatn Fjellstue, Lakselv	6	—	920	280	E 450
Ravnastua Fjellstue, Karasjok	4	—	1100	336	E 440
Roavvegiedde Fjellstue, Sirma	4	—	230	70	E 710
Rustefjelbma — see hotel and YHA lists	—	—	—	—	E 982
Sirma Fjellstue, Polmak	—	—	150	45	E 695
Sjusjavre Fjellstue, Karasjok	4	—	995	305	E 440
Skaidi — see hotel and YHA lists	—	—	333	100	E 715
Skipagurra Gjestgiveri, Skipagurra	13	6	33	10	E 695
Skoganvarre — no rooms	—	—	230	70	E 800
Solovomi Fjellstue, Alta	8	—	1240	378	E 585
Storfossen Fjellstue, Karasjok	4				E 425
Tverrelvdal Fjellstue, Alta	4		165	50	E 105
Valjok Fjellstue, Karasjok	4		360	110	E 325

(x) Owned by DNT or associated clubs.
(y) Privately owned, but DNT members are admitted at reduced rates.

GLOSSARY—HOW TO READ
NORWEGIAN MAPS

The following abbreviations are used frequently in this book: E(ast), L(eft), MR (map reference), N(orth), R(ight), S(outh) and W(est).

Most survey maps have a legend which is printed in Norwegian only. Visitors may find it rather confusing to see that the same word is not always spelt the same way. The present word for road is «veg», but before the war it was spelt «vei» and on really old maps it is even spelt «vej». In some parts of Norway a church is called «kirke», but in other parts they say «kyrkje».

It is also worth knowing that the prefix or suffix «en» (or «et») in Norwegian place names indicates the indefinite or definite articles «a» or «the», for instance as follows:

en elv — a river
elven — the river
Flåmselven — the Flåm river

et vatn — a lake
vatnet — the lake
Møsvatnet — the Møs lake

Below is a translation of the words most frequently used in Norwegian map legends.

ankerplass — safe anchorage
annekskirke — parish church
avstand — distance
barskog — coniferous forest
bekk (bæk) — brook
bilferge — car ferry
bode (boe, båe) — reef, rock
bode i sjømålet — reef or rock at sea level
bode under vatnet — concealed reef or rock
bre (bræ) — glacier
bruk — croft, small farm
bygdeveg — local road
bygrense — town boundary
bygsel — small farm
dobbeltspor — double track
einspora — single track
enkeltsporet — single track
ekserserplass — army camp
elektrisk leidning — electric cable
elektrisk sporveg — tramline
elektrisitetsverk — hydro electric plant
elv (ælv) — river
fabrikk — factory
feleger (fælæger) — cattle shed
ferge (ferje) — ferry
fiskarbu (fiskerbod) — fishing shack
fjell (fjeld, fjæld) — mountain
fjøre — beach (tidal)
flyplass — airport
fylkesgrense — county boundary
fylkesveg — secondary road
fyr — lighthouse
fyrlykt — light buoy
gangveg — footpath
gard (gård) — farm
god privat kjøreveg — good private motoring road
grense — boundary
grenserøys — frontier cairn
gruve (grube) — mine
haug — hill
havstrand — beach (facing ocean)
herad (herred) — rural district
heradsgrense — rural boundary
heradsveg — local road
høgd — hill
hotell — hotel
hovedveg (hovedvei) — main road
hovudkyrkje (hovedkirke) — county church
husmannsplass — croft, small farm
hytte — hut
jarnveg (jernbane) — railway
jarnveg under bygging — railway under construction
kapell — chapel

kirke (kyrkje) — church
kjerreveg — restricted road, cart-track
kløvveg — cattle trail
kobberverk — copper mine
koye (koie) — hut, shack
kvern — grain mill
kyrkje — church
lauvskog — deciduous forest
leirplass — camping site
lite synlig sti — faintly visible footpath
luftfyr — beacon (for aircraft)
lykt — light, lamp
lysbøye — light buoy
målestokk — scale
mindre bruk — small farm
mylne — small power station
myr — marshland
nut — peak
pensjonat — pension
plass (plads) — small farm
prestegård — vicarage
prestegjeldsgrense — parish boundary
privat kjøreveg — private motoring road
riksgrense — frontier
riksveg — main road
sag — saw mill
seter (sæter) — mountain farm
sjø — lake, sea
sjømerke — sea buoy
skjerp — mine
skole (skule) — school
skyttarbu (skytterbod) — shooting hut or lodge
slaggrunnslinje — danger line
småbruk — croft, small farm
sokn (sogn) — rural district
soknegrense — rural boundary
soknekyrkje (sognekirke) — parish church
sportshytte — tourist hut (private)
sporveg — tramline
stasjon — station
statsalmenning — crown land
sted (stad) — place
steinbrot (stenbrudd) — quarry
sti (stig) — footpath
stoppested — halt
større fabrikk — larger factory
sund — sound
taubane (togbane) — chairlift
teglverk — tile works
telegrafline (linje) — telegraph wire
tertiærjarnveg — narrow gauge railway
tjern (tjønn) — tarn

trådlaus stasjon — radio station
trallebane — trolley track
trigonometrisk punkt — trigono-
  metric point
turisthytte — tourist hut
turiststasjon — tourist hut
tvispora — double track
ur — scree, boulders

vardesett sti — cairned footpath
vatn (vann, vand) — lake
veg (vei, vej) — road
veg under bygging — road under
  construction
vegskille (veidele) — road junction
villa — villa
vinterveg — winter road

ALPHABETICAL INDEX

Please note that the letter «å» is listed as if it where spelt «aa» as in olden
days, and the letter «ø» is listed as «ö».

198

Printed in Norway 1963
A.s John Griegs Boktrykkeri, Bergen